PHARAOH'S PEOPLE

PHARAOH'S PEOPLE

Scenes from Life in Imperial Egypt

T.G.H.JAMES

TAURISPARKE
PAPERBACKS

Published in 2003 by Tauris Parke Paperbacks
an imprint of I.B.Tauris & Co Ltd
6 Salem Road, London W2 4BU
175 Fifth Avenue, New York NY 10010
www.ibtauris.com

In the United States of America and in Canada distributed
by Palgrave Macmillan, a division of St Martin's Press
175 Fifth Avenue, New York NY 10010

First published in 1984 by The Bodley Head Ltd.

ISBN 1 86064 832 0

A full CIP record for this book is available from the British
Library
A full CIP record for this book is available from the Library of
Congress

Library of Congress catalog card: available

Printed and bound in Great Britain by MPG Books Ltd,
Bodmin

CONTENTS

For Diana

ACKNOWLEDGMENTS

Thanks are due to the following for permission to reproduce photographs and line drawings:

Deutsches archäologisches Institut, Abteilung Kairo, fig. 27

The Egypt Exploration Society, pls. 13 (*bottom*), 14 (*top*); figs. 4–12, 26

The Metropolitan Museum of Art, New York, pl. 9 (*bottom left*); figs. 2, 3, 13–22, 25

The Trustees of the British Museum, pls. 2 (*top right*), 3 (*bottom*), 5 (*top and bottom*), 6 (*top*), 7 (*bottom*), 9 (*top and bottom right*), 10 (*bottom*), 11 (*top, centre, bottom*), 13 (*top*), 14 (*bottom*)

The drawings for figs. 1, 23, 24 were made by Christine Barratt

LIST OF PLATES

LIST OF FIGURES

PREFACE

In 1837 John Gardner Wilkinson published *The Manners and Customs of the Ancient Egyptians*. The three substantial volumes of this work incorporated the results of his pioneer Egyptological studies, which he had pursued, mostly in Egypt, from 1821 to 1833. These years had witnessed the decipherment of the hieroglyphic script and the opening of Egypt to travellers and scholars, and Wilkinson was among the earliest to exploit the newly won knowledge and the opportunity to work in Egypt as a serious student. His book represented the first attempt to present the history and culture of ancient Egypt in a form firmly based on the evidence provided by the monuments, by the objects discovered in early, primitive excavations and in the plundering of ancient sites, and by the writings of classical writers who were at that time still considered as reliable witnesses of life in ancient Egypt. *Manners and Customs* was a great success, and it remained the standard work on ancient Egypt until the end of the nineteenth century. It is still not without value.

Wilkinson was able to be comprehensive in his approach to ancient Egypt. Every aspect of life was included—history, geography, religion, state organization, architecture, the fine arts, crafts, social life. The work was an omnium gatherum of noble proportions. But in the century and a half which have intervened since *Manners and Customs* was published, knowledge of ancient Egypt has grown immensely, and the content of Wilkinson's work is now comprehended by a huge library of specialized publications. In this present book, therefore, it is impossible to be comprehensive. Within the narrow limits of daily life, strictly interpreted, the material available is vast, even if one allows for the inadequacies of the record to which attention is drawn in the Introduction and Chapter One. Within the chosen period—the mid-Eighteenth Dynasty, when Egypt first became an imperial state—I have in consequence selected those topics for discussion that allow the construction of a modest edifice of information inhabited mostly by those Egyptians placed on the lower rungs of the social ladder.

Such people rarely speak directly to us across the thousands of years which have passed since they lived, but there is much indirect evidence, and a little which is startlingly direct. My starting-point has been this evidence and its reliability; then the bureaucratic society of which these people form part is examined through the work and obligations of the vizir, and the exercise of the surprisingly (but perhaps superficially) fair legal system. The importance of writing and the position of the scribe in this fairly literate society are set in measure against the life on the land, and the lot of the craftsman, whose skills were great, but not always appreciated. Finally, an attempt is made to describe the living conditions of the dwellers in town and country, and the ways in which they conducted the business of daily life in an economy based on barter. Throughout I have made use of ancient texts of all kinds, most of which I have newly translated for this book. Certain conventions used in these translations need to be explained. Round brackets are used to contain words added to make sense of a passage and also words of uncertain restoration, the latter usually accompanied by a question mark. A question mark between round brackets indicates uncertainty over the preceding word or words, or over the sense generally. Square brackets are used to contain explanatory glosses and also words restored where the original text is missing.

I have tried to resist the temptation to draw sweeping general conclusions from limited evidence, perhaps not always with convincing success. My hope has been that the flavour of life in imperial Egypt might be tasted, and that the taste will not be wholly misleading, too spiced by imagination, or sweetened by sentimentality. The majority of the ancient Egyptians lived close to the soil and were pretty down-to-earth. They apparently exercised a fairly astringent practicality in an environment which was not particularly hostile. In this series of essays my eyes have been sighted low to catch the rare glimpses of the humble going about their business; but they have not always managed to avoid sweeping up occasionally to gaze at the not-so-humble.

In the years during which this book has been in preparation I have received constant encouragement from my wife. Her understanding of people, projected critically back to antiquity, has helped me immeasurably to appreciate the ways of thought, the patterns of behaviour and the foibles of the ancient Egyptians. Jill Black of the Bodley Head has exercised patience beyond reasonable expectation and applied the right kind of stimulus with the lightest of touches when progress was slow. I am greatly in her debt. I am further grateful to my colleague Professor Edward Wente of the Oriental Institute, the University of Chicago, who read my text in typescript and made many useful suggestions. To my colleagues in the Department of Egyptian Antiquities in the British Museum I owe much from daily discussions on every kind of Egyptological topic over many years.

INTRODUCTION

The kings of Egypt ruled an undivided nation in antiquity for three thousand years, with occasional, relatively short, periods of anarchy and foreign domination, before their country was absorbed into the ambit of the Graeco-Roman world. In this book a picture will be built up of Egyptian society during the central point of that long rule, the mid-Eighteenth Dynasty (c. 1500–1400 BC), a period for which, in Egyptian terms, there is abundant evidence. Yet there will still be many qualifications to be applied to the conclusions reached, for the evidence remains patchy and partial in spite of its apparent abundance. To compose an account of even a well-documented period of Egyptian history reveals the weaknesses which bedevil the work of the Egyptian historian in general. The history of Egypt can be compared with a document of great length, large parts of which are missing, while the preserved portions are rendered imperfect by lacunae, obscure sections and places where the text is difficult to establish with certainty. Sir Alan Gardiner, the most devoted of Egyptologists, who never failed to appreciate the inadequacies of his lifelong field of study, was brutally honest in his verdict on the surviving Egyptian record: 'What is proudly advertised as Egyptian history is merely a collection of rags and tatters.'[1] What he means—and he makes it quite clear in his subsequent remarks—is that the raw material for the writing of a satisfactory Egyptian history, covering the whole of the three-thousand-year span, is insufficient and sketchy.

And yet the ancient Egyptians did more than most pre-classical peoples to make some record of their achievements, to perpetuate the knowledge of private and public events, to project their own existences into the future through the magic of the written word. The desire to record great and glorious deeds is an understandable human weakness, and the ancient Egyptians were no more reticent than others in proclaiming their victories while disguising, or ignoring, their failures. The public statements of kings and great nobles, confident and vainglorious at the best of times, achieve particular weight and authority when they are inscribed in fine monumental hieroglyphs accompanied by larger-than-life reliefs of dramatic actions on the walls of great temples. How much of the truth do they incorporate? Much, certainly; but in emphasis and interpretation they are often undoubtedly slanted away from reality. Confidence in what may be related is frequently sapped by the repetitive and unconvincing phraseology of bombast lavishly used to support the bare account of a foreign campaign or military exploit, which in itself may have been little more than a small excursion beyond the frontiers of Egypt.

In the first chapter of the book a survey is made of the kinds of written evidence used by the historians of ancient Egypt, and an attempt is made to assess the degree of confidence which can be placed on the different categories of text. There are the great, apparently factual, royal inscriptions mentioned above; caution, but not total disbelief, should temper the historian's use of such texts. Where there are other sources by which some check can be made, the claims of a king may be shown to be not wholly untrue, or the product of boasting. The inscriptions of non-royal persons, often the great officials who carried out the policies of the kings, can be, on the other hand, remarkably disappointing for their lack of factual content. Only when an official recorded activities outside the boundaries of Egypt did he feel able to provide a meaty account of his achievements.

Happily, however, much of the source material of the historian is to be found not in formal inscriptions, whether royal or non-royal, but in documents prepared for official archives, or written as records of private transactions. Such writings, by their very nature, were not designed for purposes of propaganda and self-glorification, and are intrinsically more trustworthy. No one, however, should naïvely believe that an account written on papyrus in the hieratic script is *ipso facto* wholly honest. Judgements remain to be made; every document needs cool evaluation. In addition, we shall be considering the many ephemeral documents which have survived—letters, memoranda, accounts, records of disputes—rich material for the study of social life during this remote period. The telling items used in illustration in this book may not in every case be datable precisely to the mid-Eighteenth Dynasty; but the conservatism of Egyptian society renders the anachronistic use of evidence rather less improper than would be the case in attempting, for example, to illustrate life in England during the sixteenth century by reference to the writings of the Age of Enlightenment.

In building up the picture of life in Eighteenth-dynasty Egypt in the chapters which follow, use is made of all the kinds of document mentioned. But as the principal intention in this book is to throw light particularly on the existence of the less-than-great, most use will be made of the non-royal and non-official texts. Another source of information to be tapped is more pictorial than textual; it is the evidence drawn from the scenes of daily life found in the tombs of the Eighteenth Dynasty which depict the behaviour and labour of the peasants and artisans who populated the environment of the tomb-owners in their lives on earth, and in their posthumous existences. In the New Kingdom the dominant necropolis in Egypt was that of Thebes, situated in the foothills, rocky bays, and waterways or *wadis*, leading up to the mountain, shaped somewhat like a pyramid, known today as El-Qurn, 'The Horn'. Here in these hills was the visible West, the place to which a man travelled when he died. As the tombs of Western Thebes and the inhabitants of the necropolis region are central to the contents of this book, let us take a closer look at the place and, in particular, at the tomb of the vizir Rekhmire, the scenes from which will serve as illustrations for many of the subjects dealt with in the chapters that lie ahead.²

Western Thebes, this eminently suitable locality, was first used as a burial area in more than a casual manner during the late Old Kingdom when the town of Wese, later to develop into the great complex of temples and administrative buildings generally known by its Greek name, Thebes, was little more than a small provincial centre. Later large rock-cut tombs with imposing funerary temples were constructed for kings of the Eleventh Dynasty in the dramatic setting of the bay in the cliffs now called Deir el-Bahri. This was the place called *Djeser-djeseru*, 'Holy of holies', during the Eighteenth Dynasty, when Queen Hatshepsut had her own funerary temple built there under the direction of her favourite, Senenmut, about whom we shall learn much more shortly. At Deir el-Bahri also the great officials who served the kings of the Eleventh Dynasty had their tombs excavated in the rocky slopes which formed the wings of the royal funerary stage.

After this auspicious beginning the Theban necropolis was little used during the remaining dynasties of the Middle Kingdom, but it was re-established as a cemetery for kings and high officials during the

Seventeenth Dynasty (c. 1650–1554 BC) when the power of native Egyptian monarchs was confined to the southern part of Upper Egypt. Subsequently, during the Eighteenth, Nineteenth and Twentieth Dynasties, for almost five hundred years, Thebes remained probably the most important city in Egypt and frequently the principal seat of government, although not always the favoured residence of the king. Throughout this period the kings were buried in a part of Western Thebes now called the Valley of the Kings. Most of the Theban necropolis, however, was used for non-royal burials. Here were laid to rest the great officials who manned the bureaucracy of Thebes; and in the neighbourhood of the workmen's village at Deir el-Medina, the craftsmen who were responsible for these royal and noble tombs inserted their own sepulchres.

In the decoration of the non-royal tombs some of the most charming vignettes of Egyptian life may be seen. The tomb was the dwelling-place of the dead man's spirit, and the decoration aimed at creating the proper environment in which the deceased might hope to pass eternity. The apparently confused view of the after-life held by the Egyptians should be viewed as a practical expression of their view of earthly life transposed to a less substantial realm. In truth the ancient Egyptian did not expect an after-life of transcendental existence in the company of the sun-god, as did his king. He hoped to extend his life on earth into a posthumous existence which would be, ideally, the same in kind, and possibly in degree. The noble on earth should be the noble in the Field of Reeds—the Elysian Fields for him. He would continue to administer the affairs of Pharaoh as on earth; he would visit his estates, oversee the work of his servants, join in celebrations, and partake of banquets with his family and friends. The aspiration is naïve. With it was joined a more spiritual hope by which he might expect, provided that he had played his cards correctly and surmounted all the obstacles, to achieve a blessed justification for his life in the presence of Osiris and his assessors. In the decoration of his tomb, the practical and the spiritual aspects were usually represented in scenes which could be expanded or contracted in their content according to the size of the tomb.

At this point, perhaps, it ought to be explained that in talking about the tomb we are specially interested in the part of the tomb-complex which had little to do with the actual burial. In the Theban necropolis the modern tourist does not visit the Tombs of the Nobles, but the decorated rooms, the adjuncts to the burials, which are cut into the hillside and approached from a platform or court. The burial itself may be at the end of a descending passage leading deeper into the cliffs from these rooms; it may equally be at the bottom of a shaft sunk vertically either from within the decorated rooms, from the court outside, or from some other adjacent spot. The decorated rooms are commonly called the chapel of the tomb, because in one of them was placed the offering-table on which the daily food and drink offerings needed by the deceased in his after-life were laid out. For general convenience, however, it remains less pedantic, and certainly more helpful, to continue to use the word 'tomb' for whatever part of a private person's funerary monument might be visible and accessible.

This small excursus into burial architecture and terminology is not wholly unnecessary because when we come to examine the tomb of Rekhmire which is to provide much material for our study, we learn that its burial shaft and chamber have never been found. A doubt has been cast on whether Rekhmire was ever buried in Thebes, for there are clear signs of purposeful damage to the paintings of the decorated rooms which have been interpreted as indications of a fall from favour. If such a disgrace befell Rekhmire in his mature lifetime it is not at all unlikely that he would have been denied burial in the Theban necropolis, and that the actual burial chamber was never prepared. As the burial chamber in a Theban noble's tomb was usually undecorated, or only sparsely decorated, its cutting could be left to a late stage in the preparation of the tomb. The decorated rooms, on the other hand, formed the 'public' part which might be visited by relatives, friends and colleagues in the days and years following the interment. Here not only would the daily offerings be made by the appointed '*ka*-servant' or funerary attendant (paid from a prearranged endowment), but the importance of the deceased tomb-owner would be observable in the scenes which embellished the walls. The really great men who helped Pharaoh in the government of Egypt, and in so doing controlled the well-developed bureaucracy, made it a matter of pride and importance to ensure that their tombs truly proclaimed their greatness. This was certainly the case with Rekhmire; and whether he fell from grace or not, whether he was buried in the Theban necropolis or not, his tomb in its decorated chambers has—in modern times at least—wholly proclaimed his greatness (*Fig. 1*).

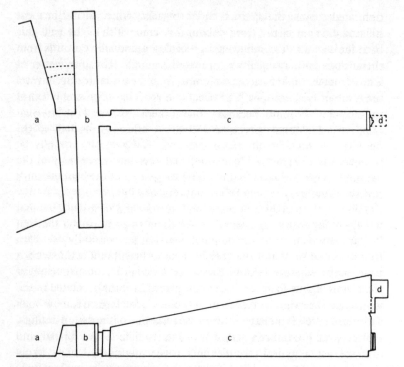

Fig. 1 The tomb of Rekhmire; plan and section: a. court; b. transverse hall; c. corridor; d. statue niche.

When Rekhmire was permitted to begin the construction of a tomb for himself, the Theban necropolis was still relatively unexploited as a burial ground, and he was able to select (or have selected by royal favour) a choice site, not very high up in the hillside in a central position, in that part of the necropolis known now as the hill of Sheikh Abd el-Qurna. A wide court was prepared, initially no doubt as a working area, its western side being formed by the exposed rock of the hill, roughly cut in a vertical manner to form the façade of the tomb. The doorway giving access to the decorated rooms of the chapel, which lie on the same level as the court, is set centrally in the façade. The short entrance corridor lies askew to the façade, and the transverse hall into which it leads runs at about 15° from the parallel to the façade. This hall is about 20.5 m. long from north to south, about 2.3 m. wide, and a little over 3 m. high. In line directly from the entrance and running at right angles to the hall is the corridor or gallery which forms the most striking element of the tomb. About the same width as the hall, this corridor is about 26 m. long, and its roof slopes gradually upwards from entrance to end, rising from 3 m. to 8 m. high. The impression of soaring height and spaciousness given by this unusual feature invests the tomb of Rekhmire with a special quality. The surprising effect of the rising ceiling presents the unsuspecting visitor with a visual experience which can be compared with that created by the first sight of the Grand Gallery in the Great Pyramid—if lesser can properly be compared with greater. There are many who find the majesty of the pyramid's gallery diminished by the stark quality of the bare masonry and the oppressive quality of the atmosphere, but can appreciate the airy lightness of Rekhmire's corridor enlivened by its gaily painted walls, illuminated by the shafts of sunlight directed by mirror through the narrow entrance by the obliging (if suitably rewarded) custodian. At the very end of the corridor, at the most westerly point in the tomb, a niche prepared for a statue of Rekhmire is set at the unusual height of about 6 m. above floor level. In antiquity, after burial, a statue in the tomb-chapel served as a representative of the deceased, and, if his body were destroyed, as his substitute for the reception of the daily offerings. No trace of Rekhmire's statue was ever found. If he did fall into disgrace before his death and was not buried in his tomb, then it is likely that no statue was ever placed in the niche. Alternatively, it might have been removed at that time, had it earlier been installed.

Whether Rekhmire was buried in this tomb at Thebes, or not, is not a primary concern for us at present. What attracts and holds the attention of the visitor to his tomb is the remarkable series of paintings on the walls of the hall and the corridor. In these, and in the inscriptions which accompany them, we can find the blueprints, as it were, for his work as vizir, some indications of his way of life in public and in private, a remarkable review of some of the agencies and offices over which he had control, and (which is not to be considered here) a very detailed depiction of the ceremonies, rituals and other activities which were to take place after his death in the period leading up to his expected burial in the Theban necropolis. In the transverse hall the scenes and inscriptions deal with Rekhmire's official activities as vizir, general episodes in his private life and his management of the estates belonging to the domain of Amun, the imperial god, whose temple was already by the middle of the Eighteenth Dynasty a great and growing shrine in

Thebes. Scenes showing the preparation of provisions for the great temple occupy part of the south wall of the corridor, and they are succeeded in a westerly direction by a richly detailed series of 'artisans' scenes in which the artists and craftsmen of the god's workshops are shown hard at work under the watchful eye of Rekhmire. On the corresponding sections of the north wall of the corridor a large formal banquet takes place, and some scenes deal with Rekhmire's attendance at the coronation of King Amenophis II, the successor of Tuthmosis III, under whom his career as vizir came to an end. A part of the east end of this wall remains undecorated, perhaps a further indication of the abrupt end of Rekhmire's high office and royal favour. The west ends of both walls of the corridor, which rise to a lofty height, are occupied by ritual banquet scenes and burial ceremonies. Such, in brief, is the summary of the decoration found in this tomb; indeed, a fitting scheme for a man who occupied the highest rank in the official bureaucracy of Egypt in the days of triumphant empire.

There are other tombs at Thebes and elsewhere in Egypt splendidly decorated with similar scenes. The repertory of the scenes, however, is only broadly the same; in detail they differ considerably from tomb to tomb. In this book we shall be specially interested in detail. Illustrations of activities and occupations will therefore be drawn from the tombs that present the most suitable examples. But the majority will come from Rekhmire's tomb, which, conveniently, is numbered 100 in the modern list of private tombs in the Theban necropolis.

NOTES

1 Sir Alan Gardiner, *Egypt of the Pharaohs*, 53.
2 The tomb is fully published by Norman de G. Davies, *The Tomb of Rekh-mi-Rēʿ at Thebes*.

1

THE WRITTEN RECORD AND ITS VALIDITY

Copy your fathers who were before you; (achievement?) is deter-
mined by knowing. See! Their words are made lasting in writing.
Open (the writings) that you may read and emulate what is known.
So the expert becomes the one who is instructed.

These words are taken from a composition attributed to an Egyptian
king of the First Intermediate Period (*c.* 2075 BC) who set down a series
of thoughts and precepts for the edification of his son and successor,
Merikare.[1] The authenticity of its origin is much disputed, but it is
agreed that it was composed at least as early as the Twelfth Dynasty (*c.*
1991–1785 BC), although the principal manuscript by which it is known
was written in the Eighteenth Dynasty (*c.* 1450 BC). The authorship of
this *Instruction for Merikare* will probably never be established, but its
existence in a papyrus copy made many hundreds of years after its
composition confirms what the quotation above proclaims. The
ancient Egyptians believed passionately in the power of the written
word. Much of the content of this book is drawn from the legacy of
Egyptian writing. We should, therefore, at the outset consider the
nature of the written record, and the extent to which the various kinds
of text may be trusted. We shall examine, in specific examples,
hieroglyphic inscriptions, both royal and non-royal, and records,
official and private, written in the cursive hieratic script on papyri and
other materials.

The historian of ancient Egypt always approaches the formal, royal,
hieroglyphic text with caution. Nevertheless, some credence must be
placed on such texts otherwise the whole fabric of Egyptian history has
to be treated as some elaborate lie, perpetuated down the centuries by

master deceivers. The reality of events related in the great inscriptions which adorn the outer walls of temples, in particular, can often be confirmed partly or in whole by independent testimony acquired elsewhere, from subsidiary Egyptian sources, or—better still—from foreign records. But the determination of what may be accepted is not a simple matter of trimming away the verbiage and the vaunting. The variable process of interpretation must intervene, and herein lies both the particular fascination and, equally, the frustration of the writing of Egyptian history.

When the great Ramesses II engaged the Hittites in battle at Qadesh on the Orontes in about 1285 BC, the outcome was probably no better than a shaky draw as far as both sides were concerned. Most historians would agree probably that in the long term the Hittites were the victors marginally, although their success was not sufficiently decisive to enable them to follow it up. For Ramesses and the Egyptians the avoidance of utter defeat and humiliation was so important that it was turned into victory, at least as far as the written record was concerned. So near to disaster had the Egyptians come that Qadesh could not be treated as anything but a triumph for royal valour and Egyptian arms. In consequence, the official record concocted to commemorate this dubious victory was cast in the form of an elaborate, quasi-literary composition which was carved on temples throughout Egypt, the words embellished with quite remarkable scenes illustrating the environs of Qadesh and notable incidents in the contest.[2] This romanticized record of the Battle of Qadesh cannot be treated as a truthful account of what happened, and I doubt whether many ancient Egyptians would have accepted it wholly as an historical narrative. It was composed to glorify King Ramesses II, to extol his exploits, and, by the magic of being carved on stone, to transmute a near-failure into a success. And how successful it was—one of the greatest pieces of propaganda of all time! For the rest of his long reign the memory of Qadesh sustained and nurtured the reputation of Ramesses. The great battle scenes impressed his contemporaries, and continued to hood-wink succeeding generations. On this basis he became Ramesses the Great, Ozymandias King of Kings, the Rhampsinitus of Herodotus. Not until modern times, when the Hittites were rediscovered, their records translated, and the extent of their power revealed, was the myth of Ramesses' greatness thrown into doubt. So much for the historical value of the Qadesh texts! Yet it would be wrong to maintain that these texts are wholly untrustworthy. The broad facts concerning the Qadesh campaign—its time, its occasion, its place of engagement, details of the organization of the Egyptian army taken by Ramesses into Asia, the dispositions even of the opposing forces, and perhaps some of the incidents in the encounter itself—are probably reported with a fair degree of accuracy. But how can truth be separated from fiction?

Presented with compositions like the Qadesh narrative, the historian is faced with the task of trying to determine what can be accepted. If there is independent source material the task is greatly eased, and in the case of Qadesh there is the native Hittite tradition to use as a check and counter to ancient hyperbole and simple misrepresentation. Unfortunately, the unreliability of the Egyptian source which is revealed by this process engenders a lack of trust in Egyptian historical texts. Once confidence is shaken the questioning of every fact, every detail, tends to follow, and the use of the texts as source material for history is distrusted. It should not, however, be so, and it must not be so. The written records of an ancient culture must form the primary source for the history of the culture. If they are held to be a tissue of lies or, at least, a romantic account of what may have happened in the past, then they are good for little more than the story-book.

It seems to be generally true that the reliability of an Egyptian historical text depends to a marked extent on the measure of success accompanying the events recounted. The less there is to be ashamed of, the more easily may the truth be recounted. But even in the best of times the composers of royal records were quite unable to resist high-flown language in describing the exploits of their divinely royal masters. King Amenophis II, the son and successor of Tuthmosis III, appears to have been exceptionally athletic and accomplished in warlike activities. Inscriptions set up to recount particular achievements of his reign never fail to draw attention to his Olympic abilities. But nothing surpasses the praise on an inscription found at Giza near the great Sphinx.[3] Of his lord the writer declares:

> Now when his Majesty ascended the throne as king, as a fine young man, he had his wits about him. He had completed eighteen years, establishing his strength by valour. He knew all the crafts of Montu [the god of war]; there was not his like upon the battle-field. He is one who knows how to handle a span of horses, without his like in this vast army. None can draw his bow; he cannot be

approached in running; strong of arm, who does not weary when he takes the oar.

Later the writer describes how the king set up a copper target, and shot his arrows right through. A fine granite relief retrieved from the core of the Third Pylon in the Temple of Karnak shows this same king in his chariot shooting arrows through a target which is precisely a large copper ingot.[4] It may not be necessary to believe the exaggeration of the words, or the imagination of the representation, which together make Amenophis II a champion among men. Yet there is probably some truth in the tradition, and it should not wholly be discounted.

Royal inscriptions, however, do not alone make up the historical record. Non-royal persons of importance, rank and influence were in no way slow to ape the commemorative propensities of their monarchs. In times when it was customary for the tombs of commoners to be decorated with scenes which, regardless of their magical and religious intention, provided vivid illustrations of contemporary life in Egypt, individuals who had much to be proud of often left records of their achievements in inscriptions in their tombs. These inscriptions, often erroneously (although understandably) described by scholars as biographical, contain much of the boasting quality of royal texts but, inasmuch as they were designed less for overt purposes of self-advertisement than their royal counterparts and more for the post-humous record, they tend to be more factual and particular in their descriptions of the great events in which their protagonists took part. Frequently also they include mentions of events, national and local, incidents in great campaigns and domestic activities, which find no place in the grandiose records of royalty. What went on to the south of Elephantine in Nubia during the time of the Old Kingdom is largely known from the descriptive texts carved in their tombs by the nobles of Elephantine, who controlled Egypt's southern frontiers and conducted expeditions into the dangerous land of Nubia on behalf of their lord, the King of Egypt, and, on the side, for their own personal benefit. Of these influential officials, the one whose inscription is the most memorable, not only for the kinds of special information it provides, but also for its preservation of a unique personal document, is Harkhuf who held the title, among others, of 'overseer of dragomans [or interpreters]'. Three times during the reign of Merenre, a king of the Sixth Dynasty, Harkhuf was sent on punitive and trading expeditions into Nubia. The brief mentions of the forays tell little more than their destinations, durations and broad results, but such meagre details alone form much of the stuff of Egyptian history for the remote period of the Old Kingdom. The exceptional bonus of Harkhuf's tomb inscriptions, however, is to be found in the account of yet another Nubian expedition undertaken in the reign of Pepi II, the successor of Merenre. Pepi became king (*c.* 2250 BC) while he was still a child, and it was as a child that he reacted to the news, sent in dispatch by Harkhuf, that a dwarf had been brought back among the trophies of this last expedition. At once the young king wrote an answer to Harkhuf, who in due time had the whole document carved on part of the façade of his tomb which looked out over the Nile from the high cliffs on the west of the river.[5] The text is laid out in precisely the form of a dispatch written on papyrus, beginning with the characteristically formal address which includes the date: 'Year 2, month 3 of the season *akhet* (commonly translated "autumn"), day 15'. Having acknowledged Harkhuf's dispatch and noted its report, the king continues:

> You said in this your dispatch that you have brought a dwarf [possibly, more correctly, pygmy] . . . like the dwarf brought by the God's Treasurer, Bauwerdjed, from Punt in the time of Isesi. And you said to My Majesty 'Never has his like been brought by anyone else who has reached Yam formerly' . . . Come northwards to the Residence immediately. Hurry, and bring with you this dwarf . . . If he goes down into a boat with you, choose trusty men to be beside him on both sides of the boat in case he falls into the water. If he sleeps by night, choose trusty men to be beside him in his tent. Make inspection ten times a night. My Majesty longs to see this dwarf more than the spoils of the mining country and of Punt. If you reach the Residence with this dwarf safe and sound with you, My Majesty will do more for you than was done for the God's Treasurer, Bauwerdjed, in the time of Isesi.

In this royal letter an individual voice can be recognized in a way that very rarely happens with ancient texts. The young king's spontaneous enthusiasm emerges fresh and unspoiled by maturity; after more than four thousand years it surprises and delights us, just as it must have surprised and delighted the successful adventurer, Harkhuf. It is small wonder that he cherished the document, and arranged for it to be written up on the front of his tomb, where all who passed could see it and read of his royal favour.

To record something in writing was to perpetuate it, and perpetuation of worthy things was in itself a good act in addition to what it might do for the posthumous benefit of the person concerned. Virtue, of course, can equally involve self-interest, and the line is fine and difficult to detect between a good act performed for its own worth, and one executed with calculation for the good it may bring its doer. Khnumhotpe, the provincial ruler of the Oryx nome in Middle Egypt during the reigns of Ammenemes II and Sesostris II of the Twelfth Dynasty, approximately 350 years after Harkhuf's moment of success, found worth mentioning what he had done for his ancestors' memories within the catalogue of his own not insignificant achievements:[6]

> I caused the names of my fathers which I had found destroyed upon the doors [i.e. in the inscriptions on the jambs and lintels of the doors of important buildings] to live again, recognizable in (their) signs, accurate in (their) reading, without substituting one for another. Truly he is a worthy son who has restored the names of his ancestors.

Again Khnumhotpe had reason to show some complacency, and his weakness in this respect need attract no more than moderate censure. For modesty was not particularly applauded in ancient Egypt, even though the boastful man might not be considered quite well behaved: 'Publish your good acts throughout the world so that all men may congratulate you', are words from a long composition of moralistic instructions, which needed little emphasizing.[7] It was important to do good, but it was equally important that it should be known as widely as possible.

As the Egyptians could write, they could record, and in Khnumhotpe's remarks about his ancestors' names, the written word is emphasized. What was written was rendered eternal, until someone came along and destroyed it. Consequently, the text carved on stone seemed more endurable than the composition written on papyrus. The commemoration of deeds was, therefore, a public activity insofar as the carved text in tomb or elsewhere was more certainly to be read and admired than any papyrus document placed wherever it might be in public or domestic archive, tomb or temple. What a private person, no matter how important he was, achieved in his lifetime could only properly be recorded in his tomb. Very occasionally a phrase or two of self-advertisement might be introduced into the commonplace texts addressed to deities, offering adoration or seeking benefits, that were carved on the votive statues placed in sacred precincts. These statements were, however, often framed by the limits of convention and generality, seemingly personal and particular in reference, but clearly trite and unspecific when placed in comparison with the texts of contemporaries, or even of individuals of earlier times. No private inscription, any more than any royal inscription, can be taken in isolation; what one man may say of his career and achievements can only be assessed when the words are examined in the context of the statements of the other known texts of his time.

Few non-royal individuals who exercised official power during the New Kingdom appear to be better known than the great functionary, Senenmut, the favourite agent of Queen Hatshepsut. This queen, the widow of King Tuthmosis II, was presented with the opportunity of seizing supreme royal power in Egypt when she found herself the guardian of her nephew, King Tuthmosis III, when he became king as a minor in about 1490 BC.[8] In a very short time, according to the conventional interpretation accepted by modern historians, firstly as royal regent, and secondly by assuming the forms and trappings of divine royalty, she usurped the government of the country and assigned her nephew to a position of subservience. For approximately twenty years she sustained her supremacy, supported by a group of devoted—and, no doubt, self-seeking—officials, of whom the most prominent seems to have been Senenmut. His principal office, that of 'steward of Amun', was not counted among the very highest official positions of the time, but his influence depended not on the rung he occupied on the ladder of the administrative hierarchy, but on his personal relationship with the queen and with her daughter, Neferure. A measure of Senenmut's power, and a very positive indication of the special favour he enjoyed, are provided by the large number of votive statues of himself which he was able to place in the great sanctuaries of the Theban area, and the two tombs which were prepared for him in the Theban necropolis.[9] And yet, how very little is truly known of this great man! How uninformative are the inscriptions which he felt able to have carved on his statues—statues which were, perhaps in all cases, made while he was alive and in power, and therefore striking testimonies of his favoured position! If one of them may be taken as an example of this reticence, let it be the quartzite squatting, or block, statue in the British Museum, which comes possibly from the Great Temple of Amon-Re at Karnak.[10]

The principal text is contained in nine lines carved on the front of the statue. In it the word 'king' refers to the female Hatshepsut:

> A boon which the King gives (to) Amun, Lord of the Seats of the Two Lands, chief of all the gods, that he may give all that proceeds from his offering-table of every day, on the day of the sixth-day festival, the month-festival, and the half-month festival, and on every festival of heaven and of earth, on the first-day-of-the-year, and on every calendar festival which happens in this temple; (may he also give) his sweet breath, which proceeds from him, and his favour which exists on earth; (all this) for the spirit of the hereditary prince, the count, follower of the King on his journeyings since his childhood, confidant of the King, the one who is in attendance on his feet, who is clear-sighted on the way to the palace, who adorns the Horus who is in this land [i.e. the King], the one who is intact of body, whom his lord has made intact, who understands thoroughly the character of the Lord of the Two Lands, who is pre-eminent of voice in privacy, vigilant in matters commanded him, who alone did what was profitable in the opinion of all, the overseer of all the building works of the King, the guider of him who works with his hands, who is skilled in every secret, who guides the man who knows towards what he does not know, the chamberlain, chief steward, and nurse of the Princess Neferure, the praised one of the Lady of the Two Lands, Senenmut, justified.

The platitudes are continued in a second text which is carved on the upper surface of the statue-base, and around the sides of the base:

> Hereditary prince, count, treasurer of the King of Lower Egypt, chief steward of the princess: He says, '. . . repeated for me the favours of the God's wife, Hatshepsut, may she live; magnified and enriched, I was promoted before the companions, knowing

1 (above) Qurna, the modern village set within the Theban necropolis.
(below) The open court and entrance of the tomb of Rekhmire.

that I was distinguished with her; they set me to be chief of her house, the Palace (may it live, be prosperous, be healthy) being under my supervision, being judge in the whole land, overseer of the granaries of Amun, Senenmut.' He says, 'O God's fathers, ordinary priests, lector priests of Amun, as you praise your gods, you will hand down your offices to your children inasmuch as you say a king's-boon-to-Amun prayer for the spirit of Senenmut.'

Taken in isolation, even in isolation from among the other inscriptions on monuments and statues made for Senenmut, this figure and its texts present a man who clearly occupied a place of highest authority in Egypt during the reign of Queen Hatshepsut. At their face value the texts place him above his fellows in the official hierarchy, without equivocation. But if the texts on the other statues of Senenmut, and on the statues of other Egyptian officials contemporary with Senenmut, and of earlier and later periods, are taken into consideration, much of what is proclaimed about him on the British Museum block-statue is seen to be conventional verbiage. No doubt, the fact that Senenmut was allowed (or felt able) to put such a self-congratulatory collection of epithets, honours, and dignities, on his statue, provides strong confirmation of the eminence of his status. Nevertheless, there is not very much here that others had not been allowed to say about themselves, and nothing is so undistinguished when it comes to praise as the conventional phraseology of praise. What the historian of ancient Egypt looks for in the inscriptions of non-royal persons—and he usually looks in vain—are the unusual statements which can be seen to be particular, to be descriptive of the activities of single individuals. When Senenmut states that he was 'overseer of all the building works of the King', he announces no more than his occupation of a particular office. But something more positive about his achievements as Hatshepsut's 'Minister of Works' can be gleaned from elsewhere. In an inscription roughly carved on a granite outcrop overlooking the Nile at Aswan,[11] Senenmut is shown facing Hatshepsut, 'presenting this work

2 *(above left) Hatshepsut's obelisk in the temple of Karnak.*
  (above right) Quartzite block-statue of Senenmut (BM 1513).
  (below) Hatshepsut presents her obelisks to Amon-Re; a block from the dismantled chapel of the queen at Karnak.

to the God's wife, Mistress of the Two Lands together'. The description of 'this work' is contained in four lines of writing underneath the scene:

> Coming by the hereditary prince, count, great favourite of the God's wife, by whose utterance the Lady of the Two Lands is pleased, the treasurer of the King of Lower Egypt, chief steward of the Princess Neferure, may she live, Senenmut, in order to inspect the work on the two great obelisks of Heh. It happened just as it was commanded that everything be done; it happened because of the power of Her Majesty.

Obelisks formed important features of Egyptian temples, particularly during the New Kingdom. They were elongated derivatives from the *ben-ben*, the cult object of the worship of the sun-god Re at Heliopolis—great shafts of Aswan granite, pointing skywards, with pyramid-shaped tops which in antiquity were often sheathed in precious metal to reflect the rays of the sun.[12] Two pairs were prepared for Queen Hatshepsut, for erection in the Great Temple of Amon-Re at Karnak. Of the second pair, placed in position between the fourth and fifth pylons of the temple in the sixteenth year of her reign, one still stands, a monument of lasting beauty and dignity to the queen. Its shaft is 29.5 metres tall, and the fine hieroglyphs of its inscriptions are as clear and crisp as if they had been cut last year, not 3,460 years ago.

It is now generally thought that this pair of obelisks is not to be identified with the two whose preparation was supervised by Senenmut, because they were erected late in Hatshepsut's reign when Senenmut was either dead or disgraced.[13] His responsibility seems to have been exercised on the pair which was set up elsewhere in the Temple of Karnak in a place before which a small temple was shortly afterwards to be built by Hatshepsut's nephew, Tuthmosis III. The bases of the two obelisks of this second pair are still in position, and many fragments, including the pyramidions, have been found; their sizes suggest that these obelisks may have been even taller than those set up in Year 16.[14]

The cutting and shaping of unflawed shafts of granite into obelisks perhaps as long as 30 metres were not everyday acts of engineering, executed in as routine a way as the regular quarrying of building blocks, or even of other large architectural elements, like architraves, lintels and columns. The successful completion of the whole complex operation of installing a pair of obelisks included the selection of suitable lengths of stone in the bed of the quarry, their extraction, their removal from the quarry to the river, their transference to barges for the journey to the temple site, their conveyance from the barges to the site, and their ultimate erection and carving. The successful achieving of such a sequence was certainly something worthy of record, and indeed Hatshepsut made sure that the record was made. In her mortuary temple a series of reliefs, subsequently deliberately defaced and now difficult to make out, commemorates the bringing and erection of two great obelisks from Aswan to Thebes.[15] These are now thought to be the obelisks the bases alone of which survive. As Senenmut is rightly considered to have been the official most responsible for the design and the building of this funerary temple at Deir el-Bahri, it is fair to conclude that the many unusual episodes pictured in the decoration of the temple were inspired, or at least supervised, by him. It is equally likely that the scene showing the transportation of obelisks contains direct reference to the very obelisks whose extraction from the Aswan quarries was organized by Senenmut.

In at least one other place there is a record of this pair of obelisks. Blocks from a red quartzite chapel set up by Hatshepsut in Karnak, probably in the second year of her usurpation of royal power, include one in which the queen is shown presenting the obelisks to the god Amun for his temple.[16] The review of these various pieces of inscription and representation shows beyond doubt that the obelisk episode was thought worthy of prominent record in important royal buildings. Yet it is not mentioned by Senenmut in any of the inscriptions (some of which are much longer than that quoted above) carved on his votive statues. It is not at all clear why this should be the case, but it must be concluded that some form of inhibition, felt if not specified, deterred even important state officials from enumerating their deeds and achievements in the inscriptions which could be publicly scrutinized during their lifetimes. The privilege of being allowed to have a statue of oneself carved, and then placed in the court or some other part of a temple, was something granted specially by the monarch. The placing of such a statue could not be done on one's own initiative. In commemorating the royal gift through the conventional phrases used to introduce the inscription carved on these statues honour was done as much to the monarch himself as to the subject of the statue. In consequence, the content of an inscription on a private votive statue was commonly non-committal, perhaps trite, and almost certainly only moderately informative. If the historian had to rely on private statues alone for the material from which he might construct his narrative, then for most periods of Egyptian history the record would be even thinner than it actually is. Happily, however, that is not the case. The obelisk episode, as it is reported in the inscriptions and representations which have survived from antiquity, provides an instructive example of what may be discovered about the episode itself, about the individuals principally involved in it, and about the interpretation of ancient written sources, both those that are explicit and those that are uninformative.

If Senenmut may be considered a little further, his case can be seen to be quite unusual. He emerges, in spite of the inhibitive nature of the written records, as a man who not only achieved great power and a privileged position, but also wanted posterity to see precisely what he had achieved. His many votive and other statues in themselves (without regarding their texts) proclaim his importance. And it may be said with confidence that the twenty-three statues, and fragmentary statues so far found, probably do not comprise all those that were made for him in antiquity.[17] Seven statues show Senenmut with the Princess Neferure, indicating a very close relationship with the royal house at the domestic level. Throughout the funerary temple of Hatshepsut at Deir el-Bahri figures of Senenmut are carved in niches and on the reveals of doors—places where they would have been concealed from view when doors were opened.[18] This almost unparalleled demonstration of private publicity was undertaken with the apparent permission of his sovereign, but it seems not unlikely that Senenmut exploited this permission well beyond Hatshepsut's intention. Furthermore, Senenmut is commemorated in a shrine at Gebel es-Silsila and in two tombs in the Theban necropolis.[19] Gebel es-Silsila, the site of important sandstone quarries, and a cult-centre for the worship of the Nile in flood, was no doubt visited by Senenmut in his capacity of Minister of Works. Like others of his contemporaries, he arranged for a shrine to be cut in the cliff overlooking the Nile; it contained a figure of himself, now badly damaged, but in its wrecked condition still suggesting that the child Neferure was shown on his lap. Of the two tombs, one was of the conventional kind prepared for high officials of the period, while the other was somewhat in the form of a modified royal tomb. Unfortunately the decoration of the former has mostly been destroyed by acts of vandalism over the centuries; the decoration of the latter was never completed. Of particular interest is the quartzite sarcophagus which was found in fragments in the first of these tombs; in form it followed the pattern used by royalty during the Eighteenth Dynasty.[20] All in all Senenmut was no ordinary official.

The purpose of this extended discussion of the monuments of Senenmut, and of the obelisk episode in particular, has been to demonstrate the character of much of the written evidence which has survived from ancient Egypt. In the case of Senenmut, his period is one from which many records have been preserved; yet how little they tell of specific events. Further, how little can be learned from them of the personalities of individuals. The banal platitudes and stereotyped phrases of honour and praise for the most part conceal successfully the characters of the high officials who controlled the administration of Egypt under monarchs whose qualities are almost equally delineated in two rather than three dimensions. There can be little depth to the characterization of these people, because they allowed so little of themselves to be included in their inscriptions. A man like Senenmut, who was less than royalty, even though exceptionally important, still allowed himself to be described for posterity in bland, conventional terms, allowing very little to elevate him above the generality of his fellows. He could say that he was more important than they, but he could in no way challenge the position of his sovereign. And as all his greatest works were done for his sovereign, the credit belonged to her.

One only of Senenmut's monuments and records specifically associates him with an important event in Hatshepsut's reign, and that is the inscription at Aswan in which he declares his part in the quarrying of the two great obelisks. This inscription is one of many found in the neighbourhood of Aswan, which was not only a quarrying region, but also the border country between Egypt and Nubia. Egypt, the ancient and complete Kingdom of the Two Lands (Upper and Lower Egypt), found its southern boundary here, and the cataract district of the Nile provided, in the many rocky islands and granite outcrops, abundant places where the leaders of expeditions into Nubia or of commissions in the quarries could leave memorials of their activities. Many of these memorials are precise and specific in their statements of embassies accomplished and of foreign adventures brought to successful conclusions; in them the parts played by high officials are stated without equivocation. Such directness is not found in the inscriptions set up by similar officials during their lifetimes within the land of Egypt proper.

It looks as if the inhibitions which caused the exercise of restraint at home were felt to be less oppressive outside Egypt. Indeed, in all places outside Egypt to which the Egyptian kings sent expeditions in antiquity, carved records are to be found, set up by the leaders of the various expeditions. The practice was particularly common in remote mining and quarrying regions, visits to which involved difficult journeys and many incidental hardships. The exploitation of mineral resources, including the quarrying of stones, was practised under royal monopoly. Expeditions were usually in the charge of important officials, particularly treasury officials. The mining districts in Sinai from which turquoises (and possibly copper) were obtained, the stone quarries of the Wadi Hammamat in the Eastern Desert, and the amethyst mines of the Wadi el-Hudi (also in the Eastern Desert, south-east of Aswan), are specially rich in records of expeditions, and the records are in many cases very informative.[21]

Ostensibly these records were set up in the name of the reigning monarch, but there can be little doubt that the wording of the texts was composed by the individual expedition leaders, or at least written under their instructions. They are, in consequence, far less formal than the impressive stelae set up by Egyptian kings in the course, or at the end, of foreign military expeditions. The treasury official in command of a work-force of miners, a small detachment of troops, and some service personnel, operating far from metropolitan Egypt, and unsupervised by critical officials of higher rank, felt surely a rare emotion of unfettered power. This feeling, and the observation of the records left behind by his precursors who had visited the scene of his commissioned activity, encouraged him to set up his own triumphant record, and emboldened him to include matter which reflected more worthily on himself than on his royal master.

The most historically informative inscriptions of this kind were put up by the leaders of expeditions during the Middle Kingdom, a time when the Egyptian bureaucracy blossomed and flourished with remarkable freedom. One of the most attractive of these inscriptions at Serabit el-Khadim in Sinai commemorates a visit to the mines by the treasury official Harwerre in the sixth year of King Ammenemes III of the Twelfth Dynasty (c. 1836 BC):[22]

> The majesty of this god [i.e. the king] sent the god's treasurer, the intendant, and leader of the gangs, Harwerre, to this mining

land. This land was reached in the third month of winter, certainly not the time of year for visiting this mining land. This god's treasurer says to the officials who may visit this mining land at this time of the year: 'Don't be put out by it. See! Hathor will bring it out all right. Look at my case! I have proved it will happen so. I arrived from Egypt very put out myself, for in my view it would be difficult to find (good) colour [i.e. of turquoise] while the desert land was hot in the summer, when the mountains burnt (one) and the colour was upset. In the morning I (set out?) from Rokhet, and I harangued the craftsmen about it continuously: "How fortunate is he who will be in this mining land!" But they said: "There will always be turquoises in the mountain, but at this season colour is sought (in vain). We have commonly heard similarly that raw material [ore?] is forthcoming at this season of the year, but that colour is certainly lacking from it at this miserable time of summer." But I persisted in setting out for this mining land, my purpose determined by the power of the king. Then I reached this mining land, I began the work at an opportune moment, and my force returned quite complete, without any loss occurring. I was not put out in the face of the labour, for I arrived at just the right moment to start. I broke off in the first month of summer, and brought away this precious stone. I did much more than anyone who had come previously, and much more than all that had been commanded. There was no need for expressions of regret; the colour was good; "The-eyes-are-in-festival" [probably the name of the mine] yielded better than in the regular seasons. Make repeated offerings to the Lady of Heaven; propitiate Hathor; if you do so it will be to your good; if you do more than that, it will turn out good for you. I carried out my expedition very well, and no voice was raised against my work, which I executed with success . . .'

The last few lines of this record are now lost, but it is not likely that they contained more than additional expressions of gratitude to the deity, of honour to the king, and of self-glorification of Harwerre. The lowest part of the stone face carrying this text contains a listing of the junior officials and supervisory craftsmen who supported Harwerre in his endeavour. The most formal part of the inscription, which was on the other side of the monument, has largely been defaced by weathering; it contained the date (happily mostly preserved), the titulary of the reigning monarch, and scenes of offering to the deity of the mining region, the goddess Hathor. It is, however, the greatest piece of good fortune that has allowed the preservation of the quite remarkable testimony of Harwerre concerning his expedition to the mines. It may not have been particularly unusual in the manner of its composition and the nature of its content, for many other inscriptions, set up by other expedition leaders during the Middle Kingdom, but now badly damaged, give hints of equally informal statements. Nevertheless, Harwerre's record is practically intact, and it gives a lively account of an expedition which seemed doomed to failure by mistiming, but which in the end turned out well. The understandable pride of the leader of the expedition in his handling of the matter makes little allowance for the fact that he was acting under orders. The successful outcome was scarcely to be predicted, unless the whole bias of the report is wrongly weighted. Yet much can be deduced from this inscription of Harwerre and from others which record similar expeditions, not only about the mounting and organization of mining activities, but also about the conditions under which they were conducted. And something of humanity can be discerned in the attitudes of expedition leaders to the forces under their command.

By their very nature, however, monumental texts, whether royal or private, formal or informal, metropolitan or provincial, suffer the limitations imposed by the spaces available for their carving, and by the laborious nature of the hieroglyphic script. Even the seemingly lengthy records of conquest and of campaigning set up by King Tuthmosis III at Karnak, or by King Ramesses III on the extensive walls of his funerary temple of Medinet Habu, are characterized by brevity of expression and absence of incidental detail. And it is an interesting observation that in general the more confident and successful the monarch, the more laconic are his formal records. It is hardly surprising that this should be so, for failure or near-failure, if it has to be recorded at all, needs to be explained away. Hence the unusually long-winded compositions which Ramesses II had composed to cover up his near-failure at the Battle of Qadesh; and also the numerous publications of these compositions on prominent walls in temples, some of which were visible even to the Egyptian populace at large.

In the case of the Annals of Tuthmosis III, the record of his campaigns and conquests between the twenty-second and forty-second years of his reign (the years that followed the domination of Queen Hatshepsut) provides a graphic example of the tendency to brevity which accompanied success. The text was put together from the written records of the successive campaigns, preserved, no doubt, on papyri in the official archives; it was specifically not a transcript of the original documents, but a digest prepared as a memorial to the triumphs of the great king. Carved on the walls surrounding the innermost part of the Temple of Karnak, where it would not have been visible to any except initiated priests, it is not particularly well preserved; but enough has survived to indicate both the flavour of the whole and the nature of the intention.[23] Its last words state precisely:

> Lo! His Majesty commanded that the victories be set up, which he accomplished from Year 23 down to Year 42, when this inscription was set up in this sanctuary, that he might achieve long life for ever.

The abbreviated nature of these Annals is clearly confirmed by a statement made in the course of an enumeration of booty and tribute obtained during the seventh campaign in Year 31:

> They are more numerous than anything, than even the knowledge of this Majesty's army, without overstating the case. They are fully recorded in the daily account of the royal palace—may it live, be prosperous and healthy. Their full number is not given in this inscription so as not to make the words too many, and in order to render them effective in this place in which they are made.

Nevertheless, within the tight limits of the wall-space available for the carving of this retrospective record, the concision was in places relaxed, always, of course, to the advantage of the victorious monarch. In no place was the record allowed to spread so much as in the account of the Battle of Megiddo which was fought in the course of the first victorious campaign beginning in Year 22 (about 1468 BC). Tuthmosis III began his programme to re-establish the power of Egypt in Asia by leading his army against a coalition of Palestinian and Syrian princelings who had raised the standard of rebellion (or, perhaps more strictly, had declared their independence), and had gathered their forces by the town of Megiddo in northern Palestine. It was the beginning of the long series of campaigns which, for Tuthmosis, confirmed his reputation as a mighty warrior. It is, therefore, not surprising that the officials who laid out the texts to be inscribed as the monumental record of his campaigns, chose—perhaps with a persuasive nod from the direction of the Palace—to emphasize the events of the initial campaign. In so doing the stage was set, the pattern of campaign and victory established. For the years that followed success in detail need not be written into the inscription.

So for this first campaign the monumental record contains not only a careful account of the actual military proceedings but also some reporting of the councils of war in which the strategy of the campaign was discussed. The officers of the army were shown debating with the king the route by which the advance should proceed. They question the king's choice, and urge him to follow another road. But the king stands firm in his decision, and the officers at last concur: 'See! We are in the following of Your Majesty wherever Your Majesty goes. The servant will accompany his Lord.' This discussion may appear to be more apparent than real. The king consults his officers, but he has no intention of following their advice. The outcome of the battle accords with his strategy; his merit, therefore, appears all the greater. The modern reader, unfortunately, must wonder to what extent the written record has been subjected to a form of editing to produce precisely the reaction the king would want. Contrivance of this kind is a subtle form of propaganda, and it is fascinating to see its apparent use in an historical inscription of three thousand five hundred years ago.

Without the need to impress the spectator of a publicly exposed inscription, the official record inscribed on papyrus and deposited in the state archives was, we may suppose, more prosaic and less heavily weighted with verbose pomposity and blatant *parti pris*. That official records were less flamboyant in their style and content can, sadly, only be supposed because no documents of the kind envisaged as the basis for the carved record of Tuthmosis III's campaigns have survived. The one great royal record on papyrus that has been preserved contains unfortunately not a narrative of campaigns and conquest, but a list of temple donations made by King Ramesses III during his long reign (*c.* 1193–1162 BC). And this document, the Great Harris Papyrus in the British Museum, was written immediately after the death of the king for deposit, probably, in his tomb.[24] So it cannot be treated as a true archival record.

In the field of official, other than royal, records the position, happily, is very different, for many documents have survived from antiquity, preserving accounts of judicial and other proceedings which were the concern of royal officers. The bulk of those now to be found in museums throughout the world comes from Thebes; they are dated to the later dynasties of the New Kingdom. It is known that many of those that have survived came from the archives preserved in the administrative complex of buildings which was established around the funerary temple of Ramesses III in that part of Western Thebes known today as Medinet Habu. Here, during the Twentieth Dynasty and later (after c. 1150 BC) all the senior officials who controlled the running of the huge necropolis of Thebes (which included the Valleys of the Kings' Tombs and Queens' Tombs) had their offices. The records of their activities were, as we shall see later, deposited in archives from which they could be retrieved by properly authorized persons if ever they might be required for reference or study. From the dates when many documents, which must have come from the Medinet Habu archives, entered the collections of the modern world, it seems certain that deposits of documents were discovered during the middle years of the nineteenth century. Whether by chance, or in the course of illicit excavation, the discoveries could not have been made under much less satisfactory conditions, for no record was made of the nature of the archival arrangements, and no one knows how many documents survived the casual circumstances of their discovery.

Odd things happened to some of the papyrus rolls retrieved in these early days of uncontrolled ransacking. One of the strangest stories attaches to one of the papyri named after the first Baron Amherst of Hackney. It consisted of the lower half of a roll containing records of the legal examination of prisoners implicated in a series of robberies in royal and private tombs in the late Twentieth Dynasty. It had been acquired in Egypt in the mid-nineteenth century, the precise date unfortunately not now being known. In 1913, a few years after Lord Amherst's death, his papyri were purchased by Pierpont Morgan, and they now reside in the Pierpont Morgan Library in New York City. Many years later, Jean Capart, the great Belgian Egyptologist, made a remarkable discovery. On 5 February 1935, he went to the Musées Royaux d'Art et d'Histoire du Cinquantenaire in Brussels to examine a group of Egyptian antiquities presented by King Leopold III. Among them was a wooden figure of a kind sometimes used to contain funerary papyri deposited in tombs. The cavity in this figure was plugged with a piece of cloth, and when it was removed, a roll of papyrus was found inside. Amazingly it turned out to be not a funerary papyrus, but the missing half of the Amherst Papyrus in almost perfect condition. The figure had been obtained in Egypt by the Duke of Brabant, later King Leopold II, on one of his visits in 1854 or in 1862–3. It is usually thought that the men who looted the Medinet Habu archive building took this papyrus (now known as the Leopold II and Amherst Papyrus), and cut the roll in two, either as part of the physical division of spoils, or in order to sell the parts piecemeal. For some reason one half was inserted into a wooden funerary figure in no way connected with it, and there it remained, overlooked and forgotten, passing perhaps through the hands of several owners before it emerged to the delight of scholars in 1935.[25]

Indeed, the Leopold II and Amherst Papyrus remains a delight to scholars. Superficially it is a splendid-looking document (it was briefly united and photographed after the discovery of the Brussels half), written in a bold, flowing, hieratic script, the hand of a master scribe. It is assessed to be a true archival document, a piece of the raw material of history, bearing a text which records events as they happened, and not presented to honour, in distorted terms, the actions of a king. It contains, moreover, statements of such unusual interest that they place it in the first rank of human documents. The stone-mason Amen-panufer under examination before the vizir and other high officials explains how he, with some others, 'fell into the habit of robbing tombs'. Three years before this examination they had gone to rob tombs 'according to their regular habit', and had entered the burial chamber of King Sobkemsaef II, a king of the Seventeenth Dynasty, who had been buried approximately four hundred and fifty years before that time:

> . . . We took lighted candles in our hands, and we went down, and we demolished the rubble we found at the entry to his recess, and we found this god [the king] lying at the rear of his place of burial. And we found the burial place of the royal consort Nubkhas, his consort, by his side, protected and guarded with plaster and covered with rubble. We broke through it also and found it [the queen's coffin] resting there likewise. We opened their outer and inner coffins, in which they were, and we found this noble mummy of this king equipped with a small curved sword, a large number of amulets and ornaments of gold on his neck, and his gold mask on

him. The noble mummy of this king was completely decked out with gold, and his coffins were overlaid with gold and silver, inside and outside, and inlaid with all kinds of decorative stones. We gathered the gold which we found on this noble mummy of this king, with the amulets and ornaments on his neck, and (the gold of) the coffins in which he rested; and we found the consort in precisely the same state. We gathered all that we found on her also, and we set fire to their coffins. And we took the furniture we found with them—things of gold, silver and bronze—and divided them between ourselves: we made the gold which we found on these two gods, from their mummies, amulets, ornaments, and coffins, into 8 parts. 20 *deben* of gold fell to each one of us, 8 men, making 160 *deben* of gold, not counting the fragments of furniture.

Continuing the evidence, Amenpanufer recalls that the district officials got to hear of these thieving expeditions, and some days after the desecration of Sobkemsaef's burial he was taken into custody to the office of the mayor of Thebes. By bribing one of the officials with his share of 20 *deben* of gold he managed to secure his release.[26] Joining up with his confederates he received a compensatory share, and together they set about robbing the tombs again, as he said, 'up to today. And a large number of men of the land rob them likewise, being in effect partners (of ours).'

Not many ancient Egyptian documents provide equally graphic, and eminently trustworthy, accounts of happenings which illuminate so brilliantly the shadows of remote antiquity. This is not to say that we should unreservedly accept the details of the evidence given by Amenpanufer. Given some years after the robbery, and extracted almost certainly under duress, it comes out clear and in order, at least as set down by the court clerk. It was probably tidied up a bit for the record. Nevertheless, the habitual practice of tomb-robbery among artisans working in and about Thebes in the late Twentieth Dynasty is made very clear, and need not be doubted. What further documents remain hidden away, like the Leopold II Papyrus (or half-papyrus)? The unexpected has happened so often in the course of modern Egyptology that it might be postulated with some hope of fulfilment that the share of documents taken by one of the men who plundered the Medinet Habu archives may yet lie forgotten and undisturbed in some cache.

The stone-mason Amenpanufer was a craftsman who had turned his skills to improper use. Ancient Thebes was full of craftsmen whose services were needed for the maintenance and continuation of life in one of the most extensive cities of antiquity. They were also needed for the provision of tombs and tomb-equipment for the life hereafter. An élite corps of craftsmen was maintained at royal expense especially to work on the tomb of the reigning monarch. A 'model' village was provided for them, and there they lived, with their families, a segregated, almost imprisoned existence. Among their number, apart from builders and excavators of tombs, were the artists and craftsmen who decorated the tombs, and the scribes who saw to the administration of the work, and the day-to-day matters arising from their life and employment. The standard of literacy found among the inhabitants of this village (the place today is known as Deir el-Medina) seems to have been exceptional, and a measure of its virtual universality, at least among the senior craftsmen of all trades, is provided not only by the wealth of inscribed objects found in the houses of the village, but also by the many thousands of inscribed limestone flakes and potsherds recovered from the village and its vicinity.[27]

These casual writings, the memoranda and jottings of a literate community, written informally on what are regularly called ostraca now, cover almost all aspects of daily life for which writing was needed. They bear accounts, notes of work in hand, work completed, lists of workmen and of their tools and rations. They were used also by student scribes for the writing out of practice passages from the classics of Egyptian literature. All in all they provide the modest aspect of ancient records, the proper counter to the great royal inscriptions and the official records of the archives. In so many of the ostraca-texts we may taste the true flavour of life in ancient Egypt outside the ambit of court and the nobility. One text demonstrates the difficulty of getting what is rightfully owed when the borrower is a policeman. The workman Menna describes how he endeavoured to get payment for a pot of fat he had sold to Mentmose, a police officer:[28]

Year 17, day [blank] of the first month of summer in the reign of Usermare-Miamun [Ramesses III]. On that day the workman Menna gave the pot of fresh fat to the chief of Medjay [police] Mentmose, who said: 'I will pay you for it with barley from this brother of mine who will be responsible. He is my guarantor. May

46

Pre [the god Re] keep you in health!' So he said to me. Three times have I reported him in the court before the scribe of the tomb Amennakhte; he has up to today given me nothing. And see! I reported him to him [i.e. the scribe of the Tomb] on the fifth day of the second month of summer in the third year of King Heqmare-Setpenamun [Ramesses IV], that is eleven years later. He took an oath by the Lord, saying: 'If I do not pay him for this pot before the last day of the third summer month of the third year, I shall receive a hundred blows with the stick, and shall be liable to pay double.' So he said before the three domestic captains, the external agents, and the whole gang [of workmen].

Why the record of such a transaction and its subsequent complications should have been written down on an ostracon is not at all clear; but it is for us enough to appreciate its contents and to marvel at the preservation of such a small nugget of historical gold. And it is not alone. While very many of the ostraca from the workmen's village carry literary and religious texts, many hundreds bear business documents of the various kinds mentioned earlier. Together they bring one close to the daily activities of people who, while not being exactly simple, were in no way part of the governing class. From most of the other periods of Egyptian history similar texts have survived, both in the form of ostraca and written on papyrus, but never in such profusion as those of Deir el-Medina.

It needs no special advocacy to demonstrate the value of this kind of documentation for the writing of social and economic history—the kinds of history which are not commonly expected for the most ancient literate cultures. Sadly, the great bulk of non-official, non-literary, documents belongs not simply to a fairly short span of about 300 years—short, that is, by the side of Egypt's 3,000-year dynastic history—but also to one place—the Theban necropolis—and within that area to a fairly small and somewhat unrepresentative community. The picture derived from Deir el-Medina texts is, therefore, rather partial. Yet from much that it reveals of procedures in the handling of labour, the maintenance of accounts, the attitudes towards litigation and the ways by which legal redress might be sought, the ethics of economic transactions, and in other generalized activities, proper conclusions can reasonably be drawn about the same fields of action and behaviour in other sections of the ancient Egyptian community at large, both contemporaneously and for other periods. In drawing general conclusions from the particular evidence of the royal workmen's village, the similar, but scanty, texts of other periods can be invoked for comparison and for corroborative purposes. That they can so be used with some confidence is founded on the remarkable stability and conservatism of Egyptian life, particularly rural life, over the millennia. Even today, in an Egypt far removed chronologically from the end of the Pharaonic Period, where many and great changes have been wrought in recent years, it is still possible to go about the countryside and find simple practices in daily life very similar to those of antiquity. The scenes of husbandry and simple artisan activity found in ancient Egyptian tombs are played out before one's eyes in the fields, particularly in the Delta and in parts of Middle Egypt. In the course of this book from time to time in text and in illustration the present day will be used to illuminate antiquity. The sense of the past in the present is a remarkable phenomenon of Egypt, perhaps the more remarkable because there is no general feeling of identity with their Pharaonic past among the majority of modern Egyptians. But the great monuments which stand proud throughout the land accommodate themselves in the landscape with no incongruity; and even the mighty colossus of Ramesses II, until recently mounted in the square in front of Cairo's main railway station, looked in no way out of place in the bustle and traffic of an overcrowded modern city.

NOTES

1 The text of *The Instruction for Merikare* is contained in Papyrus Leningrad 1116A. For a good modern translation, see M. Lichtheim, *Ancient Egyptian Literature*, I, 97 ff. The passage quoted is ll.35 ff.

2 For a study of the whole Qadesh text, see Sir Alan Gardiner, *The Kadesh Inscriptions of Ramesses II* (Oxford, 1960).

3 For this inscription, see B. Porter, R. L. B. Moss and J. Málek, *Topographical Bibliography of Ancient Egyptian Hieroglyphic Texts*, III, 2 ed., Pt. I (Oxford, 1974), 39 f.

4 Illustrated in *Luxor Museum of Ancient Egyptian Art* (Cairo, 1979), 68 f. The probability of Amenophis II's claim is tested and found wanting by E. Edel in *Studien zur altägyptischen Kultur* 7 (1979), 39.

5 For the hieroglyphic text, see K. Sethe, *Urkunden des Alten Reichs* (Leipzig, 1932), 128–31. The whole inscription is translated in M. Lichtheim, op. cit., 23 ff.

6 The text is published in P. E. Newberry, *Beni Hasan* I (London, 1893), pls. XXV, XXVI. The lines quoted are 161–8.

7 From *The Instruction of Amenemope*, 10, 15. The text is on British Museum Papyrus 10474, and translated by M. Lichtheim, op. cit., II, 146 ff.

8 See W. C. Hayes in *Cambridge Ancient History*, II, 3 ed., Pt. 1 (Cambridge, 1973), 317 f.

9 A study of the Senenmut monuments is made by C. Meyer, *Senenmut. Eine prosopographische Untersuchung* (Hamburg, 1982). His first tomb (no. 71 in the Theban necropolis), was superseded by a second (no. 353) late in his career, that was abandoned, unfinished, presumably at the time of his disgrace.

10 British Museum no. 1513; the texts are published in H. R. H. Hall, *Hieroglyphic Texts ... in the British Museum*, 5 (London, 1914), pl. 29.

11 See L. Habachi in *Journal of Near Eastern Studies* 16 (Chicago, 1957), 92.

12 A good general account of obelisks can be found in L. Habachi, *The Obelisks of Egypt* (London, 1977).

13 Sir Alan Gardiner, *Egypt of the Pharaohs*, 185.

14 A. Varille in *Annales du Service des Antiquités de l'Égypte* 50 (Cairo, 1950), 140 ff.

15 The scenes are reproduced in drawings in É. Naville, *The Temple of Deir el Bahari*, VI (London, 1908), pls. 153–5.

16 *Luxor Museum of Ancient Egyptian Art* (Cairo, 1979), 46 f. Also Pl. 2 (*below*).

17 The statues so far known are listed by C. Meyer, op. cit., 28 ff.

18 See W. C. Hayes in *Mitteilungen des Deutschen Archäologischen Instituts Abteilung Kairo* 15 (Wiesbaden, 1957), 80 ff.

19 For the shrine, see R. A. Caminos and T. G. H. James, *Gebel es-Silsilah*, I (London, 1963), 53 ff.

20 Reconstruction published by W. C. Hayes in *Journal of Egyptian Archaeology* 36 (London, 1950), 19 ff. It is now on exhibition in the Metropolitan Museum of Art, New York.

21 For Sinai, see A. H. Gardiner, T. E. Peet, and J. Černý, *The Inscriptions of Sinai*, I, 2 ed. (London, 1952); II (London, 1955). For the Wadi Hammamat, J. Couyat and P. Montet, *Les inscriptions hiéroglyphiques et hiératiques du Ouâdi Hammâmât* (Cairo, 1912). For the Wadi el-Hudi, A. Fakhry, *Inscriptions of the Amethyst Quarries at Wadi*

el Hudi (Cairo, 1952); A. I. Sadek, *The Amethyst Mining Inscriptions*, I (Warminster, 1980). Generally, see K.-J. Seyfried, *Beiträge zu den Expeditionen des Mittleren Reiches in die Ost-Wüste* (Hildesheim, 1981).

22 *Inscriptions of Sinai*, II, p. 97 f.

23 Still to receive a full publication. For a useful translation, see J. H. Breasted, *Ancient Records of Egypt*, II, 163 ff. Records of this kind are usefully discussed in A. J. Spalinger, *Aspects of the Military Documents of the Ancient Egyptians* (New Haven, 1982).

24 A convenient text is in W. Erichsen, *Papyrus Harris I* (Brussels, 1933); a translation in J. H. Breasted, *Ancient Records*, IV, 87 ff.

25 The story of this papyrus is told by J. Capart, A. H. Gardiner and B. van de Walle in *Journal of Egyptian Archaeology* 22 (London, 1936), 169 ff.; a full translation of the text is also given.

26 A *deben* was a unit of weight, weighing about 91 grammes.

27 A good general account of the village and the workmen is given in M. L. Bierbrier, *The Tomb-Builders of the Pharaohs*.

28 See J. Černý, *A Community of Workmen at Thebes in the Ramesside Period*, 282 f.

2
THE VIZIR AND HIS ROLE

A thriving bureaucracy existed in Egypt as early as the First Dynasty; the small, inexplicit, texts found in the great royal and noble burials of that time contain titles which were subsequently to be found attached to officials serving the kings of the Old Kingdom and later.[1] Egypt was a land which, by its very geographical form, demanded careful administration. Six hundred miles of Nile Valley from Memphis, approximately at the apex of the Delta, south to Aswan was a stretch of country with length but little breadth. The Delta, on the other hand, was a vast, broad district broken up by waterways and marshy areas. Communication was tedious by land, but easy by water. If administration was not good it was difficult to maintain a centralized control over the whole land. In consequence, in periods of weak administration Egypt tended to fall apart, reverting to a string of antagonistic provinces, ruled by chiefs who attempted, usually unsuccessfully, to conduct their affairs independently of their neighbours. The periods when the central power of the king was greatest were characterized by good administration. In the Old and Middle Kingdoms much of this administration was devolved to the provinces, or nomes, and controlled by the nomarchs, the provincial governors. They, by hereditary succession, established minor principalities within the general ambit of royal power. Such were Harkhuf and Khnumhotpe, whom we have already met. Their power and independence, however, always represented a threat to the central authority, and during the Twelfth Dynasty a complete reorganization of provincial administration was undertaken by King Sesostris III. As a result the old system of hereditary nomarchs was destroyed and replaced by a bureaucratic machinery, the operators of which owed their allegiance directly to the king in his residence.[2]

This change took place in about 1860 BC, and to some extent the consequent redeployment of administrative power helped to minimize the worst effects of the dissolution of central control which occurred during the Second Intermediate Period. This was the time of the Hyksos domination of most of northern Egypt, when the southern parts of the land found stability only in Thebes, where the vizir, the principal officer of the king, kept the diminished ship of state on a reasonably even keel. His role at that time will be more fully explained shortly. The survival, if only vestigially, of this bureaucratic system certainly contributed substantially to the success of the kings of the Eighteenth Dynasty in establishing rapidly their control throughout Egypt after the expulsion of the Hyksos.

It would be quite proper to speak of the Egyptian system of bureaucracy during the Eighteenth Dynasty as a civil service. The practice of official authority was inspired by disinterested service and justice on the part of the bureaucrats in the interests of the king and of his subjects. At least, that was the declared theory. At the head of the pyramid of authority was the vizir, and he was supported in all his duties by officials who mostly bore scribal titles. Being a scribe was almost synonymous with being a civil servant and, as we shall see in Chapter Five, to become a scribe was a noble ambition, about which the scribal profession—the principal repository of literacy and learning in the land—never ceased to boast. The mastery of reading and writing were essential for the proper exercise of administration, and the scribal schools, of which more will be said later, were undoubtedly the academies for the bureaucracy. Throughout this book we shall observe scribes at work, administering justice, assessing and gathering taxes, sitting on commissions and writing reports. And all their activities in the public domain were theoretically controlled by the vizir.[3]

During the mid-Eighteenth Dynasty (c. 1450 BC), the holder of the office of vizir was Rekhmire. He occupied his high office mostly during the reign of Tuthmosis III, but he carried on into the following reign of Amenophis II, until his career ended, perhaps violently, almost certainly with disgrace. He is in many respects the epitome of the vizir, and his fame rests principally on the splendour of his tomb-chapel which has been described in the Introduction. Although the decorations on the walls of this remarkable chapel are badly damaged in part, they remain a rich source not only of textual information about the vizir's office, but also of the many crafts which enriched the material quality of Egyptian life (*Fig. 2*).

Some licence attends the use of the term 'vizir' to describe the office

Fig. 2 The vizir Rekhmire and his wife Meryt.

occupied by Rekhmire. It is properly used to denote the chief minister in a Moslem state. In ancient Egypt the chief minister was called ⟨hieroglyphs⟩ in the hieroglyphic script, *tjaty* in modern transcription. It cannot be translated directly into English; in consequence 'vizir', being a closely parallel oriental title, has been used to designate the *tjaty*; it will be used in this sense throughout. The office of vizir in ancient Egypt can be traced back to the early Old Kingdom with certainty, and possibly to the very time of the unification of Upper and Lower Egypt at the beginning of the First Dynasty (*c.* 3000 BC), but in those early times the character of the office was probably very different from what it became later. The autocracy of the king in the first half-millennium of dynastic history was absolute; the administration of the country, apart from being on a smaller scale, was developed as a kind of extension of the power of the king, who was in all senses the State. Like most high offices, the vizirate was occupied by men of highest rank, and usually relatives of the king. Very little is known about the activities of the vizir in the Old Kingdom, but it becomes clear that by the time of the Sixth Dynasty the close family links between the king and the highest officers of state had become greatly slackened. In the Middle Kingdom the deliberate policy of the kings of the later Twelfth Dynasty, though aimed at destroying the feudal authority of provincial governors or nomarchs, enhanced considerably the authority and power of the vizir; and it was this position of supremacy in the Egyptian bureaucracy which was carried forward into the regime established during the Eighteenth Dynasty.

In fact, during the period between the Middle Kingdom and the Eighteenth Dynasty, and particularly at the early part of this Second Intermediate Period, as it is generally called, the vizirate had achieved its highest point of authority *vis-à-vis* the crown. In a time which remains hopelessly obscure, the succession of Egyptian kings developed a momentum which defies rational historical explanation. In the surviving king-lists for the Thirteenth Dynasty reign follows reign with bewildering speed, and the only stability in the Theban monarchy seems to have been provided by the vizir. In the absence of really informative documents it is not possible to do more than speculate about the political situation which produced such an unusual pattern of succession. Vizirs, like the relatively well-documented Ankhu, served perhaps as many as five kings. Ankhu seems to have succeeded his grandfather and to have been succeeded by two of his sons. Later vizirs during the Thirteenth Dynasty also seem to have been directly related with the line of Ankhu.[4] On the other hand, it has been observed that the kings who succeeded each other at the same period seem rarely to have been related to each other. The traditional pattern of inherited kingship supported by vizirs appointed according to ability and not through family influence, seems to have been turned wholly upside down. It was at this time, as we have noted, that the power and prestige of the vizirs achieved their highest points, and it is possible that it was at this time also that the formulation of the duties and responsibilities of the vizir was written down, to serve as a guide for action and as a stimulation of conscience for vizirs in the future. When we move forward to the time of the vizirate of Rekhmire, we find that while the Egyptian throne has become immeasurably stronger, the office of vizir has not altogether lost the particular advantages it gained in the Thirteenth Dynasty.

In one particular, however, the vizirate in the Eighteenth Dynasty and later was very different from the office in earlier times. It was, for clearly good administrative reasons, split into two, with a vizir in the north controlling the northern part of Upper Egypt and the whole of the Delta, while the Theban vizir managed affairs in the south. It seems possible that this division dates back to the preceding Second Inter-mediate Period when the split in authority in Egypt between the Theban kingship and the power of the Asiatic Hyksos in the north represented a division in the land of Egypt similar to that found in the domains of the two vizirs of the Eighteenth Dynasty and later. Unfortunately little is known about the activities of the northern vizir, whose base was probably Memphis, the most ancient capital of united Egypt. It could be scarcely doubted that his responsibilities were quite as great as, if not greater than, those of his Theban colleague, par-ticularly as his territory was larger. The richness of material remains surviving from antiquity in the Theban area has, on the other hand, given the Theban vizirs a particular advantage in the lottery of fame. Even the succession of the northern vizirs is not established; their names, up to now at least, have not in all cases been 'made to live'—as they would have wished. Their time, however, was yet to come, for the political centre of gravity in Egypt was to shift during the Nineteenth Dynasty to the north of the country. This move was brought about particularly by the establishment of the principal royal Residence in the Eastern Delta, at a place newly named, appropriately, Piramesse, 'the House of Ramesses'. It seems certain that for the greater part of the year the king and his court lived in this place which was, in the terms of literary hyperbole, a paradise on earth, where people, herds, and crops prospered as nowhere else, a city 'beautiful with its balconies, shining with halls of lapis-lazuli and of turquoise'.[5] With the king in the north, the vizir of the north assumed greater importance than formerly.

In spite of the clear political advantage held by the northern vizir from the Nineteenth Dynasty onwards, the Theban vizir apparently retained his superior position in the bureaucratic hierarchy of the land for most of the New Kingdom, his supremacy resting on the power of tradition and his intimate control of most of the activities centred in Thebes. Throughout the New Kingdom Thebes remained the religious capital of Egypt, the shrine of Amun serving almost as the metropolitan cathedral of the land. Amun, the imperial god, received the bulk of the tribute of empire. This was true for the great days of the Eighteenth

Dynasty, and it was still so in the Twentieth Dynasty, as the donations recorded in the Great Harris Papyrus testify. To Thebes the king came for certain of the great festivals in the calendar of the religious year; to Thebes he came to render thanks to Amun for his victories in foreign lands; to Thebes he came, finally, to be buried. In all the ceremonies of life and death the vizier played a central role, and it was probably the case that he frequently deputized for the king in the great Theban occasions, if the king could not be present. Whether the king was in residence in Thebes or not, the superior position of the vizier was assured. Never was he so obviously supreme as in the Eighteenth Dynasty, and part of his strength came from the perpetuation of the hereditary principle which we have seen developing in the Thirteenth Dynasty. It would be incorrect to claim without reservation that the office was strictly hereditary at the period when it was occupied by Rekhmire; but it can be observed that his grandfather, Aametju, was vizier under Hatshepsut, that his uncle, Useramun, held the same office in the early years of Tuthmosis III, and that his father, Neferuben, was apparently northern vizier more or less contemporaneously with Useramun. The fact that the succession passed out of the family after Rekhmire's fall from office—if indeed it was a fall—demonstrates that the hereditary principle was more apparent than actual.

Although coming from a family of viziers, and therefore being well acquainted with the trappings of power, Rekhmire shows himself in his tomb to have been immensely proud of his high office, and determined to leave to posterity a fitting memorial of his greatness; and through this memorial he might hope to reap the appropriate posthumous benefits by the magical revivification of the scenes painted on its walls. In his own semi-autobiographical text, which is to be found on the south wall of the transverse hall, he sets out his virtues plainly in broad, but conventional, terms:[6]

> The hereditary prince, steward of stewards, master of the secrets, who goes into the sanctuary, from whom the god keeps nothing excluded; there is nothing he does not know in heaven or earth, or in any secret place in the underworld . . . He says: 'I was a noble, being second with the king . . . occupying a forward position in the privy chamber, praised at every moment . . . first in the estimation of the ordinary people . . . I was called again into the presence of the good god, the King of Upper and Lower Egypt, Menkheperre

[Tuthmosis III] . . . His Majesty opened his mouth and spoke his words before me . . . "You should act according to all that I say, and Ma'at [Truth and Order] will rest in her place" . . . I acted according to his orders . . . Now I was the heart of the Lord, may he live, be prosperous and healthy, the ears and eyes of the Sovereign. Truly I was his very own skipper; I knew not sleep by night as by day . . . I raised up Ma'at to the heights of heaven; I made her beauty circulate over the breadth of the land, so that she rested in their [i.e. men's] nostrils like the north wind when it has driven out evil from heart and body. I judged both [the insignificant] and the influential; I rescued the weak man from the strong man; I deflected the fury of the evil man and subdued the greedy man in his hour . . . I succoured the widow who has no husband; I established the son and heir on the seat of his father. I gave [bread to the hungry], water to the thirsty, and meat, oil and clothes to him who had nothing . . . I was not at all deaf to the indigent. Indeed I never took a bribe from anyone . . .'

With very much more in similar vein Rekhmire reviews his achievements and extols his virtues. The sentiments are, as we have already pointed out, conventional, but they are expressed here with a lavish use of hyperbole, and a variety of statement unusually rich even for an Egyptian official of the highest order. The reading of such a catalogue of virtues should be accompanied by the realization that Rekhmire composed (or had composed for him) this text for his posthumous benefit, and not in order to improve his position in the eyes of his fellows while he was still alive. It was part of his testament to posterity, and while it may, or may not, properly reflect the truth of his own official career, it undoubtedly embodies the ideas of justice, charity, understanding and kindliness which formed the guiding ethic of Egyptian public life. No finer sentiments for the inspiration of public behaviour are to be found in other literate cultures of antiquity. Ideas of vengeance and retribution are subdued almost to the point of disappearance. The emphasis rests on a positive response to the weakness and miserable state of those less fortunate in life, and on a suppression of the unfortunate characteristics which tend to accompany power and wealth. This altogether laudable order of priorities was in a sense written into the code of action by which the vizir, and, at more modest level, all government officials were expected to exercise their authority.

The small repertory of compositions which make up the 'library' of Egyptian literature contains a number of works which are termed *sebayt* (instructions) in Egyptian. These 'instructions' generally purport to represent the testaments of wisdom passed on by the wise for the guidance of the young. The most famous was ascribed to Ptahhotpe, vizir of King Djedkare Isesi of the Fifth Dynasty (*c.* 2350–2310 BC). In the preamble to the main substance of the work Ptahhotpe explains to his king why he wishes to take an assistant in his old age:[7]

> Then shall I tell him the words of the judges, the counsels of those who were of old, who formerly attended to the gods.

To this King Isesi replies:

> Instruct him then in what was said in the past that he may provide a worthy copy for the children of officials, that proper judgement and all precision may enter him. Speak to him. There never was a wise child.

Ptahhotpe then launches into his instructions. They cover both public and private behaviour, and in sum constitute a pretty general guide to action. Although Ptahhotpe is credited implicitly with their composition, it is not generally thought likely that he was in fact their author, except perhaps by tradition and reputation. The Egyptians were excessively attentive to tradition, to that wisdom inherent in knowledge that had been handed down over the generations, and which might in consequence be thought of as tested by time. They were ancestor-reverers, if not worshippers, and this reverence for the past was best concentrated when it was focused on the great men of yore— those whose reputations had survived the vicissitudes of history. The educated Egyptian of the bureaucratic ranks and above saw himself as part of the tradition and expected to continue it and, if fate worked in his favour, to be part of it in future times. Ptahhotpe, the famed vizir of Djedkare Isesi—we do not know why he was famed, but it could scarcely have been for his homely wisdom alone—was one of those so remembered, but the *Instructions* credited to him were probably put together during the Twelfth Dynasty (*c.* 1900 BC), to judge from the language, phraseology and style, and from the fact that the earliest surviving text can be dated to that time.[8] The Twelfth Dynasty was the age when many of the real classics of Egyptian literature were composed or, if not composed, put into relatively firm literary moulds from which texts emerged more or less established in the forms in which they were to survive for generations; indeed, in some cases well into the New Kingdom. Ptahhotpe's *Instructions* remained one of these classics for almost one thousand years.

Another composition which may find its origins in the Middle Kingdom, though probably not as early as the first reigns of the Twelfth Dynasty, was designed more explicitly to instruct the vizir himself in the ways and responsibilities of his high office. In Rekhmire's tomb it is inscribed in the transverse hall in the southern section and on the west wall.[9] The ceremony it is supposed to accompany is the formal installation of Rekhmire as vizir by the king. A figure of Tuthmosis III dressed in the garb of Osiris is shown seated in a kiosk. This figure, sadly, is seriously damaged, while that of Rekhmire, which stood before the kiosk, has been totally destroyed. Happily, the docket written above this destroyed figure states the purpose of the ceremony: 'Regulations enjoined on the vizir Rekhmire; admitting the court to the audience-chamber of Pharaoh, may he live, be prosperous and healthy; having Rekhmire, the newly-appointed vizir brought in.' Twenty-one long lines of the most beautifully painted hieroglyphs now follow:

> Then spoke His Majesty to him: 'See to the office of vizir; be watchful over everything done in it [i.e. in its name]. For it is the support of the whole land. Indeed the vizirship is in no way sweet; it is truly as bitter as gall.'

These words introduce the text generally known as *The Installation of the Vizir*, which is to be found not only in Rekhmire's tomb, but also in the tombs of Useramun, Rekhmire's uncle, and of Hepu, a vizir who served King Tuthmosis IV (c. 1413–1403 BC). It is indeed likely that it was also inscribed in other vizirs' tombs at Thebes during the Eighteenth and Nineteenth Dynasties, for the associated text enumerating the duties of the vizir can be found, in part at least, in the tombs of Amenemope, who succeeded Rekhmire as vizir, and of Paser, one of Ramesses II's vizirs during the Nineteenth Dynasty. This frequent use of the same texts provides a certain indication that during the great days of the New Kingdom they served as the public statements, if not the official, practical handbook, of the vizir's commission and duties. By having them inscribed in his tomb, a vizir declared for posterity the rules by which he had ostensibly managed his official duties while he was vizir. It is well worth noting, however, that the tone of *The*

Installation of the Vizir, like that of *The Duties of the Vizir* which we shall consider below, is wholly impersonal. In none of the copies preserved in the various New Kingdom tombs is the name of the tomb-owner incorporated into the text. There can be no doubt that a standard form existed which was simply copied straight on to the walls of the tombs of vizirs. Like Ptahhotpe's *Instructions*, it had become fixed and established at an earlier date, and was transmitted like holy writ, the vademecum of the highest official of the land. Its moment of crystallization remains uncertain, but it has been suggested that it may have taken place in the Middle Kingdom, perhaps in the later Twelfth Dynasty, when the internal government of Egypt was reorganized to the detriment of the hereditary provincial nomarchs, and to the advantage of the central administration.[10] Again, the time might have been during the Thirteenth Dynasty when the vizir himself seemed to embody the continuity of the Egyptian state, as ephemeral monarchs succeeded each other with bewildering rapidity. At such a time the specification of a vizir's appointment might have seemed all the more urgent, because of the danger that he might overreach his position in the presence of a weak monarch. Before considering the *Installation* text in full, we should also observe that all the copies are in Theban tombs constructed for southern vizirs. Yet the content of the text makes it clear that its application was universal for the whole land of Egypt. From this observation it may be (perhaps erroneously) concluded that the text was written down first at a time when only one vizir was to be found in Egypt, either because such was the regular practice at that time, or because Lower Egypt was then under foreign rule. These questions about the origins and composition of the text are of small concern in face of the essential practicality of what is said. After the initial words spoken by the king—a little extended beyond what has already been quoted—no space is wasted; the king gets down to brass tacks:[11]

> See! The petitioner both of Upper and of Lower Egypt, of the whole land, comes prepared to receive judgement in the hall of the vizir. Then should you see that everything is done in accordance with what is specified by law, that everything is done in a precise manner in letting a man plead his innocence. See! As far as a magistrate who gives judgement in public is concerned, water and wind proclaim on everything he does. See! There is no one who does not know what he does . . . See! A magistrate's refuge lies in acting according to the regulations in doing what is specified. A

petitioner who has been judged should not be able to say: 'I have not been allowed to plead my innocence.' See! It is an utterance which is in the Book of Memphis, a declaration of the Lord, the clemency of the vizir . . .[12]

Do not make judgement (improperly?); God hates biased behaviour. This is an instruction, and you should act accordingly. See equally the man you know and the man you do not know, the man who is near you and the man who is far away. The magistrate who acts in accordance with this (instruction) will be successful here in this place. Do not dismiss a petitioner before you have considered his words. If there is a petitioner who makes petition to you, do not reject the things he has to say as being things already said. You should dismiss him only after you have let him hear the reasons why you dismiss him. See! The saying is: 'The petitioner prefers the consideration of his utterance to the judgement on the matter about which he has come.' Do not lose your temper with a man improperly; lose your temper only in a matter worth losing your temper over. Establish fear of yourself that you may be feared; for a real magistrate is one who is feared. See! The worth of a magistrate comes through behaving justly. See! If a magistrate makes himself feared a million times, there will be an element of guilt in him in the understanding of the people. They do not say of him: 'He is a man.' See! It is said: 'A magistrate who speaks lies goes forward according to his worth.' See! You will succeed in exercising your office and in acting justly. See! What is wanted is that justice be done through the pronouncements of the vizir. See! The vizir has been its true protector since (the time of) the God. See! It is said about the chief scribe of the vizir: 'Scribe of Justice'—so 'tis said. Now the court in which you make judgements contains a hall with records of all judgements. He who will act justly before all people is the vizir. See! A man continues to exercise his office as long as he acts according to his commission. A man's reputation remains inasmuch as he does what he has been told to do. Do not act as you wish in matters about which the law is known. See further! It is appropriate for arrogance that the Lord prefers fear to arrogance.[13] You should therefore act according to what has been enjoined on you . . .

Implicit in this 'instruction' given to the vizir at the time of his installation by the king is a general legal philosophy which lays emphasis on duty, natural justice, open judgement, and the observance of the law. The vizir should act within the terms of his commission, meting out judgements not only with an even hand, but also in such a way that his motives are clear and not open to question. In so acting he should also pay strict attention to the great body of case law preserved in the archives of the vizir's office. The precise definition of law in ancient Egypt is difficult to achieve because the evidence is both thin and scattered over many centuries. It has, in addition, an elusive quality which hinders precision of definition. Clearly there was no strict legal code such as was found in some other ancient cultures of the Near East. Egyptian law was an integrated system of statute, precedent, practice and, to a limited extent, religious principle.[14] In subsequent parts of this book the application of the system in civil matters touching upon the lives of ordinary people will be demonstrated. For the present it may be sufficient to show how law and justice were regarded at the highest level in the land. The ethic is embodied in the statement we have just seen being laid down formally as an instruction on Rekhmire. How it was observed in practice can be seen in the second text enumerating the duties of the vizir, which in Rekhmire's tomb is inscribed on the east wall of the south part of the transverse hall. Like the text of installation, it is found in other tombs, as we have already mentioned, and it may equally be regarded as an historical statement of the vizir's duties, compiled probably during the late Middle Kingdom.

The Duties of the Vizir takes its place in the decoration of the tomb as part of a scene in which Rekhmire was shown engaged in exercising his highest function. On the right he sat in a hall or kiosk.[15] His figure is completely destroyed, but the accompanying text makes clear what he was doing: 'A sitting to hear the petitioner in the hall of the vizir, by the prince, count, treasurer of the King of Lower Egypt, (many titles and epithets) . . . mayor and vizir [Rekhmire], justified, born of Bet, justified, begotten of the priest of [Amun], Neferuben, justified, son of the mayor, Aametju.' Rekhmire, then, was seated ready to pass judgement on the petitioners who came before him; and some of these were shown, along with court officials, in the precinct of the court—a scene also badly damaged, though possibly not maliciously damaged like the figure of Rekhmire. The subsequent text is entitled *Regulations for Sitting* [i.e. in judgement] *for the mayor and vizir of the Southern City* [i.e. Thebes] *and of the Residence* [i.e. of the King] *in the hall of the vizir.* What follows includes in some detail the way in which the vizir should behave, how he should conduct his day, what he should do in particular circumstances. It may not cover all the duties which a vizir might expect to fulfil, but it encompasses enough to ensure that the vizir was responsible for most of the bureaucratic functions of government. He was undoubtedly expected to be a very busy man. First are laid down the precise manner in which the vizir should present himself in his hall, what he should wear, and who should attend him; also in what order men should present themselves to him. Then the text continues:[16]

The sealing of strongrooms at the correct hour should be reported to him, and their opening at the right hour. The condition of the fortresses of the Delta and the North should be reported to him, and the issuing [perhaps 'expenditure'] of all that is issued from the King's House. And the entry of all that should come in to the King's House should be reported to him. Furthermore, everything that comes into and everything that issues from the floors of the Residence should be reported to him, whether they come in or go forth. It is his agents who arrange entry and issuing forth. The overseer of sheriffs, sheriffs and the overseer of estates should report their affairs to him.

Now he should go in to greet the Lord—may he live, be prosperous and healthy—every day when the affairs of the Two Lands have been reported to him in his house. He should go into the Great House [the Palace] when the overseer of treasurers stands at the northern flagstaff. And the vizir should move forward in a brisk manner in the doorway of the great gate. Then the overseer of treasurers should advance to meet him and report to him as follows: 'All your matters are in a good state and prosper. All functionaries have reported to me as follows: "All your matters are in a good state and prosper. The King's House is in a good state and prospers." ' And the vizir should report to the overseer of treasurers as follows: 'All your matters are in a good state and prosper. Every department of the Residence is in a good state and prospers. The sealing of the strongrooms at the correct hour has been reported to me, and their opening at the right hour, by every functionary.' And after the one has reported to the other, i.e. the two officials, then the vizir should send (someone) to open every door in the King's House to allow all that should enter to come in, and all that should go forth (to go forth) likewise. It is his agent who should arrange that it should be properly recorded in writing.

Let no official have the power to judge in his [the vizir's] hall. If an accusation should occur against one among the officials belonging to his hall, then he should have him brought to the judgement hall. It is the vizir who should punish him in return for his wrongdoing. Let no official have the power to beat (anyone) in his hall. Any judgement which may be the concern of the hall should be reported to him, that he may place it in it [the hall].

Any agent whom the vizir may send on a mission to an official, from the highest to the lowest, let him not be enticed, and let him not be bullied by the official. He should speak the vizir's message, standing in the presence of the official, speaking his message and going out to his appointed place. It is his agent who should bring mayors and district governors to the hall of judgement . . . Now as to the behaviour of the vizir in judging in his hall, if anyone is not efficient in carrying out any duty, he should judge him in the affair, and if he is not able to remove the guilt in hearing the details about it, then an entry should be placed in the criminal register which is kept in the Great Prison. So too if he is not able to remove the guilt of his agent. If their misdeeds occur a second time, a report should be made setting out that they are in the criminal register, and stating the matter on account of which they were placed in the register, according to their offence.

Any documents for which the vizir may send from any hall [i.e. court], provided that they are not confidential, should be taken for him along with the register of their curator, on the seal of the judges and the scribes attached to them, who were in charge of them. Then he should open it [the document] and after he has seen it, it should be taken back to its place, sealed with the vizir's seal. Now if he asks for a confidential document, let it not be released by the (archival) curators. But in the case of any agent sent by the vizir about it on behalf of a petitioner, he [the curator] should let it go to him.

3 (above) The island of Siheil, with inscriptions on the rocks.
(below) Part of the Abbott Papyrus which contains the report of the examination of the tombs in the Theban necropolis (BM 10221).

Now anybody who petitions the vizir about lands, he [the vizir] should order him (to appear) before him over and above listening to the overseer of farm lands and the assessor of the land register(?); he may grant a delay of two months on his behalf for his lands in the South and in the North; but for his lands which are in the neighbourhood of the Southern City [Thebes] or of the Residence, he should grant a delay for him of three days, which is what the law lays down. He should hear in judgement any petitioner in accordance with this law which is in his hand.[17]

Further, it is he who should bring together the district-assessors, and it is he who should send them that they may report to him the condition of their districts. All conveyances should be brought to him, and it is he who should seal them. It is he who makes distribution of land in the form of plots of land. In the case of any petitioner who says, 'Our boundaries are shifted,' then it should be seen that it has happened under the seal of an official. If it has happened, then he [the vizir] should take away the plots of lands of the assessors who had them [the boundaries] shifted. Now in the case of any unusual event and its outcome, whatever may be seen in it, and whatever any petitioner may put in writing, he should not be allowed to petition a judge. Any petitioner of the land should be reported to him [the vizir] after he has put (his affair) in writing.[18]

It is he who dispatches any agent of the King's House, sent to mayors and to district governors; it is he who dispatches any courier and any expedition of the King's House; it is he who appoints from the magistrates those who are to be the administrators(?) of the North, the South, the Head of the South, and Tjau-wer. They should report to him whatever has happened through them at the beginning of each season, and they should bring him the written accounts thereof (of what has happened) through them and their assessors.

It is he who should arrange the mobilization of troops and (their)

4 *(above) Ploughing with a pair of oxen in the Faiyum.*
   (below) The workmen's village at Deir el-Medina.

moving in the suite of the Lord when he travels downstream and when he travels upstream. It is he who should make up arrears which occur in the Southern City or in the Residence in accordance with what is declared in the King's House. There shall be brought to him the Controller of the Ruler, established in his court, together with the council of the army, so as to give them the instructions for the army.

Now let every rank [i.e. officials of every rank] come in, beginning from the lowest rank, to the hall of the vizir that they may greet each other.

It is he who should dispatch (men) to cut down sycamore trees when it is specified in the King's House. It is he who should dispatch regional officers to construct dykes throughout the whole land. It is he who should dispatch mayors and district governors to (arrange) the cultivation in the summer. It is he who should appoint the overseer of sheriffs in the hall of the King's House. It is he who should appoint the assessor [?judge] of mayors and district governors, and his named representative to visit the South and the North.

Every plea should be reported to him. The condition of the southern fortress should be reported to him, and the apprehending of anyone who might . . . It is he who should take action against(?) anyone who plunders a nome, and it is he who should judge him. It is he who should dispatch troops and the scribes of the land register(?) to conduct the business of the Lord.

Nome records should be (lodged) in his office for the hearing of cases concerning any land. It is he who should fix the boundaries of every nome and of every marshy district in the Delta(?), every divine offering and every contract. It is he who should make every public proclamation, and hear every complaint. It is he who should hear the case when a man goes to law with his fellow.

It is he who should appoint everyone who has to be appointed to the hall of judgement. Every enquiry from the King's House should come to him. It is he who should carry into effect [lit. 'hear'] every decree. It is he who should hear the case over any deficiency of divine offerings. It is he who should levy any tax in the form of revenue for anyone who should pay it to him. It is he who should make every . . .[19] in the Southern City or in the Residence. It is he who should seal it with his seal.

It is he who should hear all pleas. It is he who should arrange the exaction of the dues of the administrative districts(?), and to him should the Great Council report its taxes . . . [It is he who should arrange every . . .] which is brought to the hall of judgement, and every presentation (of dues) to the hall of judgement. It is he who should hear cases about them. It is he who should open the Treasury together with the Chief Treasurer. It is he who should examine the tribute of . . .(?) . . . It is he who should draw up inventories directly before all cattle of which inventories are to be drawn up. It is he who should examine water supplies on the first day of every ten-day period. . .[20]

[It is he who should hear every petitioner] for every plea of the hall of judgement, whether he be mayor or district governor or common person; all their dues should be reported to him by every overseer of land and every sheriff . . .

The last sentences of this long text are badly preserved in all four copies which have survived, and no consecutive translation can be given. Among the matters mentioned, of which sufficient can be made out, are the vizir's role in receiving reports about natural phenomena affecting the life of the country—the rising of Sirius (the Dog Star),[21] the loosing (i.e. the beginning) of the inundation of the Nile and, possibly, rain-storms. Some function in the equipping of ships and of dispatching agents when the King is on campaign is also set out. The last readable sentence declares that it is 'the door-keeper of the hall of judgement who should report concerning him everything that he shall do, and concerning hearings (of pleas) in the hall of the vizir'. The final words, which could scarcely have made more than one sentence, are lost. So ends the long and important composition known as *The Duties of the Vizir*.

Earlier writers have commented on the abrupt way in which this remarkable text ends.[22] It is not brought to a tidy ending with some general remarks on the whole. Although all four surviving versions are incompletely preserved, it is generally clear that they all offer the same text, even to the extent of showing close parallels in the writing and spelling of words—matters which in ancient Egyptian can exhibit considerable variations without conveying differences of meaning. It is therefore safe to assume that the scribes who were employed to lay out the text of *The Duties of the Vizir* in the four tombs were provided with copies derived from a common original—the very papyrus, possibly, on which it had first been written down during the Middle Kingdom.

It is worth considering for a moment the circumstances in which the text was composed and then written down to become the classic statement of the duties of Egypt's first official. Whereas *The Installation of the Vizir* has many of the characteristics of the type of composition called 'Instruction', *The Duties of the Vizir* is less literary, altogether more practical. It contains the matter of what should engage the vizir's attention both day by day and in general plan. But it is a haphazard composition in many respects. Some aspects of government are dealt with neatly and coherently, others are divided between different parts of the work, and a few, in particular the strictly legal duties, are reiterated to some extent in several places. It does not give the impression of having been composed as a whole by a single person at one particular time; it appears rather to be a *mélange* of disconnected statements concerning duties from which a coherent document might be compiled. What is more, it does not by any means cover the whole range of the vizir's duties, as one may judge from observing the multifarious activities involving the vizir which are depicted on the walls of Rekhmire's tomb-chapel. There is no mention of his supervision of what went on in the vast temple workshops and the estates of the capital, for example; scarcely anything is said of his advisory function with his king—a matter which must have absorbed a very great part of his time. The text is in fact only a partial enumeration of duties, reflecting, possibly, a state of affairs in which the vizir's duties were circumscribed by the contraction of the Egyptian state. Such a situation obtained during the late Middle Kingdom after much of the northern part of the country had fallen under the sway of the Hyksos princes.

What does emerge clearly from a reading of *The Duties of the Vizir* is that his role was concerned almost entirely with matters governed by administration in the strictest sense—civil order, the assessment and collection of taxes, the maintenance of archives and the organization of their retrieval for consultation, the appointment and supervision of officials, the examination of land claims, and, by extension, the protection of property, the inspection and surveillance of provincial government, the monitoring of natural phenomena which affected the life of the country, including the state of the inundation and, subsequently, of crops, and, above all, the exercise of law in what in Britain would generally be classified as civil cases. These were the kinds of case that really mattered in ancient Egypt—perhaps they are so in all developed societies. Disputes over land and other property, the contesting of wills and matters involving inheritances, in fact the whole range of actions considered as torts in English law, formed the province over which the Egyptian legal system exercised its principal jurisdiction. The exercise of justice in criminal matters could be dealt with in an altogether more summary manner, as was the traditional procedure in the ancient world.

To regard the vizir as the pharaonic prime minister in the modern sense would not, however, be strictly adequate because many of the functions of government, both administrative and executive, were not his concern. He seems to have had little to do with the conduct of foreign affairs, which, during the Eighteenth Dynasty, was concerned mostly with the mounting of expeditions for military reasons, and the sending of missions to mining areas. Yet he was not wholly uninvolved in the consequences of such actions; he received emissaries and deputations from foreign countries, presided, in the absence of the king or simply as his proxy, over the receipt of tribute brought back from campaigns or presented to Pharaoh by ambassadors. A large section of the southern part of the west wall of the transverse hall of Rekhmire's tomb is devoted to a series of scenes which make up the greatest representation of the presentation of tribute and plunder from abroad to be found in the whole of the Theban necropolis. The installation of Rekhmire as vizir is shown, as we have already seen, on the right (northern) end of this wall. In sequence to the left, Rekhmire was painted accompanied by attendants. His figure is completely destroyed, but the informative texts painted above him explain what he is about:[23] 'Receiving the tribute [or "produce"] of the southern foreign land, together with the tribute of Punt, the tribute of Retjenu, the tribute of Keftiu, together with the plunder [or "booty"] of all foreign lands, brought for the might of his Majesty, the King of Upper and Lower Egypt, Menkheperre [Tuthmosis III], live for ever, by the hereditary prince, count . . . mayor of the city and [vizir, Rekhmire].' Four scenes arranged in parallel, horizontal registers, show the reception of tribute from the various countries in the order (from top to bottom) Punt, Keftiu, the southern foreign land, and Retjenu, with a fifth scene devoted to captive foreigners—the 'booty of all foreign lands'.[24] The wealth of detail which makes this whole series so fascinating does not concern us here. It is also not our concern to enter into the scholarly debate about the occasion in the reign of Tuthmosis III (or in Rekhmire's career) when this great ceremony took place.[25] May it just be said that the degree of precision in dating postulated by some scholars seems hard to support in face of the generality of reference which must be assigned to most scenes of activities depicted on the walls of the Theban tombs of the nobles during the New Kingdom. We can properly maintain, on the basis of the scene just described in briefest summary, that there was at least one occasion when Rekhmire acted for his king in the receipt of tribute from foreign countries. There is, however, a good chance that the five registers of tribute and plunder represent a pictorial summing up of numerous occasions on which embassies were received in Thebes during the absence of the king, or when prisoners and other booty were brought to the capital at the close of successful campaigns (*Fig. 3*).

From the details given in *The Duties of the Vizir* text it is apparent not only that the vizir was the final arbiter of most of the internal government of ancient Egypt, but also that he was thought of as the one

Fig. 3 Tribute from the 'southern foreign land': ivory, ebony, animal skins, a baboon and a leopard.

official who had to shoulder the responsibility of bureaucratic action. In the course of this book some shreds of reality will be produced to substantiate the theoretical claims of this idealized text. Prescribed duty and the reality of actions are two different things. In this difference may lie the true hypocrisy of the politician and the government official. To what extent was the reality of official behaviour in ancient Egypt a poor thing when set beside the high idealism of the prescribed text? I believe the answer which will emerge will hardly be surprising. The population of ancient Egypt, and the officials who ruled it in the name of the king, were not particularly different from other peoples, ancient or modern. There were, however, certain aspects of the settled life of the Nile Valley—generally conservative and undisturbed for many generations at a time—which encouraged a more placid and benevolent attitude to humanity than might be found in countries afflicted by endemic warfare and poor living conditions. In Egypt, where society was nurtured in such relatively comfortable conditions, the virtues of moderation and justice were more easily practised and sustained than in lands torn by conflict. Benevolence and a regard for one's fellow man cease to be luxuries of daily life when the act of living is unmarked by the struggle to survive. When *The Duties of the Vizir* was put together, it is not at all improbable that the lofty ideals incorporated in the text were scarcely realizable in the land of Egypt. The very act of composition suggests that all was not well; to find it necessary to set down precepts for action which would have seemed self-evident in happy times, incorporates a kind of condemnation of the moment of composition. Nevertheless, the enumeration of duties, with the principles of action which they embody, was of lasting value, and was recognized as such in the Eighteenth Dynasty when it was not so difficult to be magnanimous and considerate. For Rekhmire, no doubt, it may have been no act of hypocrisy to have the text inscribed in his tomb. And there is no reason to suppose that his fall from grace was due more to the corrupt use of his position than to political misjudgement.

NOTES

1 The evidence for high officials in the earliest historical period is summarized by I. E. S. Edwards in *Cambridge Ancient History*, I, 3 ed., Pt. 2 (Cambridge, 1971), 35 ff.

2 See W. C. Hayes in *Cambridge Ancient History*, I, Pt. 2, 505 ff.

3 On the Eighteenth-dynasty bureaucracy, see W. C. Hayes in *Cambridge Ancient History*, II, Pt. 1 (Cambridge, 1973), 353 ff.

4 For the vizirate at this time, see W. C. Hayes, *A Papyrus of the Late Middle Kingdom in the Brooklyn Museum* (Brooklyn, 1955), 146 ff.

5 This description comes from British Museum Papyrus 10246 (Papyrus Anastasi III), p.7, ll.4–5.

6 N. de G. Davies, *The Tomb of Rekh-mi-Rē'*, pls. XI, XII.

7 For a good translation of *The Instructions* (or *Maxims*) *of Ptahhotpe*, see W. K. Simpson (ed.), *The Literature of Ancient Egypt*, 159 ff.

8 Papyrus Prisse, in the Bibliothèque Nationale in Paris.

9 N. de G. Davies, *The Tomb of Rekh-mi-Rē'*, pls. XIII, XV.

10 W. C. Hayes in *Cambridge Ancient History*, II, Pt. 1, 355.

11 The text with variants is studied by R. O. Faulkner in *Journal of Egyptian Archaeology* 41 (London, 1955), 18 ff. The version given here is somewhat abridged, and is occasionally restored, where the original is imperfect, to render it more readable. The frequent repetition of 'See!' reproduces a much worked stylistic particle in the Egyptian.

12 The *Book of Memphis* is not otherwise known.

13 I.e. the King prefers an official who inspires fear to one who is arrogant.

14 On Egyptian law in general, see A. Théodoridès in J. R. Harris (ed.), *The Legacy of Egypt*, 291 ff.

15 Davies, *Rekh-mi-Rē'*, pl. XXIV.

16 Davies, op. cit., pls. XXVI–XXVIII. The translation is completed, where the original is damaged, from parallel copies in other tombs.

17 I.e. whatever laws may be currently in force.

18 These sentences are very obscure.

19 The crucial word is lost here.

20 A ten-day period represented in effect the Egyptian week.

21 The heliacal rising of Sirius (Sothis) marked the beginning of the Egyptian civil year. On the Egyptian calendar in general, see R. A. Parker in J. R. Harris (ed.), *The Legacy of Egypt*, 13 ff.

22 E.g. Davies, *Rekh-mi-Rē'*, 94.

23 Davies, op. cit., pl. XVI.

24 Ibid., pls. XVII–XXIII.

25 See, for example, C. Aldred in *Journal of Egyptian Archaeology* 56 (London, 1970), 105 ff.

3

JUSTICE FOR EVERYBODY

In the *Installation* text the vizir is instructed: 'See equally the man you know and the man you don't know, the man who is near you and the man who is far away.' This exhortation to impartiality embodied a long-established, and much cherished, aspiration which formed one of the principal tenets of behaviour in public and private life in ancient Egypt. If a man were an official carrying out the instructions of government in his small locality, if he were the chief administrator of a province or nome, the vizir himself, or even the king, it was right for him to attend with equal attention to the pleas of the weak and of the strong. The merit of a person, or of his case, should determine how he should be treated. The Prince Merikare is instructed by his father:[1] 'Make no difference between a man of position and a commoner; but engage for yourself a man because of what he does.' Above all one should be charitable in dealing with inferiors, for they lack influence and the ability to defend themselves. 'I gave bread to the hungry and clothing to him who had no clothes. I never made a judgement between two litigants in such a way that I allowed a son to be deprived of his father's inheritance.'[2] Such was the claim made (admittedly in the much used phraseology of private tomb-inscriptions of the Old Kingdom) by Pepinakhte, one of the great nobles of Elephantine in the Sixth Dynasty. In the same vein Merikare was advised:[3]

> Act justly, that you may endure on earth. Quieten him who weeps; do not dispossess the widow; do not deprive a man of his father's property. Do not put down high officials from their offices. Avoid punishing wrongfully. Do not smite (anyone) with the knife: there is no profit in it for you. You should punish by beating and imprisonment—in this way will the whole land be ordered— except for the rebel whose plans have been discovered. God knows the disaffected, and God punishes his sin with blood.

It would, no doubt, be too much to claim that ancient Egyptians in high positions always acted according to such honourable and considerate principles, but their constant reiteration in monumental funerary texts and in established literary compositions over many centuries suggests that they were fairly generally accepted. Not only was benevolence written into the Egyptian way of life, but its complement, mercy, was practised in the exercise of justice. Harshness in meting out punishment was reserved for the really great crime, the offence against the State. Unfortunately, there is not enough in the way of real case evidence for a close study to be made of Egyptian law in action. Although it is certain that good records were kept of cases, particularly of those involving property, and that these records were stored in central archives, scarcely a document has survived which can with confidence be regarded as coming from such a depository. What is possible, however, is to observe what the attitudes and procedures were in particular cases, either recorded in inscriptions and other written documents, or embodied in literary compositions. Indeed, the evidence provided by literature is often of a particularly significant kind; for it may incorporate attitudes of mind and descriptions of procedures which are quite specific and very informative.

Justice in Egypt was not thought of as being the prerogative of the rich and powerful. It was open to the humblest, not just because the great were conditioned by training to be charitably disposed towards the weak and the poor. To some extent it was the right of all to expect equitable treatment at the hands of those who administered justice. For, although benevolence and 'fair play' were guiding principles, it could not be expected that all men would always observe them, and order their behaviour accordingly. How did the man of no influence go about getting justice if he felt unjustly treated? The availability of justice is a traditional expectation in many societies; but its actuality may seem to be almost unattainable in some. *The Story of the Eloquent Peasant* tells how one simple fellow pursued a grievance to a happy outcome. It is a Twelfth-dynasty composition—possibly of slightly earlier date—the scene of which is set during the First Intermediate Period, when the kings of the Tenth Dynasty ruled from a capital city, Ninsu, later called Heracleopolis by the Greeks, and Ihnasya el-Medina today.[4]

A peasant called Khunanpu farmed a little land in the Wadi Natrun, an area of salt flats and brackish springs lying in the desert to the west of the Nile Delta. One day he decided to take his produce down to Egypt, that is to say the Nile Valley, to trade for provisions for his family. His wife put up a hamper of bread and beer for his journey, and he set off with his donkeys well laden with a great variety of strange produce. As he travelled south-east he entered a district called Perfefi, and his way ran past the house and land of a man called Djehutinakhte, who was a serf of Rensi, son of Meru, a Chief Steward at the royal Residence. Djehutinakhte coveted Khunanpu's donkeys and devised a way by which he could confiscate them. The path which Khunanpu was following was bordered on one side by water (a canal or the river), and on the other by a plot of standing barley. Djehutinakhte spread a cloth across the path and defied the peasant and his donkeys to pass, either over the cloth, or over the verge of the barley plot. While Khunanpu argued the right of way, one of his donkeys helped himself to a mouthful of barley from the standing crop. This was precisely what Djehutinakhte had expected: 'See! I shall confiscate your donkey, peasant, because it eats my barley. It shall tread (grain) for its sin.' Khunanpu at once offered to repay what had been eaten, and he invoked the name of Rensi, a man renowned for his treatment of robbers. At that Djehutinakhte set about him with a stick, and left him, driving away all his donkeys and threatening Khunanpu with death if he continued with his complaints.

For ten days Khunanpu hung around, appealing to Djehutinakhte, but with no success. He then moved to Ninsu to carry his complaint to Rensi. Chancing upon him, he put his complaint to the Chief Steward through his favourite attendant, and Rensi agreed to put the case to the magistrates who were with him. To begin with they were unwilling to hear the case, and suspected Khunanpu's motives. Rensi, however, allowed the peasant to state his case, which he proceeded to do with a remarkable flow of fine language and well-judged flattery: he could rely on Rensi's judgement:

> For you are a father of the orphan, a husband of the widow, a brother of the divorced woman, a kilt for him who has no mother; let me extol your name in this land, according to every good law, (as being) a leader devoid of rapacity, a great man devoid of meanness, who destroys lies and nurtures truth, who comes at the voice of him who speaks. Set aside evil. I speak that you may hear. Act justly, praised one whom the praised praise. Dispel my needs.

See! I am laden with woe. See! Because of it I am weak. Look into my case. See! I am at a loss.

Khunanpu's eloquence bore fruit at once. Rensi went straight to the king and told him about the peasant's complaint and about his speech, judging, correctly as it turned out, that the king would be tempted to hear more. 'If you want me to be well,' said the king, 'make him tarry here, without answering anything he says, so that he may go on speaking. Be silent. You should bring his words to us in writing, and we shall hear them.' The king further ordered that Khunanpu and his family should be properly supported in the meanwhile. At Ninsu the peasant received ten loaves and two jugs of beer every day, while in the Wadi Natrun his wife was sent three measures of barley every day.

So Khunanpu was encouraged to pursue his complaint. Eight times more he came before Rensi, delivering at the outset imaginative panegyrics on the Chief Steward's abilities, his justice and his compassion, then proceeding to highly critical comments on his apparent reticence in the face of the peasant's pleas. The subject matter of the case he had to present against the confiscation by Djehutinakhte was scarcely touched on, for the facts were not under dispute. By eloquence would the case be carried, although no indication of that intention was conveyed to Khunanpu. Indeed, after one particularly outspoken address Rensi set two of his agents on the wretched peasant, and had him soundly thrashed. Unabashed, Khunanpu returned to the assault with a string of telling phrases:

> The son of Meru [i.e. Rensi] goes on making mistakes. His face is blind to what he sees, and deaf to what he hears; (he is) misguided over what is mentioned to him. You are a town without a governor, like a group of people without a chief, like a boat without a captain on board, like an association of people without a leader. See! You are a sheriff who steals, a town governor who receives, a district overseer who should put down theft, but has become an epitome of the thief.[5]

This outburst prompted no further action by Rensi or his agents, and Khunanpu continued his highly critical commentary on the Chief Steward. The latter, obeying the instructions of the king, made no answer, and his apparent indifference to the peasant's plight was more than adequate stimulus to further eloquence. From criticism Khunanpu turned to admonition and advice, and in his ninth petition he left Rensi in no doubt about how he should fulfil his duties. In a final jibe he declared: 'See! I petition you and you pay no attention to it. I shall go and make petition about you to Anubis.'[6]

As Khunanpu left the Chief Steward sent his two agents after him, and he reasonably assumed that he was about to be thrashed again. He no longer cared; he had done his best but had, perhaps, spoken a little too much out of turn: 'The nearing of a thirsty man to water, the approach of the mouth of a nursing child to milk, the same is the death which has been entreated, when he sees it coming, after his death has been slow in coming for him.' At least, so the peasant thought, he was to be put out of his misery. How surprised, therefore, he was to find that he had no worse ordeal to suffer than to have to stay and hear all his nine wordy petitions read back to him from the transcript that had been made. The papyrus containing the transcript was then sent to the king who was delighted with it: 'It filled his heart with joy more than anything in the whole of this land.' He instructed Rensi to make judgement in the case, and Djehutinakhte was brought before him for this purpose. The last lines of the story are only partially preserved, and the precise outcome is lost. It seems that Rensi had an inventory made of all Djehutinakhte's property, and that the whole was made over to Khunanpu as compensation for the original confiscation, and as a reward for having presented his case in such a varied and eloquent way.

It would be a mistake, undoubtedly, to draw too many conclusions from a simple reading of this story. It would, for example, be a mistake to take the treatment endured by the peasant in the name of justice as a fair representation of the regular process of the hearing of complaints during the Middle Kingdom. And yet it seems characteristic of Egyptian legal practice that procedure in any particular case was not precisely governed by set rules but, in a sense, improvised to meet each particular set of circumstances. Herein lay the flexibility of the system and also, no doubt, its tendency to inconsistency and, on occasion, lack of justice. Where the evidence could be interpreted to the advantage of either side, if properly presented, a premium was set on the ability of him who could present the more impressive case by his eloquence. If a petitioner could contrive to have his petition heard, then he was well on the way to securing a form of justice. But the path to a hearing was fraught with difficulties, especially if the petitioner were a man of no importance; for that path was supervised by the servants of the magistrate or of the court, who no doubt served the purpose of a rough-and-ready filter. The scope of a magistrate's justice could be only as wide as his servants allowed.

In the practicalities of life, however, position and influence mattered in ancient Egypt just as they have mattered in other countries and other societies since remotest antiquity. But even if a petitioner had neither position nor influence, he might yet be able to advance his case by the judicious use of bribes. That bribery was commonly practised may be reasonably concluded from the admonitions to avoid it which occur in the books of wisdom of all periods.[7]

> Do not bring down [pervert ?] the men of the magistrate's court or incite the just man to rebel. Do not pay too much attention to him clad in shining garments, and have regard for him who is shabbily dressed. Do not accept the reward of the powerful man, and persecute the weak for him. Justice is the great gift of God; he gives it to him whom he chooses.

The realities, unfortunately, tend to weigh more heavily in the balance of justice than honesty and fair play. Consequently the poor were always at a disadvantage unless they had the wit sufficient to turn the tables on their adversaries. The quandary in which Khunanpu found himself would have been beyond extrication had he not grasped his opportunity of meeting Rensi and been allowed to exploit it. That the poor and weak could obtain justice was a fundamental object of the legal process in ancient Egypt; but justice for such did not come easily. A story of much later date than that of the *Eloquent Peasant* recounts how justice was secured after many years by a son determined to avenge his father.[8]

There were two brothers called Truth and Falsehood. Truth borrowed, it seems, an implement of some kind[9] from Falsehood and in due course lost it, and was unable to return it when Falsehood wanted it back. Indeed, when another was offered to replace it, Falsehood rejected it out of hand, making absurd claims for the lost article: 'Its blade consists of the mountain of El, its handle is the wood of Coptos, its seating(?) is the tomb of the god, its thongs are the cattle of Kar.' To exact the utmost in recompense Falsehood took Truth to law, and demanded as a penalty that his eyes be put out and that he be obliged to act as his doorkeeper. Falsehood was determined to destroy Truth. Unable to deny the charge, Truth was found guilty and punished accordingly. But his sufferings did not end there. As his brother's doorkeeper he constantly reminded him of his cruelty. So Falsehood had him taken into the desert and left to be destroyed by savage lions. Truth wandered about until he was weary and hungry. As he lay asleep he was spotted by a lady who appreciated his beauty in spite of his wretched condition. She had her servants bring Truth to her house, and that night he made love to her.

The son born of this union was exceptional in all respects, and he had no difficulty in beating his fellows at work and play. They retaliated by teasing him with 'Who's your father?' and 'You certainly have no father!' Despairingly he begged his mother to tell him the answer, and she pointed out the blind man, Truth, who sat by the door of the house. The son was shocked, and brought his father into the house, questioning him 'Who blinded you?' After he heard Truth's story he set out to avenge him, taking with him provisions, a staff, sandals, a sword and a fine ox. Coming to Falsehood's land the son asked Falsehood's herdsman to look after his fine ox for a few days, giving him his other possessions as payment for his trouble.

Some time later Falsehood came to inspect his herd and saw the fine ox. 'Give that ox to me to eat,' he ordered. But his herdsman explained that he could not. Falsehood ignored his scruples and told him to replace the ox with another. When Truth's son came back and found his ox taken, he had Falsehood brought before the same court as had tried his father years before. He claimed that his ox was unique: 'If it were to stand at Balamun, its tail would reach to the edge of the Delta: one horn would rest on the western hills and one on the eastern hills; the great river is its resting place, and sixty calves are born to it every day.' When the court challenged this description Truth's son said: 'Is there an implement as big as the one described, its blade consisting of the mountain of El, its handle being the wood of Coptos, its seating(?) the tomb of the god, its thongs the cattle of Kar? Judge between Truth and Falsehood. I am his son, and to avenge him have I come.'

Falsehood then swore a solemn oath by Amun and the Ruler that if Truth were found alive he should himself be blinded and made the doorkeeper of Truth's house. When Truth was produced before the court Falsehood was sentenced to suffer a hundred blows and five open wounds, to be blinded, and to serve as doorkeeper for Truth. So was Truth avenged by his son, and his dispute with Falsehood settled.

The allegorical aspects of this story of Truth and Falsehood need not be underlined here. Its interest for us at present lies in the process by which Truth was originally punished and, subsequently, his case reopened by his son in a well-judged attempt to avenge his father.[10] It seems, on consideration, highly unlikely that the son could ever have succeeded in his purpose if he had attempted simply to have the case between Truth and Falsehood reopened. His stratagem of using Falsehood's herdsman as the unwitting agent of his own master's destruction was ingenious. The only defence which would work had to be presented as a countercharge of such absurdity that the court could be persuaded of the equal absurdity of Falsehood's original charge against Truth. In fact, the court (which in the story is actually composed—again allegorically—of the Ennead, the company of nine gods) does not comment on the charge implicit in the exposure made by Truth's son. As soon as the boy declares his purpose, that he is out to avenge Truth, Falsehood at once concedes defeat in effect, although his behaviour seems to be a calling of the boy's bluff, as it might have been interpreted. He had every reason to believe that Truth had perished in the wilderness. If he had survived, then Falsehood had no defence. And so the demonstration that Truth had survived served as the *dénouement* of the sequence of events. No hope remained for Falsehood, and he presented no defence.

The penalty Falsehood suffered—one hundred blows, five open wounds, and to be blinded—accurately reproduces, in part at least, the pattern of punishment found in Egyptian documents of the New Kingdom. A decree promulgated by Horemheb, the last king of the Eighteenth Dynasty (c. 1332–1305 BC), set out the ways by which he determined to re-establish justice and order in Egypt after the period of internal unrest—not to say anarchy—which had accompanied and followed the strange interval of rule by Akhenaten. Specific crimes against the people of Egypt are dealt with, and precise penalties prescribed. In many of the most serious cases the penalty is to cut off the nose of the malefactor and to banish him to the garrison-town of Tjel on Egypt's eastern border. In the case of wrongful misappropriation of the hides of cattle the decree states: 'As for any soldier of whom is heard said "He is going about stealing hides also", from this very day the law shall be enforced against him by beating him with one hundred blows and five open wounds.'[11]

Similarly, in a great inscription set up by King Sethos I of the Nineteenth Dynasty at Nauri, in his fourth year (c. 1300 BC),[12] shortly after the promulgation of Horemheb's decree, very analogous penalties are laid down for those men who committed specified crimes against the estates, and workers on the estates, of the temple of the great god Osiris at Abydos—Sethos' own foundation. Throughout the part of this text which deals with hurts and penalties, the latter include physical assault on the bodies of the convicted persons, and, when suitable, the deprivation of property, as happened in the case of Djehutinakhte after the successful action of Khunanpu. It has been shown that the organization of the text, particularly in the order of the listing of misdemeanours, seems haphazard and, in part, repetitious, as if the various matters had been set down as they had been presented to the writer in an initial draft.[13] Such too was the case with the *Duties of the Vizir* text. It is indeed difficult to conceive how a great inscription of this kind—the main portion alone measures 2.80m. high by 1.56m. wide—carved in a position of the utmost isolation far to the south of Egypt in Sudanese Nubia, came to be composed in such a slapdash manner. If the text had survived on papyrus it might have been considered a draft of something which would be put in fair order before official promulgation. Its lack of coherence and shape is, however, rather typical of similar texts in which the content is concerned with matters of detailed policy and its application. A reading of the whole of Sethos' Nauri Decree gives one the impression of surveying part of a formal legal code. This impression, sadly, does not survive close scrutiny and impartial consideration. The phraseology appears to be legal, but it would be more true to call it legalistic. In the case of Sethos' decree, in particular, the various 'laws' referred to seem to be rather a compounding of the idea of 'law' in general rather than specific, properly enacted, laws of universal application throughout the land of Egypt. The phrase 'the law shall be enforced on him', already met in Horemheb's Decree, means in effect 'he shall be brought to justice'; it is the equivalent of 'having the law on someone'. And just as the English term, last quoted, contains a suggestion of arbitrary punishment, as if the person concerned is accused and condemned at one stroke, so the Egyptian usage equally implies arbitrary punishment without the intervention of conventional legal process.

In the Nauri Decree this element of particular arbitrariness is especially evident because the text contains promulgations concerned only with matters connected with the temple foundation at Abydos. It is a charter for the temple, and the various prohibitions are 'bye-laws' of local application in the sense that they refer principally to the people attached to the temple and its estates. But in so far as the estates were distributed throughout Egypt and, it would seem, Nubia, these 'bye-laws' were operational far beyond the environs of Abydos.[14]

> As for any high official, any overseer of fields of this estate, any herdsman of ploughing cattle(?), any factor who shall tamper with the boundaries of the land belonging to the Abydos Temple of Sethos so as to shift the boundaries, the law shall be enforced on him by cutting off both his ears, he being made a field-worker in the Abydos Temple of Sethos. Likewise, any man who is in the whole land, who drives away any marsh-catcher of the Abydos Temple of Sethos from his snaring marshes or his fish-catching pond, the law shall be enforced on him by beating him with one hundred blows and five open wounds.

In other places the penalty is more precisely fixed according to the crime:[15]

> As for anyone who shall disobey this decree and seize a herdsman belonging to the Abydos Temple of Sethos, forcibly, or (by moving him) from district to district, on any duty, and the herdsman shall say, 'Since someone took me, ruin has befallen my cattle, to the extent of one head of the herd, or two, or three, or four,' the law shall be enforced on him by beating him with two hundred blows, together with replacing the head of the herd of the Abydos Temple of Sethos from him, as a theft, at the rate of one hundred to one.

Summary punishment was common in cases where the facts of the matter were not in dispute or, perhaps even more common, thought not to be in dispute. A felon brought before a local magistrate would have found little in the way of legal process before punishment was enacted, unless the crime was something which required investigation. Such, for example, were the proceedings concerned with the robbing of royal tombs in the Theban necropolis in the Late New Kingdom, already briefly touched on in Chapter One. In general, however, the Egyptian position in respect of criminal acts is well expressed in one of the instructions of Ptahhotpe:[16] 'Punish in an exemplary manner, instruct thoroughly; the suppression of an evil action makes for the establishment of good character; as for a (bad) matter—except for one brought about by mischance—it is what causes the complainer to become the opponent.' The principle here seems clearly to be that criminal wrong-doing should be dealt with arbitrarily and physically, because it is thus better for the correction of the criminal, and for the good name of the man who dispenses the punishment. On the other hand, legal processes ought to be invoked for the settlement of non-criminal cases.

In the practice of everyday living, the simple Egyptian peasant had much to fear from this principle of arbitrary rough justice. He could expect little sympathy from the agents of provincial and local officials bent on carrying out the orders of their superiors, and little concerned with the niceties of justice. Taxes, for example, were commonly collected with the help of sticks and staves, and recalcitrant payers were dragged bodily before the appropriate magistrate or official, when further physical persuasion was administered. The theme was one which occurred frequently enough in tomb scenes of the time of the Old Kingdom to confirm that defaulting on taxes and its subsequent punishment were characteristic events in the life of the countryside. As far as one can judge, no formal legal process was involved. The appropriate official received reports on the payment of the properly assessed taxes, had the recalcitrants brought before him, and administered the necessary punishment without argument. Presumably questions were asked and, again presumably, the punishment was graded according to the amount owed, the persistence in the fault by the individual, and the personal circumstances of the defaulter. What is not made clear is whether the summary punishment was in itself all that was exacted from the defaulter. No doubt the matter was settled according to the status of the individual and his ability to pay. We have already seen that certain felonies might be punished both by physical means and by the exacting of swingeing damages.

In a non-monetary society like that of ancient Egypt, where payment for anything could be made only in kind, and where precious metal was but one among a series of acceptable commodities used for transactions, the simple peasant or artisan had little with which he could settle an outstanding debt. His one realizable asset was his capability to work. Conscription for public service was, therefore, a common way by which punishment might be exacted; inevitably, it was a practice as commonly liable to abuse. In the scenes showing the examination and punishment of defaulters, however, it is not only the lowly and insignificant who are shown enduring rough justice. The mastaba-chapel of Khentika, a vizir under the kings Teti and Pepi I of the Sixth Dynasty (*c.* 2280 BC), shows, in one small scene, a group of five district governors brought before the vizir to answer charges of maladministration—probably failure to remit the prescribed quantities of tax, although no precise crime is specified.[17] Three of these local officials grovel in subservience before the vizir, while two bend low in obeisance, encouraged by attendants. Khentika is supported by two scribes, administrative secretaries, who are busy noting down what is going on, or calculating what is owed in each case. Two convicted miscreants, probably also district governors (although they are not identified as such), are tied fast to posts, receiving the prescribed punishment of blows delivered by two stick-wielding attendants who cheerfully call out, 'Fine gifts for yourselves (to whom) the like has never occurred.' The point seems to be that district governors were more in the habit of handing out such treatment than of receiving it. The vizir's justice may have been rough, but it was meted out to the influential as well as the humble (*Fig. 4*).

A somewhat similar scene in the tomb-chapel of Menna in the Theban necropolis is more precisely associated with the business of tax-collection.[18] Menna, a scribe of the fields of the Lord of the Two Lands (in his case, probably King Tuthmosis IV, the second successor of Tuthmosis III), was a relatively modest member of the Theban bureaucracy of the Eighteenth Dynasty, answerable to the vizir for the success or failure of his own duties. Among these duties was the assessment of standing crops for tax purposes. A painted scene shows

Fig. 4 Tax defaulters brought before the vizir Khentika.

the team of surveyors at work with measuring cord, supported by an inspector, scribes and small boys. A man and woman approach the group carrying produce: is it a bribe to ensure favourable treatment, or a simple token of willingness to pay? It is, most probably, the humble tax payment on their own modest crop. The events depicted in a scene of this kind were not all necessarily contemporaneous; here assessment and payment are shown side by side; and here also is shown the bringing of tax-defaulters before Menna. There are, as it were, two levels of miscreant: a group of four, who are well dressed and seemingly important, come slightly stooping into the presence of this self-important bureaucrat; two others, apparently peasants, are brought by boat to Thebes, forced to prostrate themselves before Menna, and suitably beaten.

The imposition of forced labour as a punishment was, as suggested above, a reasonable way of securing recompense when nothing else could be extracted. Conscription was the regular method by which adequate labour could be recruited for large and small official works in ancient Egypt. It is thought probable that the vast numbers of labourers needed to construct the pyramids of the Fourth and Fifth Dynasties were brought together by conscription during the months of inundation when work in the fields was suspended. It is known that the many field-works required after the subsiding of the inundation were carried out by labour recruited locally for the specific purpose.[19] The precise way by which individuals were selected for this annual call-up is not known; but it is understood from related funerary practices, that the

call to service was not irrevocable. It is certain that a conscripted person could nominate a substitute; it is not at all unlikely that the scribes who made the selection acted frequently unjustly, or were suitably influenced by timely bribes. Unfair or improper conscription to forced labour was a hazard to be expected by anyone who could not afford to buy exemption, or secure it through a patron. The Nauri Decree of Sethos I, already quoted, contains many sections prescribing penalties to be imposed on those foolish enough to conscript men attached to the estates of the great Abydos Temple of the king. What is abundantly clear from a reading of this informative text is that officials in high positions felt able to conscript individuals for official or personal purposes without constraint. Only specifically exempted categories were apparently able to avoid conscription; but the penalties for conscripting a person in such a category might be very harsh. Thus:[20]

> As for any Viceroy of Kush [i.e. the King's representative in Nubia], any troop-commander, any mayor, any agent, or any person who shall take anyone belonging to the Abydos Temple of Sethos forcibly from one district to another by arrangement, on *corvée* for cultivating, or on *corvée* for reaping; similarly, him who shall take any woman or man belonging to the Abydos Temple of Sethos, and similarly their servants, forcibly to perform any duty in the whole land; similarly, any charioteer, any stable-master, and any man of the royal household, sent on any mission of Pharaoh— may he live, be prosperous and healthy—who shall take any man belonging to the Abydos Temple of Sethos from one district to another, by arrangement, on *corvée* for cultivating, or on *corvée* for reaping; similarly, to perform any duty: the law shall be enforced on him by beating him with two hundred blows and five open wounds, together with exacting the work of the person belonging to the Abydos Temple of Sethos from him for every day which he shall pass with him, being handed over [i.e. the wrong-doer] to the Abydos Temple of Sethos.

Evidently, the purpose of such harsh penalties was not to protect the individual who might suffer improper conscription, but to ensure that the temple foundation at Abydos should not have its work-force diverted to other employment; and not even royal service would justify a diminution of this work-force. Nevertheless, conscription in any form was distasteful, something to be avoided if possible, and to be challenged when a successful outcome might be deemed likely. Among a number of literary pieces contained on a papyrus in Turin is one, more or less in the form of a letter, ostensibly written to a scribe in the Temple of Hauron in Memphis by a senior archivist in the office of the royal granary in Memphis, concerning the wrongful conscription of a group of men. The time of the abduction seems to have been some time during the Nineteenth Dynasty.[21] Djehutiemheb says to Bakenptah: 'I hear that you have taken the eight *corvée*-labourers who were at work in the Temple of Thoth in Memphis, and it is to drag stone for (the Temple of) Hauron in Memphis that you set them. Now it is in no way a *corvée*-work that you do; and you take them (only) for two or three days.' He goes on to complain that the nature of the work on which these eight men are engaged is not the kind of work for which men are conscripted; and, in any case, Bakenptah is not entitled to impress workers in this way: 'A shield-bearer of His Majesty or a stable-master or a follower of Pharaoh it is who commandeers the crowd of workers who are in Memphis. It is not you who shall command them in the Temple of Thoth, your god.' So the best that Bakenptah can do is to dismiss the men: 'You should let them go this day so that they may pass the night with another man who has been sent on a mission of Pharaoh tomorrow. How is the matter to be done? Immediately! Death is how I am involved with you.' Djehutiemheb seems to be saying that the improper conscription of the eight men might lead to Bakenptah's death if he does not let them go.

It would, I feel sure, be incorrect to conclude that Djehutiemheb's intervention with Bakenptah was inspired by a desire to put right a wrong inflicted on the eight men who had been improperly diverted to work in the Temple of Hauron. Let us put humanity and justice out of our minds. What is at stake here is the improper diversion of eight men from one duty, expressly described as a *corvée*-work, to another in which they were equally constrained, though not strictly by *corvée*. The men are scarcely considered as human beings; they are nameless labourers, pawns in a bureaucratic wrangle between two officials. Where in all this does the justice of ancient Egypt lie? Somewhere, presumably, in the worthy intentions of those who seek power and position, and equally in the nostalgic retrospect of lives well and honourably lived by the same men of power and position. The actuality may be less honourable, and it should not be too surprising for being so. The business of daily life in an autocratic state is generally conducted with greater regard for the machine of government than for the rights of individuals. Surely, the strong appreciation we feel in modern times for the rights of individuals arises to a great extent from the fact that these rights have so rarely been recognized in the past. In ancient Egypt a man of lowly position would not have set his rights above his duties, and his duties lay centred on the King and the State, including within these duties any obligation he might have towards his immediate master, whether it be an individual or a temple (or other) administration. If his interests were to be at variance with those of the State or of his master, he could scarcely expect to see them prosper. The most he could probably hope for was that in any particular situation he might have his side of a dispute listened to without its summary dismissal. In a straightforward case, where no special interests of his superiors were involved, he might expect some form of hearing, and look forward to the possibility of a favourable verdict. It was not that the scales of justice were deliberately weighted against the weak and unimportant. Justice in such a society was much more an expectation of consideration than a constitutional right.

Criminal cases of a modest kind, in which the safety of the State was not involved, were either settled in an arbitrary manner by local magistrates, or tried in a relatively formal process before legal tribunals which were set up on a local basis for *ad hoc* purposes. The best attested tribunal of this latter kind was summoned, as required, in the village of necropolis workmen of the Place of Truth—the artisans of the royal tombs at Thebes.[22] Some of the inscribed ostraca found in the neighbourhood of this village, known today as Deir el-Medina, contain records of cases brought before tribunals, the members of which are drawn from the ranks of the workmen themselves. The paucity of evidence from similar villages and communities elsewhere in Egypt prevents our knowing whether tribunals of this kind were generally common throughout the land during the New Kingdom. It is of course true that the community of workmen was special in more senses than one, and that it enjoyed privileges which reflected the importance of the work performed by its members. Nevertheless, it is reasonable to assume that the setting-up of 'worker courts' was not confined to this one place, and that other close communities in the land were equally able to conduct forms of legal proceedings in cases of local interest.

The 'court' or *qenbet* of workmen of the Place of Truth was convened, it would appear, to deal with specific cases as they occurred; its composition was wholly of members of the workmen's community, but the rules by which the constituents were appointed are not known. Ideally, no doubt, the list of worker-magistrates serving in any particular case should be headed by one of the two chief workmen, who were individually in charge of the 'right' and 'left' gangs of workmen; a scribe or two and a selection of more modest villagers completed the complement. The procedures of operating this court are splendidly revealed in a text inscribed on a limestone ostracon in the British Museum, dated 'Regnal Year 6, third month of summer, day 10', almost certainly in the sixth year of King Sethos II of the Nineteenth Dynasty (c. 1204 BC).[23] The workman Nebnufe made a complaint on that day to the court against the citizeness Herya in the following terms:

'I buried a tool of mine in my house after the war, and it was stolen. I made everyone in the village clear themselves in the matter of my tool. Then after some days the citizeness Nubemnehem came to tell me, "Divine power obliges me (to speak): I saw Herya taking your tool." So she said.'

Then the court said to Herya: 'Are you the one who stole Nebnufe's tool? True or false!'

What Herya said: 'False! It was not I who stole it.'

What the court said to her: 'Can you swear the great oath of the Lord—may he live, be prosperous, and healthy—concerning the tool, as follows, "It was not I who stole it."?'

Then the citizeness Herya said: 'As Amun endures, and as the Ruler—may he live, be prosperous, and healthy—endures—he whose power is more dire than death, the Pharaoh—if it is found that it was I who stole the tool . . .'[24]

After an hour in which the court examined her, the attendant Pashedu was dispatched with her, and she brought the tool which was buried at her place, together with a ritual vessel belonging to Amun-of-good-encounter, which had been buried in her house, having stolen the counterpart(?) of the ritual vessel of Amun. And yet she swore the great oath of the Lord—may he live, be prosperous, and healthy—saying, 'It was not I who stole this tool.'

Then the court said: 'Exceedingly guilty is the citizeness Herya, and worthy of death. The workman Nebnufe is vindicated.'

Her case was suspended until the vizir came.

The (composition of the) court on this day:

> The chief workman Paneb
> The chief workman Hay
> The scribe Pashedu
> The scribe Paser
> The scribe Pentaur
> The police-chief Mentmose
> The guardian Ypuy
> And the gang all together

Hence the disgust of this village—the theft of metal objects from it, with the complicity of the widow [i.e. Herya].

Let my Lord [the vizir] know the practice of the place: A citizeness Tanedjemhemes stole a metal *tjek*-vessel of one and a half *deben* here, from the village, formerly in the time of the vizir Neferronpe, although she was the wife of Pashedu, son of Heh. The vizir sent for the scribe Hatiay, and had him take her to the quay [river-bank].

My Lord should act so as to have this woman punished for stealing the tool and likewise the ritual vessel, that no other woman of her kind should do the same again.

See! I have informed my Lord.

Now it is the vizir who knows. Let him make all his dispositions as he wishes. May it be known!

The case dealt with in this text was concerned with much more than the simple theft of Nebnufe's tool. In the course of the proceedings it emerged that the woman Herya had also stolen a ritual vessel from a shrine of Amun. To theft, therefore, was added desecration. It is small wonder that the workmen's court felt unable to pass a sentence on Herya, and adjourned the matter for consideration by the vizir. The vizir, as we have already seen, was the one who had to watch over the proper administration of justice throughout the land. He, in consequence, also had the responsibility of passing sentence in cases of gravity referred to him from lower courts. It is interesting to see in the text on this ostracon that in addition to the bare outline of the case a precedent is cited from the past, and a recommendation made that severe punishment be given.

From the sketchy nature of the account of the case, and the various omissions of vital matters, like the completion of the oath, it can be assumed that what is written on this limestone ostracon represents a kind of *aide-mémoire* or memorandum from which the clerk of the court—no doubt one of the scribes from the village—would have prepared a report to be sent on to the vizir. In the vizir's office the precedent cited could be checked, and the punishment meted out on that occasion brought before the vizir for reference. Some hints at procedure can be squeezed from the text. What is clear, however, is that the proceedings were somewhat arbitrary and, from the account given, one-sided. The widow Herya, denounced by a neighbour, was evidently not allowed to plead her case in full. But it would be unfair to dismiss the proceedings as being wholly weighted against the accused. The ostracon does not carry a transcript but only a summary. Nevertheless, the general impression of rough justice cannot be denied. It was surely a case in which the humble status of the accused did little to assist her. The case cited as precedent, on the other hand, involved, it seems, a woman of superior status; yet the matter went ahead and the judgement was given against her. So status was not a sure protection.

Hay, the chief workman who formed part of the court which tried the case of Nebnufe's tool, was involved in another matter investigated by a similarly constituted court the year before. In this case his position in the ranks of the workmen seems to have helped him to obtain an outcome happier than that suffered by Herya. The brief account of this case is preserved on another ostracon from the Theban necropolis, now in the Cairo Museum:[25]

> The chief workman Hay came before the court with Penamun, Ptahshedu, Wenenufe and Tawosre, in the presence of the magistrates of the court:
>
> The chief workman Paneb
> Nebsmenu
> Amennakhte
> Nekhuemmut
> Huy
> Pashedu
> Rahotpe

Nebnufe, son of Pennub
Nebnufe, son of Wadjmose
Huy, son of Inherkhau
Meryre
Ypu
And the gang as a whole

What the chief workman Hay said: 'As for me, I was asleep in my hut when Penamun came out with his people, and they spoke about the utterance involving the greatness of Pharaoh—may he live, be prosperous, and healthy—attributed to Hay: "He has spoken curses against Sethos." '

The court said to them: 'Tell us what you heard.'

They went back on their words to get out of the matter.

The chief workman Paneb said to them: 'Tell us what you heard.'

And they said: 'We didn't hear anything.'

The court said to them, i.e. to Penamun, Ptahshedu, Wenenufe and Tawosre: 'Say: "As Amun endures and as the Ruler endures, there was no utterance [of Hay] against Pharaoh—may he live, be prosperous and healthy—and if we keep quiet about it today so as to reveal it in a day or two's time, (our) nose and ears should be cut off, [for we should have committed] an evil act." '

And they were given a hundred severe blows with a staff.

From this brief account of the case it is not at all clear what was the charge which needed investigation, and even who was in fact on trial. It was either a charge of slander by Penamun and his accomplices against Hay, or a charge of criminal blasphemy committed by Hay against the person of Pharaoh. From the way in which the investigation was conducted it seems that the workmen's court was primarily concerned with establishing the truth of the declaration by Penamun and the others that Hay had spoken against King Sethos. No effort was made— if the text conveys a fair, if abbreviated, account of the proceedings—to establish what precisely Hay was supposed to have said about the king. The court was surely relieved when the accusers refused to repeat their charge before the tribunal of magistrates. If they had maintained Hay's guilt, and declared unequivocally what they claimed he had said, then the grave charge against Hay would have had to be pursued. Further, it may be assumed that such a charge would have lain outside the competence of the workmen's court. *Lése-majesty* was not a matter for a local court, even one so unusual and favoured as that composed of workmen of the royal necropolis. In all probability it would have been passed on to the vizir's court, and that surely would have sealed Hay's fate. The modern reader can perhaps sense a closing of the ranks by the workmen-magistrates to protect an important member of their community, one of the leaders of the two main gangs of workmen. For him to have been convicted of treason might have brought all kinds of bad consequences on many families in the village. So personal interests also probably played their role in the determination that the charge of blasphemy—which would have to be investigated, or awkward questions might subsequently have been asked—should in effect be dropped through the lack of evidence. The consequent condemnation of Penamun and company through the oath of disclaim which they were required to repeat, conveniently cancelled the charge against Hay, and provided the court with a crime for which they could properly pass a sentence without reference to higher authority. We shall never know whether Hay ever did pass some foolish remark against King Sethos, but it does seem likely that his accusers were in the end made scapegoats for him.

The case of Hay versus Penamun and others provides a good example of the conduct of a criminal action culminating in the imposition of a summary sentence. Civil cases required much more careful handling, and seem to have had more involved and established procedures. As we have already noted, matters of inheritance, of land tenure, and similar, were those which particularly engaged the time and interest of Egyptian courts. And because Egypt enjoyed for very long periods settled social conditions, it was possible to bring to court cases which needed the consultation of old documents and the invoking of events lying far in the past. The most instructive case of this kind, for which good textual evidence is available, dates from the reign of Ramesses II (*c.* 1250 BC) and concerns events the earliest of which go back to the first years of the Eighteenth Dynasty (*c.* 1550 BC).

Mose, a scribe of the treasury of the god Ptah, whose great shrine was in Memphis, achieved sufficient status in his life to be allowed a fairly substantial burial in the great Memphite necropolis. The tomb was at Saqqara and the chapel, built above ground, was decorated with fairly conventional ritual scenes.[26] Two walls, however, were almost wholly occupied by a long and remarkable text in which the protracted legal proceedings concerning the inheritance of some land were set out for posterity.[27] The matter must have occupied a central position in Mose's life, and its successful outcome (for we must assume this to have been the case, although the end of the affair is lost) must have represented a triumph possibly beyond Mose's expectations. Its importance for Mose is indisputable; the future fortunes of his family surely depended on the success of the action. Unfortunately, as is so often the case with Egyptian texts, the background is generally unknown; in only one or two particulars, through the extraordinary chances of survival, can the story revealed in the tomb-inscription be supplemented.

The land about which the dispute occurred was part of a gift given by Amosis, the first king of the Eighteenth Dynasty (c. 1554–1529 BC) to an ancestor of the parties in the case called Neshi, who is given the title 'overseer of ships', perhaps the equivalent of 'flotilla commander'. Neshi is not a very common Egyptian name, but one person so called has been rescued from oblivion in recent years. A great inscription found at Karnak in 1954 recorded part of the history of the campaign conducted by Kamose, the last king of the Seventeenth Dynasty and predecessor of Amosis, to free Egypt of the Hyksos.[28] The last lines of the inscription read:

> His Majesty ordered the prince and count, who is privy to the secrets of the palace, and chief of the whole land, the treasurer of the King of Lower Egypt, instructor of the Two Lands, leader, overseer of (royal) companions, overseer of treasurers, the valiant one, Neshi: 'Let all that My Majesty has accomplished in victory be recorded on a stela resting in its place in Karnak in the Theban nome for ever and ever.' He then declared before His Majesty: 'I shall act in accordance with all that is commanded.' And the favours of the king were commanded.

A small figure of a man carved by the side of these words represents, according to the short accompanying text, 'the overseer of treasurers, Neshi'. The suggestion has been made that this Neshi, so honoured by Kamose, was the man who subsequently was honoured again by Kamose's successor, Amosis, and given a grant of land in the region of Memphis.[29] A doubt should, however, be recorded, for the Neshi of Mose's inscription was a 'flotilla commander', which was scarcely as high a rank as those held by the Neshi of the Kamose text. The search for the historical Neshi need not stop at this point. From surviving examples of inscribed funerary cones, used to decorate the façades of New Kingdom rock-cut tombs, there is good reason to think that another Neshi, also a 'flotilla commander', was buried in Thebes.[30] The precise date of his burial, which certainly occurred in the first half of the Eighteenth Dynasty, is unestablished, but there is some reason to think that this other Neshi could have served in Amosis' successful campaigns against the Hyksos, and have been suitably rewarded with a gift of land. It would, further, not be at all unreasonable to suggest that this Neshi was the grandson of Kamose's Neshi.[31] More than this can scarcely be proposed. One other helpful coincidence is worth mentioning. In the Mose inscription the land is placed in what is called 'the village of Neshi'. Just such a place is mentioned in a long document dated to the reign of Ramesses V of the Twentieth Dynasty (c. 1155 BC), approximately one hundred years after the date of Mose's lawsuit, and four hundred years after the grant of land was made to Neshi. This village in the Wilbour Papyrus (as the document of Ramesses V is known) has been placed about fifty kilometres to the south of Memphis.[32]

Mose went to law because he was convinced that he had been done out of his inheritance of part of the estate granted to Neshi by King Amosis. From the various depositions of witnesses and participants recorded in the long inscription it appears that for over two hundred years the estate of Neshi passed down from generation to generation in the hands of single successive trustees who administered it on behalf of the members of the family who were entitled to share in the product of the estate. The trustee who was occupying this position in the reign of Horemheb, last king of the Eighteenth Dynasty (c. 1332–1305 BC), was Khay, son of Userhat. His position was challenged in the Great Court in Heliopolis (an ancient and most important religious centre not far to the north-east of Memphis) by Werenro, Mose's grandmother. An officer of the court was sent to the village of Neshi, and as a result the estate was placed under the trusteeship of Werenro. Shortly afterwards Takharu, Werenro's sister (or female relative),[33] challenged the settlement, again before the Great Court, and after a further investigation on the ground by an officer of the court, the inheritance was divided, apparently for the first time, between the six individual heirs.

Subsequently, Werenro with her son Huy (Mose's father), again took up the matter, but it seems that they were unable to bring the case to court before Huy died. Mose, as Huy's heir, inherited his right to part of the Neshi estate, but was presumably a minor at this time. His mother Nubnofret therefore undertook the cultivation of the land, but was prevented from doing so by the old opponent Khay, who was her cousin by marriage. In order to prove her claim she asked: 'Have brought to me the registers from the Treasury and also from the Department of the Granary of Pharaoh—may he live, be prosperous, and healthy—I am fully certain in saying I am the daughter [i.e. female descendant] of Neshi.' Khay brought the case before the Great Court in Year 18 of Ramesses II, and produced with the collusion (or through the deceiving) of a court official a register said by Nubnofret to be forged. On the instruction of the vizir, who was now in charge of the case, the parties were taken to Piramesse, the Delta Residence of Ramesses II, and the two registers requested by Nubnofret were produced and consulted. 'Who is your heir among the heirs who are in the two registers we have to hand?' asked the vizir. Nubnofret said: 'There is no heir among them'. 'Then,' said the vizir, 'you are in the wrong.' Having thus established what appeared to be the truth of the matter, the vizir ordered a redistribution of Neshi's land, and Khay was granted thirteen *setjat* of land—approximately nine acres.

So the matter stood when Mose assumed control of his family affairs, probably on coming of age. Determined to regain control of his proper inheritance he set about proving the legitimacy of his claim. The last parts of the long text are sadly damaged, but the fragments at least show how he obtained depositions from people who could testify that he was descended from Neshi, and that his direct ancestors had cultivated parts of the Neshi estate. Among the witnesses were people in official positions, a priest of the Temple of Ptah, a bee-keeper of the Treasury of Pharaoh, and a stable-master; also ordinary folk, including several women. The outcome is assumed to have been favourable, as was stated at the beginning of our discussion of the case. The text's end is not needed to confirm this; the presence of the text in the tomb of Mose speaks for itself.

5 (above) Limestone ostracon containing an account of the legal proceedings against the woman Herya (BM 65930): front (left) and back (right).
(below) A garden pool from the tomb of Nebamun (BM 37983).

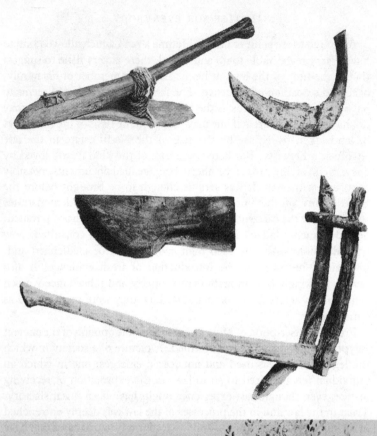

Although Mose achieved in his lifetime a rank which allowed him to have a very respectable tomb and burial, there is very little to suggest that at the time of the lawsuit he, or any other member of his family, occupied a position of influence. The famous ancestor Neshi seems to have provided such status as the family possessed, and even this may not have been very great if one may judge, on the basis of the nine acres of land taken by Khay, by the size of the Neshi estate in the late Eighteenth Dynasty. But here was a case of the kind dearly loved by lawyers, involving property, inheritance, falsified documents, possibly suborned witnesses. It was serious enough to be brought before the Great Court of the northern vizir in Heliopolis. It demonstrates something of the care with which a case of this kind might be pursued; how documents lodged in official archives might be consulted; how legal decisions taken by such high courts could be challenged and, ultimately, reversed by the introduction of fresh evidence. It also reveals strikingly how in matters of property and inheritance women were able to act as freely as men, and how they were readily used as witnesses.

From the inscription of Mose a very favourable opinion of the ancient Egyptian legal system may be formed. A picture of a society in which the legal system was used and not feared emerges; one in which an individual felt prepared to go to law, in the expectation of receiving justice, even though past experience might have been unsatisfactory. Trust in the law and in the processes of the law was deeply entrenched in the minds of the Egyptians, and the accounts of actual cases that have survived from antiquity generally confirm this trust. Justice was for everyone, and even if the practice of justice did not always favour the poor and lowly, it seems that the poor and lowly always hoped that the law might be on their side. To be fair and unprejudiced was the declared aim of the law. So the vizir was commanded: 'Do not make judgement improperly(?); God hates biased behaviour . . . See equally the man you know and the man you don't know, the man who is near you and the man who is far away.'

6 (above) Hoe, sickle, winnowing scoop, wooden plough; the sickle has flint blades (BM 22863, 52861, 18206, 50705).
   (below) Quarrelling girls and resting workers in the harvest field; from the tomb of Menna.

NOTES

1 L.62f. of Papyrus Leningrad 1116A; see n.1 to Chapter One.

2 From the tomb-inscription of Pepinakhte; see K. Sethe, *Urkunden des Alten Reichs* (Leipzig, 1932), 133, ll.2–5.

3 Papyrus Leningrad 1116A, ll.46–50.

4 *The Story of the Eloquent Peasant* is known from several (but no complete) papyrus texts. For a useful bibliography and a translation, see M. Lichtheim, *Ancient Egyptian Literature*, I, 169 ff.

5 'Thief' is a free translation of the Egyptian for 'the one who does'.

6 The god of embalmment and of the necropolis. The implication here may be that he will make petition in death.

7 From *The Instruction of Amenemope*, 20.20–21.8. On this text, see n.7 to Chapter One.

8 *The Blinding of Truth by Falsehood* is contained in British Museum Papyrus 10682. For bibliography and translation, see M. Lichtheim, *Ancient Egyptian Literature*, II, 211 ff.

9 Usually taken to be a knife, although more probably an axe.

10 For the legal implications of the story, see A. Théodoridès in *Revue d'Égyptologie* 21 (Paris, 1969), 85 ff.

11 The decree is published in W. Helck, *Urkunden der 18. Dynastie* (Berlin, 1958), 2140 ff. A translation in J. H. Breasted, *Ancient Records*, III, 22 ff. The words quoted are in l.27 of the text.

12 For the text, see K. A. Kitchen, *Ramesside Inscriptions*, I (Oxford, 1975), 45 ff.; a translation by F. Ll. Griffith in *Journal of Egyptian Archaeology* 13 (London, 1927), 193 ff.

13 Sir Alan Gardiner in *Journal of Egyptian Archaeology* 38 (1952), 24.

14 Nauri Decree, ll.50–53.

15 Nauri Decree, ll.66–71.

16 See n.7 to Chapter Two.

17 T. G. H. James and M. R. Apted, *The Mastaba of Khentika called Ikhekhi* (London, 1953), pl.IX.

18 Theban Tomb no.69; see B. Porter and R. L. B. Moss, *Topographical Bibliography of Ancient Egyptian Hieroglyphic Texts*, I, 2 ed., Pt. I (Oxford, 1960), 134 f. The scene discussed is part of (2).

19 H. Schneider, *Shabtis*, I (Leiden, 1977), 9 ff.

20 Nauri Decree, ll.42–7.

21 From Turin Papyrus 1882; see A. H. Gardiner, *Late-Egyptian Miscellanies*, 123.

22 J. Černý in *Cambridge Ancient History*, II, Pt. 2, 624; also A. Théodoridès in *Revue Internationale des Droits de l'Antiquité* 16 (1969), 103 ff.; M. L. Bierbrier, *The Tomb-Builders of the Pharaohs*, Chapter 6.

23 British Museum no. 65930 (Nash ostracon 1); see J. Černý and Sir Alan Gardiner, *Hieratic Ostraca*, I (Oxford, 1957), pl.XLVI, 2. It is discussed by A. Théodoridès, op. cit., 128 ff.

24 The consequence is not written down.

25 Cairo 25556, published by J. Černý in *Annales du Service des Antiquités de l'Égypte* 27 (1927), 200 ff.; discussed by A. Théodoridès, op. cit., 123 ff.

26 The tomb fragments are now mostly in the Cairo Museum, and published by G. A. Gaballa, *The Memphite Tomb-chapel of Mose* (Warminster, 1977).

27 The text was first and most fully discussed by A. H. Gardiner, *The Inscription of Mes* (Leipzig, 1905); see also Gaballa, op. cit., 22 ff.

28 Now in the Luxor Museum, no. J.43; see *Luxor Museum of Ancient Egyptian Art* (Cairo, 1979), 36 f. The inscription is published in L. Habachi, *The Second Stela of Kamose* (Glückstadt, 1972).

29 The identification was due in the first place to G. Posener in *Revue d'Égyptologie* 16 (Paris, 1964), 213 f.; see also Habachi, op. cit., 44, 50; and Gaballa, op. cit., 28.

30 Habachi, op. cit., 57. For the cones, see N. de G. Davies and M. F. L. Macadam, *A Corpus of inscribed Egyptian funerary cones* (Oxford, 1957), no. 138 (where the name is read Seshi).

31 Boys in ancient Egypt were commonly called after their grandfathers.

32 A. H. Gardiner, *The Wilbour Papyrus*, II (Oxford, 1948), 32 f., 178.

33 The Egyptian language was weak in terms of relationship. Thus the word for 'sister' could at times be used for 'wife', and for other female relatives.

4
THE BUCOLIC MODE

Even the most city-bound person has some feeling for, if no understanding of, the rural life. It may show itself in the simple wish to escape
the constraints of the city, a desire to commune with nature in the
vaguest and most sentimental sense. It may be seen in an inclination to
dispense with the artificialities of town life, as they appear to be. Some
feel a simple urge to return to the earth, to grow things and practise
husbandry. This urge to return to the earth is commonly a chimera.
Nevertheless, there is an elemental quality about this attraction to the
rural life—an attraction which includes not only the openness and
beauty of natural surroundings, but also the actual activities of
agriculture. The fascination of making things grow, both plants and
animals, is deeply rooted in the human spirit, but its manifestation may
not always be greeted with pleasure.

An ambivalence of attitude towards the life on the land was as
common in antiquity as it is today. The truth of the matter is that
agriculture involves hard, physical toil, and this was so even in ancient
Egypt where the business of husbandry was in most respects easier than
elsewhere, both in the ancient and the modern world before the
introduction of labour-saving machinery. A thriving agricultural
economy meant simply a thriving economy; and for much of antiquity
the ease and success of agriculture in Egypt were the envy of other races
and the prime reasons for invasion and infiltration. In periods of
famine, or even at times of seasonal shortage, small groups of foreigners
might make their way into Egypt in search of pasture to feed their
flocks. An efficient bureaucracy also helped to minimize the effects of
occasional droughts and of low or extra high inundations of the Nile. In
difficult circumstances Jacob sent his sons to Egypt: 'I have heard that
there is corn in Egypt. Go down and buy some so that we may keep
ourselves alive and not starve.'[1] The same reason, at an earlier time, had

prompted Abraham to make the same journey: 'There came a famine to the land, so severe that Abraham went down to Egypt to live there for a while.'[2]

The reactions of Egyptians to self-invited visitors of this kind seems to have been generous and humane, certainly at the local level where general instructions had to be interpreted and applied. The direct evidence is slim, but the presence of large numbers of Asiatics in Egypt at certain periods may well have been due to the gradual infiltration over many years of foreigners who chose to stay on after the emergency caused by external famine had passed. The Hyksos domination of Egypt during the Second Intermediate Period probably came about in this way. Yet the movement of migrants continued in later times as if no lesson had been learned. A frontier official writing to his superior during the reign of Merneptah of the Nineteenth Dynasty (c. 1224–1214 BC) includes in his report:[3]

> Another message to my lord: We have finished letting the Beduin tribes of Edom pass the fort Merneptah-Hetephermaat—may he live, be prosperous and healthy—which is in Tjeku, to (visit) the pools of Pithom of Merneptah-Hetephermaat which are in Tjeku, in order to let them and their flocks live, by the great favour of Pharaoh—may he live, be prosperous and healthy.

Regularity in agricultural expectation was without doubt the most important element in the Egyptians' attitude to life and death. Nowhere was the annual cycle of the seasons so clearly marked as in Egypt, where the Nile flood arrived with predictable regularity, determining by its height the success of the harvest and, incidentally, confirming the good will of the gods towards the country. The Nile was special among rivers, and in consequence Egypt was special. It was not like other countries, and the Egyptians, in recognizing this special character, extended it also to themselves, the inhabitants of that land. By further extension, the ideal nature of life in Egypt—a model of rural bliss—provided the pattern for the after-life to which the properly qualified Egyptian might attain. After surviving judgement in the halls of Osiris, the divine king of the after-life, the Egyptian expected to pass his time in the Field of Reeds, a kind of Elysium, which was visualized as an other-worldly Egypt, watered by an other-worldly Nile. Here he engaged in agricultural activities of ploughing and reaping as if he were a peasant on the land. In the copy of *The Book of the Dead* written for the scribe Ani, the painted vignette showing Ani so engaged is accompanied by a text (part of Chapter 110) which says:[4]

> The start of the spells of the Field of Offerings, the spells of going out by day, of entering and leaving the necropolis, of being looked after in the Field of Reeds, which is in the Field of Offerings, the city of the Great One, the Lady of the Winds, being strong there, being a spirit there so as to plough there, to reap there, to eat there and to drink there, in fact, to do everything that is done on earth.

The centrality of agriculture in Egyptian life, made explicit by this statement of what was thought proper for a fulfilled after-life, is understandable and yet surprising. For no matter how important cultivation was for the continuation of life in Egypt, it must be supposed that most of the people who expected to enjoy an eternity in the Field of Reeds had never put hand to plough during their earthly lives. Yet, so fundamental were the processes of agriculture, together with irrigation and other rural activities, that they are specifically mentioned at the time of judgement when the dead Egyptian presented himself before Osiris and his panel of forty-two assessors. Among the denials of moral laxity and lack of proper religious observance, the deceased plaintiff declares: 'I have not reduced the acre, I have not made inroads on fields [i.e. of other people] . . . I have not removed herds from their pastures . . . I have not misdirected water in its time, I have not dammed running water.'[5] The maintenance of these agricultural proprieties in daily life can have posed negligible problems for the well-placed Egyptian official, but in detail, as we shall see later, the proprieties were essential to the good economy of the country. And it is this basis of sound agricultural policy which prompted both the inclusion of the principles of good husbandry in the properly conducted life on earth, and the expectation of a way of life dominated by ploughing and reaping in the after-life. It is not a reflection of a sentimental and romantic attitude towards rustic pursuits on the part of the well-placed ancient Egyptians.

Indeed, the enjoyment sought by well-to-do Egyptians in the attractions of nature was largely confined to the pleasure to be found in a well-tended garden, a pool, an arbour and the discreet attention of servants. To be a farmer was not at all a thing to desire. Apart from the misery of seasonal catastrophe, which seemed to characterize life on the land for the bureaucrat and the noble, there was far too much hard work involved. 'Be a scribe,' says one of the well-copied passages used possibly as instructive exercises in the scribal academies of the New Kingdom. It continues:[6]

> It saves you from hard work and preserves you from every kind of labour. It protects you from carrying a hoe and a mattock(?), that you may not carry a basket.

The miserable life of the farmer is described in fuller detail in another passage of the same kind:[7]

> Let me set out for you the farmer's state—that other hard calling. When the water is full he irrigates [the fields ?], servicing his equipment. He spends the day cutting tools for cultivating barley, and the night twisting ropes. His midday hour even [his dinner-time ?] he is in the habit of spending in farmer's work. He sets about equipping himself to sally forth to the field like any warrior. The field is parched and set out before him; he goes out to recover his team. Many days later, after tracking the herdsman, he recovers the team. He comes leading it and he makes a path for it in the field. At dawn he goes out to begin work early, and he does not find it [the team] in its place. He spends three days looking for it, and finds it (stuck) in the mud. But he does not find any hides on them [i.e. the animals of the team], because the jackals have bitten them.

After a further list of natural calamities, the writer of this encouraging essay adds:

> The scribe moors at the river bank. He estimates the harvest tax, attended by lackeys carrying staves, and Nubians with clubs. They say: 'Produce barley!' but there is none, and he [the farmer] is beaten violently. He is tied up and cast into a pool. He is ducked and thoroughly soaked, while his wife is tied up in his presence, and his children are in shackles. His neighbours desert them, and are fled. It is the end; there is no barley. If you are mindful, be a scribe.

It was, we may suppose, proper to encourage the trainee scribe—the budding bureaucrat of Egypt—in this heavily prejudiced way. What young man in his right mind would renounce a comfortable desk for the life on the land? But, in case the student-scribe wearied of the precise training he was obliged to follow, and thought with envy of the farmer's freedom, a discouraging account of rural life had to be placed before him. The procedure is familiar; but criticism served thick and indiscriminate does not encourage belief. To what extent did the disagreeable picture paraded before the student-scribe correspond with the reasonable experience of an Egyptian farmer? Not much, it may be said, as far as the farmer, the land-owner, was concerned; but quite considerably, it may also be said, as far as the peasant, the field-worker, was concerned. What may be learned for the New Kingdom from the depictions of agricultural life in the decorated tombs of the Theban necropolis, is in a general sense too ideal. The concept of tomb decoration implies the representation of what might be thought best for the tomb-owner. The decoration presented life on earth for life in the hereafter—life in microcosm, ideal and successful, in which the snags represented were modest, doing little or nothing to jeopardize the posthumous existence of the tomb-owner. If encounters with the law, for example, were shown, like the apprehension and bringing to justice of the tax-dodgers in the tomb of Menna,[8] it was usually to show up the tomb-owner's own righteousness, or to illustrate his own position as a legal officer of some kind. It would not have been right to show a tomb-owner as a malefactor, even in a small way, on the walls of his tomb, for the tomb served as part of his equipment for achieving his destiny. And for that his record had to be impeccable.

What then can be learned about Egyptian agriculture from tomb scenes? From the time of the Old Kingdom, when the tombs of non-royal persons were first provided with scenes of everyday activities, agricultural scenes were commonly included, and, as early as the Fifth Dynasty, achieved a kind of order or pattern (almost a stereotype) which persisted in the standard repertoire of tomb scenes down to the New Kingdom and later. The principal theme was the cultivation of the staple crops, cereals and flax, the former for food and for brewing beer, the latter for the production of linen, the chief textile material of ancient Egypt. These crops are precisely those shown in the vignettes illustrating Chapter 110 of *The Book of the Dead*, mentioned earlier— the bases of life for the Egyptians. But whereas, in the vignettes of the religious papyri, the cultivators are the deceased for whom the papyri were written, frequently accompanied by their spouses, those who work the land in the tomb scenes are peasants labouring on the estates of the tomb-owner, also deceased. How confused then were attitudes to

fields.[12] What particularly enlivens the pictures of peasants at work is the inclusion of texts containing remarks attributed to some of the labourers. The upper part of the wall containing the principal scenes is divided into three rows or registers of small-scale scenes, overshadowed by a figure of Paheri on the left, shown at much larger scale. He is said to be 'seeing the seasons of drought [harvest], the season of coming-forth [cultivation], and all the activities going on in the fields', and he is characterized by the epithet, 'he who makes inspection in the land of the southern province'. What he inspects is laid out in the three facing registers which need to be taken in the order bottom to top, reading, as it were, from the right (*Figs. 5–12*).

The first group shown in the lowest register consists of six men engaged in ploughing by hand. Two pairs drag forward the plough which is controlled by an elderly man, his age and somewhat superior status indicated by his thin, wispy hair and his paunch, the latter always a sign in Egyptian scenes of a reasonably prosperous life. A young man completes the group; he walks behind the plough casting seed into the furrow. The plough is very simple, consisting of a pole, at the lower end of which a wooden share is loosely attached, and prevented from forming too wide an angle with the share by a twisted rope. From the same end of the pole rises the handle used more to hold the ploughshare down in the furrow than to control the direction. The old man clearly presses down as they move forward. The design of this typical Egyptian plough is primitive, but very effective; from the few surviving examples it is clear that only occasionally was the share more than a pointed piece of wood, perhaps fire-hardened; rare examples show traces of bronze blades, and these were not shaped to turn the sod to the side as modern ploughshares do. The men who draw the plough use, it appears, two different means: the forward pair pull apparently on a crossbar inserted at right angles through the top end of the pole, while the second pair drag on ropes or thongs fastened in some way to a point about half-way along the pole. It is rather unusual to have a plough drawn by man-power, a task usually performed by cattle, as we see further along the same register. Nevertheless, the labourers appointed to this work do not appear to be too dispirited. They declare (the words are written above them, rather like a strip-cartoon 'balloon') 'Let us work. Look at us. Do not fear for the fields; they are in splendid condition.' Meanwhile their enthusiasm is echoed by the young man broadcasting the

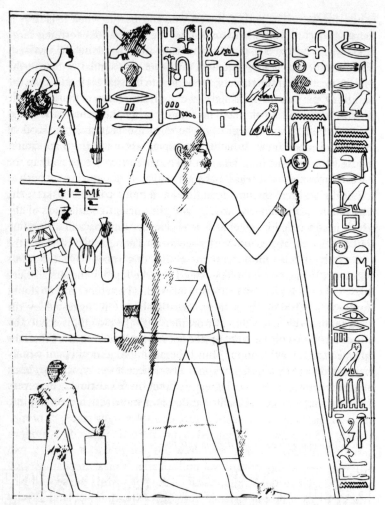

Fig. 5 Paheri inspects the work in his fields, accompanied by attendants with various supplies including napkins, sandals and a stool.

grain: 'The year is good, free from difficulties; all crops flourish and the calves are better than anything.' The old man at the plough answers: 'What you say is quite right, my son' (*Fig. 6*).

Moving left along the register we come to two pairs of labourers using hoes to break up the ground further, after the ploughs have made the initial furrows. The soil of Egypt, fine and friable when it is dry, is heavy and glutinous when soaked by the inundation, forming large clods which had to be broken up by hand after the plough had passed. The form of hoe shown here is in principle very similar to that of the plough except that the part corresponding to the share is longer than the handle. One pair of hoes have the connecting ropes found on the plough; the second pair show no ropes, probably because each hoe is fashioned out of a single piece of wood with a natural angle. Hoes of both kinds are known in actual examples surviving from antiquity. Those with separate handles and blades, frequently—especially in the New Kingdom—have paddle-shaped blades, so designed to act both as a useful clod-breaking implement and as a tool for filling baskets, the equivalent of the modern shovel, and the ancient counterpart of the *turiya* used in Egypt today as a dual-purpose digging and shovelling tool. The artist who executed this scene has distinguished carefully the two types of hoe; those with the connecting ropes have the joints between the handles and blades clearly marked, while the single-piece hoes, very correctly, have no joints marked. The serene, but no doubt implausible enthusiasm in their back-breaking toil suggested by the comments of the first group of workmen with the plough, is echoed by one of the men with the single-piece hoes: 'I shall do even more than the (allotted) task for the noble.' But his crawling eagerness is not wholly welcomed by one of his fellows on the two-piece hoes: 'My friend, buck up the work so that you let us go home in good time.' It is very satisfactory at last to find a little touch of dissatisfaction creeping into

Fig. 6 Ploughing by hand and digging with hoes.

the idyllic picture which would provide Paheri with the stage-set for his posthumous existence.

More ploughing is shown next in the register. Two groups manage two ploughs, here represented one behind the other, but in reality probably ploughing parallel furrows. These ploughs are drawn by pairs of oxen, and from the represented detail it can be seen that the pole in each case is attached to a transverse rod which is fastened by rope to the horns of the oxen.[13] This method of attachment, apparently not uncommon, at least on the basis of the New Kingdom evidence, seems to have gained favour over the older and more obvious use of a yoke fitted over the necks of the animals. Each plough is controlled by one labourer, pressing down on the handle to keep the share in the ground, and each is accompanied by another man dispensing the seed. The man in control of the second plough uses a two-thonged whip to urge on his team, while a child apparently performs the same duty for the first group. Deliberate damage to part of his figure obscures precisely what he holds in his raised hand, but a whip or goad may be supposed. This damage to faces and, in certain cases, to hands also, occurs throughout the tomb; it is a form of mutilation probably inflicted on the reliefs by squatters who used the tomb as a house in later times. Such squatters, not necessarily early Christians, as is often claimed, feared the active hostility of the people shown in the reliefs, animated by magical means—the reverse, as it were, of the expectation of Paheri who had

Fig. 7 Ploughing with teams of oxen. Paheri's chariot awaits his return.

the reliefs carved that they might, again by magical means, be animated for his own benefit after his death. This disfigurement, happily, rarely conceals in this tomb what was originally depicted (*Fig. 7*).

A text running above the two ploughing teams expresses the general pleasure of the men in their work: 'A fine day; it is cool; the cattle are drawing (the plough); the sky favours us; let us work for the noble.' But even where the façade of eagerness and diligence appears sound and smooth, all is not necessarily well. The suggestion of guilt creeps into the words which the second ploughman calls out to the first: 'Hurry up, leader; drive on the cattle. See! The mayor stands, looking on.' It is the old cry 'Look busy!' And indeed, Paheri has come to the fields to see how the work goes. To the left of the labourers ploughing and hoeing stands Paheri's chariot drawn by two horses and attended by his charioteer Khenmem. He holds the reins and a whip in one hand and a bow in the other, and he seems to be having some difficulty in controlling the team: 'Stand still! Do not struggle, excellent team of the mayor(?), beloved of your master, about whom the mayor boasts to everyone.' The claim may not have been idle, for horses were still something of a novelty in Egypt in the early fifteenth century BC. Paheri may well have been the first mayor of Nekheb to have a chariot drawn by horses, and would no doubt have taken as much pride in driving with them around his province as a country land-owner might have shown in his primitive motor car in the late nineteenth century. While

the charioteer/chauffeur waits restraining the lively horses his master
has walked through the fields to the river bank, alerting his field-
workers and stirring up their enthusiasm, as we have seen. At the end of
his walk he is shown standing (at the other end of this register),
observing the loading of boats. This event in fact took place at a
different time in the annual cycle of agriculture, and we shall return to it
later on. The need to show as many activities as possible within a small
spatial compass led to the juxtaposing of many successive, rather than
contemporary, events, and it is sometimes difficult to determine the
order in which the scenes on a wall should be read. For the owner of the
tomb the apparent confusion was no confusion at all; the general
panorama of activities made up in sum his posthumous expectation. He
himself would expect to read out his own prescription for eternity from
this 'blueprint'.

In the overall description of the agricultural scenes in Paheri's tomb
the great man is said to be observing the seasons of 'drought' and
'coming-forth', and 'all the activities going on in the fields'. The
Egyptian year had three four-month seasons named after the phenomena which characterized them in terms of the land. The summer season
was the time when the whole of Egypt was flooded by the Nile in
inundation, when there was no activity on the land; it was 'inundation'
(akhet). Next came the season when the waters returned between the
banks of the river, when the land came forth from the flood, soaked and
ready for cultivation; it was 'coming-forth' (peret). After this season
came the time when the land slowly dried out, when the pools and lakes
left behind by the flood evaporated, when the crops ripened and were
harvested; it was 'drought' (shemu). In the scenes so far examined in
Paheri's tomb we have been concerned with the activities of the season
of 'coming-forth' which began, in modern terms, in about the middle of
October, lasting until mid-February. The first part of this season was a
time of very great activity on the land, for apart from ploughing and the
planting of crops, there was the annual chore of putting the land in
order after the devastation of the flood.

The good management of land was one of the greatest achievements
of the ancient Egyptians. From the earliest historic times there is
evidence of the appointment of officials with duties specially concerned
with the control and maintenance of the river-banks, canals, and the
supervision of the orderly division of the land.[14] The ease of cultivation
in the Nile Valley, due to a superfluity of water and a rich soil, led to the

early settlement of the country. As the population grew and became organized, first on a provincial basis, and later on a national scale, some of the major administrative tasks were concerned with the organization of land and the control of water. It was the boast of a good provincial governor that he was able to maintain good land- and water-control within his province even when matters were bad elsewhere. Amenemhet, governor (nomarch) of the Oryx province (nome) in Middle Egypt in the reign of Sesostris I of the Twelfth Dynasty (c. 1971–1929 BC) set out some of the achievements of his career thus:[15]

> When the years of hunger happened, I then cultivated all the fields of the Oryx nome as far as the southern and the northern boundaries, giving life to its inhabitants and providing its food. No man went hungry in it. I gave to the widow as equally as to her who had a husband. I made no distinction between the great and the small in all I gave. Then came great inundations, bringers of crops and of all things; but I did not exact the arrears of land-tax.

In Amenemhet's claim we can find an echo of pride in local achievement, which harks back particularly to the sad days of the First Intermediate Period, not a century before, when Egypt had no central government, when there was no co-ordination of water-control throughout the land. It was almost a case of every nome for itself, and if a nome had an efficient and caring nomarch then there might be some hope that good administration would minimize the effects of the breakdown of the national system. But over a long period the success of land administration and agriculture in ancient Egypt depended on the efficiency of the whole system; weak links were very damaging, and in years of small inundations they became disastrous.

There is much evidence to show that a number of low Niles occurred during the First Intermediate Period and the Eleventh Dynasty, and that much hardship followed—'years of hunger', as Amenemhet called them. A small farmer of the Theban area, writing to his family during the last years of the Eleventh Dynasty, scolds them for complaining about short rations, and reminds them of what he has done to sustain them in times of shortage:[16]

> See! The whole land is perished while [you] are not hungry. When I came hither southwards I had fixed your rations properly. [Now] is the inundation [very great ?] See! [Our] rations are fixed for us

according to the state of the inundation. Be patient, you lot(?).
See! Up to today I have gone out of my way to feed you.

After listing the members of his household and specifying their rations
individually, this farmer, named Hekanakhte, continues:

If you avoid being angry about this, (consider): the whole
household are like my children—everything is mine—(for it is
said) 'half-life is better than death outright'. See! One says
'hunger' about hunger. See! They are beginning to eat men here.
See! There are no people to whom those rations [i.e. those he has
listed earlier] are given anywhere. You shall conduct yourselves
with stout hearts until I have reached you.

In this letter, which was not a statement of achievement for the ears of
posterity (like a tomb inscription), or a model for student-scribes to
copy, Hekanakhte addressed his family alone, and what he said about
poor conditions may be believed, although the reference to cannibalism
might border on hyperbole. Here on the smallest personal level we find
a man of responsibility who by good management helped his people to
survive the effects of low Niles and poor harvests. His claim is very like
that of Ankhtifi, nomarch of Edfu and Hierakonpolis during the First
Intermediate Period. In his tomb at Moalla, just a few miles south of
Thebes, after making the conventional claims of supporting the weak,
humble and helpless, he describes how people came from far to the
south and far to the north to obtain grain from him in time of famine:
'The whole of Upper Egypt died from famine (to the extent that) all
men ate their children. But death from hunger never happened in this
nome.'[17]

Good management, therefore, helped when nature failed to produce
the ideal conditions needed for successful harvests in Egypt. When the
general administration of Egypt was good it was easier to carry out a
national strategy in time of trouble. This is evident in the steps taken by
Joseph in the seven lean years—'years of hunger'; it is evident in the
claims made by individual nomarchs. When the general administration
collapsed the good nomarch alone succeeded. It is noticeable, however,
that the best direct evidence of years of famine comes from texts of
those periods when central administration was weak or even non-
existent, like the First Intermediate Period. At times of good government things were automatically better, and it is striking that there are

no statements about the occurrence of hunger and bad Niles during the Eighteenth Dynasty.[18] It may be that the incidence of low Niles was less at this time than in earlier periods, but a more important factor was the high degree of good government during the Eighteenth Dynasty. Not much was left to chance and, if we may believe the statements made in the *Duties of the Vizir* text we examined earlier, the lessons of good land management had indeed been learned. By regular reports from all over the country the vizir should know the state of affairs at every season. 'It is he who should dispatch mayors and district governors to (arrange) the cultivation in the summer.' He oversees the fixing of district boundaries, and looks into cases involving estate boundaries. 'It is he who should examine water supplies on the first day of every ten-day period.'

In the course of the year no time was more crucial for the success of the crops than the weeks following the withdrawal of the flood-waters. It was then that the proper execution of the national plan for irrigation had to be implemented at the local level. The effect of the annual inundation was to swamp most of the cultivated land, leaving villages, the tops of dykes (along which roads and paths passed) and naturally produced high places clear of the water, except in years of very high Niles. Much of the inundated land remained flooded after the waters receded, forming the 'basins' or depressions which provided the key and opportunity for successful irrigation throughout the Dynastic Period and later. The proper exploitation of the 'basins' depended on a good, working system of canals and dykes to contain and direct water as needed. The extension of cultivable land consequently was effected through the intelligent use of the system. Here lay the opportunity for the local administrator to improve the agriculture of his district, the prosperity of the local inhabitants and his own reputation. The success of central government followed the successful operation of the system in all its local parts. In the difficult times of the First Intermediate Period a nomarch, Akhtoy, of the XIIIth Upper Egyptian nome, made clear in his tomb inscription how he had, through good water discipline and new works, done wonders for his land and his people. Tiresome small gaps in the text make a full running translation impossible, but enough has survived to make Akhtoy's claims quite clear:[19]

I made a monument in [Siut?] . . . I provided (?) a canal of 10 cubits (in width) which I cut for it from the plough lands, and I set its

sluice in order . . . I nourished my city; I made the ordinary
workman into someone who ate barley; I made spittle possible in
the middle of the day[20] . . . I made a dyke for this city. Upper Egypt
was in a sad state without a sight of water. I confirmed the
boundaries of . . . with my seal. I turned the high ground into
marsh. I made it possible for the inundation to flow over the old
high points. I made the arable lands [well watered?], while
everything on both sides (of my territory) was parched. [Everyone
enjoyed ?] the inundation to his heart's desire, and water was given
to his neighbour; he was kind to them.

Akhtoy then specifies more precisely how prosperous everyone became
as a result of his prudent actions. What emerges abundantly clear from
his inscription is that in matters of irrigation success was not just a
matter of chance. Steps could be taken to counteract the effects of poor
floods; equally, steps could be taken to maintain and develop a
successful water economy. And even when the river behaved as
expected all could not be left to chance, for the flood was a flood, and
flood-waters by their very nature caused destruction.

Work on the land is continuous, the seasonal activities following in
regular succession with varying degrees of difficulty and intensity. In
Egypt the long summer 'vacation' during the period of inundation led
on to the most intensively active season in which the land was prepared
for planting. Preparation included the rehabilitation of the orderly
features of the valley landscape after the flood's devastation. In the
quickest possible time the canals and smaller water-channels were dug
out to their proper depths, and the dykes and other elevated land
'dividers' repaired and raised to their proper heights. The water sluices
were put in order and the boundaries of estates confirmed by the
planting of markers. And all this had to be completed before the drying
out of the land so that ploughing and sowing could take place. The
ordinary work-force of field-workers was scarcely large enough or
concentrated enough to complete this annual emergency programme
on its own. The problem of labour was solved by the standard Egyptian
practice of *corvée*—statute labour, or the raising of gangs by decree. For
this duty any man might be eligible unless he was specifically excused
because of his rank or because he served some particular institution like
certain temples.[21] The precise details of the means by which the gangs
were raised are not known, although it is generally thought that the

conscription was organized and supervised at the local level. A suggestion of central control in such matters can be found in the *Duties of the Vizir* in the words: 'It is he who should dispatch regional officers to construct dykes throughout the whole land.' The compulsion implicit in this annual recruitment for work on the land after the inundation is vividly preserved both in the conception of the *shabti*-figure and in the texts which were commonly used magically to vitalize the *shabti* in the after-world.[22] From the time of the early Middle Kingdom the well-placed Egyptian who could look forward to a reasonable burial and the prospect of a posthumous existence in the Field of Reeds took care to ensure that he would not be recruited for field-work by *corvée* in the after-life. By the time of the Eighteenth Dynasty all properly equipped funerary kits included one or more *shabti*-figures—small statuettes showing the deceased owner as a wrapped mummy. At first they were unencumbered but later they were shown carrying the tools of the field-worker, the hoe and the mattock, with a carrying-basket. Most figures were inscribed with texts designed to activate them on behalf of their deceased owners. After an initial exhortation, in which the deceased is designated 'the Osiris X', he says:

> O this shabti! If the Osiris X, justified, is numbered to do any work which is customarily done in the necropolis, as a man at [i.e. performing] his duties—now an obstacle is implanted against him therein—to make the fields flourish, to irrigate the riparian lands, to ferry sand of the east to the west, 'I shall do it; here I am,' you shall say there.

This text, which occurs in many variant forms from the Middle Kingdom down to the end of the Pharaonic Period, makes it reasonably specific that a man might expect to be called up for labouring work in the after-life. In the version given here,[23] which was common during the Eighteenth Dynasty, the parenthetical clause, 'now an obstacle is implanted against him therein', demonstrates with no possibility of doubt how disagreeable the Egyptian considered it was to have his name on the call-up list for the agricultural *corvée*. In consequence, the *shabti*-figure by invocation is ordered to answer on behalf of the deceased person, for whom he is to act as a surrogate in the specified duties. During the early and middle Eighteenth Dynasty the *shabti* might be provided with actual miniature tools and baskets, but subsequently these implements were incorporated in the figure, as mentioned above.

Few texts describe the lot of the field-worker, especially the conscripted labourer, apart from those pieces of composition designed to show how superior is the calling of the scribe. The scribe was likely to be exempted from the call-up and able, therefore, to take special pride in his station in life. But, in spite of the distinctly biased nature of these texts, there is no reason to believe that they greatly overestimate the misery of the man who might be put to work on the land under duress, either because of the call-up or for some other reason, such as criminal punishment. The position of men taken prisoner in war, or of those who might be in some state of slavery, should perhaps be discounted here, for they, unlike the conscripted labourer, would have less reason (in relative terms) to consider their lot unfavourable. In terms of treatment, however, it is unlikely that there was much discrimination between the conscripted freeman and the prisoner or slave when duties were allocated and control exercised. A papyrus in The Brooklyn Museum bears, among other texts of the late Middle Kingdom, a list of seventy-six people, mostly men, who were in trouble for having deserted apparently from their conscripted duties. Not only were they liable for stiff penalties in consequence but, in the case of their failure to surrender, hostages were taken from their families. A number of laws concerning desertion by conscripted and other field-workers are mentioned:[24]

> The law concerning deserters;
> The law concerning deliberate desertion for 6 months;
> The law concerning deliberate desertion from work;
> The law concerning the man who runs away without doing his duties;

The distinctions between the various 'crimes' covered by these laws are not specified in the document, but it seems clear that simple desertion was probably held to be less heinous than premeditated desertion. Presumably a man might down tools and take to his heels after suffering some particularly disagreeable insult or punishment from an overseer or farm manager; he would be thought less culpable than the man who planned his flight in advance. References to work and duties underline the importance placed on the fulfilment of conscripted services. The system might appear to be unjust to those who suffered under it, but it was probably considered the only sure way of securing the continuance of good land economy in antiquity. No doubt there were gross abuses, both in the management of the *corvée* and in the treatment of the conscripts; some who were 'numbered' would avoid the call-up either by bribery or by obtaining a deputy; some land managers would consider the conscripts as tied labourers or serfs. We should perhaps not exaggerate the bad aspects of the system, for it lasted in antiquity for thousands of years, and persisted in a modified form until the nineteenth century when it was abolished under the British administration.[25] Unfortunately, no matter how necessary the system may have seemed in antiquity, the pain and discomfort suffered by the conscript, partly by necessity, and occasionally through ill-treatment, were inescapable. Hard labour is hard labour; and the work performed on the land after the flood was certainly hard labour. In the Eleventh Dynasty the small-holder Hekanakhte by letter urges those who work on his fields (including members of his family) to work hard so that they may earn their keep:[26]

> You are to give rations to my people while they are doing work. Take great care; hoe all my land; sieve with the sieve; hack with your noses in the work. See! If they are diligent God will be praised for you and I shall not have to make things unpleasant for you.

This direction means hard labour certainly; but work on the land has always been so. At least in Egypt the climate was relatively kind, particularly in the fall of the year when the conscription of labour was greatest.

This season, that of 'coming forth' for the ancient Egyptians, was the time of greatest activity on the land because it witnessed not only the rehabilitation of the land in the valley, but also the ploughing of the land and the sowing of the principal crops. These last were the activities we witnessed in the scenes from the tomb of Paheri at Elkab. The subsequent season of 'drought' or 'drying-out' brought the harvest, scenes of which are also shown on the same wall of Paheri's tomb, in the two registers above the scenes of ploughing and sowing. Again the realities of life on the land are somewhat modified, and if the representations are not wholly idyllic, they are not far from the ideal. The labourers in the fields are willing workers, and they include a sprinkling of faithful old retainers. There are no signs of conscripted labour, of serfs and slaves, of prisoners from the local gaol, or of prisoners of war. The work goes ahead as the master would wish for his eternal existence, with enthusiasm and success, and only an occasional grumble.

Of the two registers devoted to the harvest, the lower shows the cutting of the crops, while the upper presents the recovery and storing of the grain. Two sorts of crop are being harvested, barley on the right and flax on the left. Barley is reaped with elegantly shaped sickles held in what seems to be a rather awkward manner by the reapers. Inspection of actual sickles preserved from antiquity shows that the eccentric angle at which the handle is set in relation to the line of the blade is well designed for use, but not quite in the manner represented here. From the earliest times the sickle was made of wood and set with short, shaped blades of flint, bevelled and notched or serrated, easily capable of cutting the stems of standing crops with a properly judged, semi-rotary, slash. Ancient sickle blades frequently show a polish imparted by their considerable use on crops. The action of cutting is much better shown in the comparable scene in the tomb of Menna, a scribe of the fields of the Lord of the Two Lands in Upper and Lower Egypt, a man who, presumably, knew more than a thing or two about the techniques of field-work, who saw that the artists working on his tomb scenes took care to reproduce them faithfully.[27] In Paheri's tomb the sickles are shown schematically, in the form in which they are drawn in the hieroglyphic script, and as the artist no doubt could best represent them. Paheri's reapers work in pairs: the first two pairs cut the barley, grasping the heads in their left hands and cutting the straw just below the heads. This unusual way of reaping was characteristic of

Fig. 8 Harvesting barley with sickles. Refreshment for Paheri.

Egyptian practice throughout antiquity, and it possessed certain advantages over the reaping of the whole standing crop. In the first place only the essential part of the crop had to be carried to the threshing floor, and, as we shall see, the method of threshing would not have left the straw in a state fit for much else than bedding or for being chopped up. Further, the standing straw could be recovered later from the fields in good condition, to be used for many purposes, both agricultural and industrial. Apart from basket-making and brick-making, straw was used as a principal fuel for firing pottery kilns. But undoubtedly the main reason for reaping barley in this manner was the practical one of economy of effort. The second two pairs of reapers have completed cutting the heads from their stint, and pause in their work. Between them and the first two pairs stands a single reaper, his sickle tucked under his arm, drinking from a jar. It contained, presumably, water, but it is not clear whether the jar came from the alfresco bar on the right of the register presided over by a servant who fans a jar and a jug on wooden stands with a palm-frond fan. The elegance of the booth nearby, containing more pots on wooden stands (above) and pottery stands (below), suggests that it was set up for the refreshment of Paheri himself during his visit to the fields. The attendant holds a folded cloth in one hand, which surely identifies him as a servant from Paheri's household and not one of the field-workers. It would certainly have been the case that the field-workers would have made their own arrangements for water to drink, although their food was probably provided by their master. Food and clothing was about as much as they could expect as payment for their services (*Fig. 8*).

A short line of inscription set above the barley reapers contains what is described as an 'answering utterance', perhaps some kind of antiphonal work chant. It follows the pattern of the words put into the mouths of the men ploughing with oxen in the register below. The reapers proclaim: 'This day is fine; go out on the land; the north wind is risen; the sky favours us; our work is what binds us together.' The reapers, content in their work, apparently, are followed in the field by two females, neither of them fully grown, perhaps a young woman and a girl. They bend down to glean what may have been dropped and left behind by the reapers. One, presumably the older, grumbles at the reapers: 'Give me a handful, or you will make us come (again) in the evening. Don't repeat the malicious acts of yesterday today.' She implies that the reapers, or at least one of them, are being mean and ungenerous to the gleaners. A sympathetic reaper, no doubt, allowed a certain amount to fall deliberately to be picked up later by the gleaners. In this way a fair sub-harvest might be made without too much backbreaking toil; otherwise the gleaners would be obliged to return in the evening to scour the field for a few heads of grain accidentally overlooked. The first gleaner here carries a kind of pannier on her back, while the girl has a basket in one hand. Gleaning was undoubtedly an important way of supplementing modest rations, and was probably carried out as a jealously guarded right by specific families in particular fields. It was an activity which led to squabbles, and in the tomb of Menna two young girl gleaners are shown pulling each other's hair, while the grain they have collected lies spilled between them.

The left-hand side of the register of harvesting in Paheri's tomb is occupied with the flax harvest, and its successive scenes are separated from the barley harvest by a woman who is shown coming to the fields carrying containers, now damaged, filled, in all probability, with food for the workers. The flax is harvested quite differently from the barley; here the stalks form the important part of the crop. So the flax is pulled bodily from the ground, the roots tidied up and then taken to be combed and further prepared. Three men and one woman pull up handfuls of stalks, one man up-ends the stalks to clear the bottoms, and an old man (shown with thin wispy hair) binds up the stalks into bundles. The bundles are then carried to another elderly workman who strips the seed heads from the stalks with a special toothed instrument, a kind of long-handled comb operated with his foot. Alone among the labourers shown in this register, the old man throws himself into his work with apparent enthusiasm, shouting to the man who brings the bundle: 'If you bring me 11,009 (bundles), I shall comb them.' The other answers: 'Buck up, don't gabble, you bald old man of a field-worker!' Here are the traditional, back-answering, jolly rustics, cheerfully grumbling, representing the rough but contented myth of rural bliss. Such modest expressions of discontent give a slight touch of verisimilitude to the schene of bland harmony on the estates of Paheri (*Fig. 9*).

Harvesting of flax was not necessarily contemporaneous with the harvesting of barley. It might be pulled when the crop was young or old, the time being determined by the use for which the fibrous stalks were to be employed.[28] The older the crop, the coarser the subsequent thread. On the other hand, the older the crop, the riper the seed heads; and from the seeds oil could be extracted, linseed oil. There is no documentary evidence for the use of linseed oil before Graeco-Roman times, but it is unlikely that the Egyptians of earlier times would have neglected such an obvious source for an oil which could be used in lamps at least.[29] In addition, the use of a special tool and a separate process to remove the seeds suggest that this by-product, as it were, was something to be utilized and not just thrown away. But the important product from flax was linen, one of those basic commodities which stood high in the list of things of value in the prevailing barter system. In one of his letters to his family, the small-holder Hekanakhte, whom we have already met, says:[30] 'Get Heti's son Nakhte to go down with Sinebnut to Perhaa to cultivate [for us] 5 acres of land on rent; and they shall take its rent from the cloth woven where you are.'

Fig. 9 Harvesting flax.

The processes whereby flax stalks were turned into yarn were long and complicated, and they are not shown as a sequel to the harvest of flax. The harvesting of barley, on the other hand, was followed immediately by the threshing, winnowing, measuring and storing of the grain. The top register of the west wall in Paheri's tomb takes us through these stages. Although Paheri's eternal harvest seems to be going well (as it must for his eternal well-being), it has its problems, though none that cannot be resolved if everyone tries hard. The register shows first two labourers bringing the cut barley from the fields. It is carried in a pannier supported by a pole on their shoulders; it seems to be made, if one may judge from the empty one being carried back to the fields by the next pair, of netting on a wooden or wicker frame. But time is short, the harvest has come close to the rising of the river. The overseer raises his switch and shouts: 'Buck up, move your feet, the water is coming and reaches the bundles (of barley).' The labourers answer: 'The sun is hot! May the sun be given the value (or price) of barley in fish!' By this they seem to mean that what may be lost to the sun in the way of barley caught by the flood may be made up in the shape of fish brought by the flood—an extension of the barter system to the natural world. The implication of what they say is also that it is too hot to hurry and that fish may compensate for what they fail to gather from the crop of barley, an ancient case of 'swings and roundabouts'.

Fig. 10 Bringing the barley to the threshing floor; threshing with cattle; winnowing.

The next pair of labourers return to the fields, one carrying the empty pannier and the other the pole. The latter says: 'Doesn't the pole spend the whole day on my shoulders? How strong is my heart!' He challenges the overseer with a declaration of his continuous activity and resolve. We may imagine what the overseer's reply might be (*Fig. 10*).

The panniers of cut barley are brought from the fields to the threshing floor, a circular space of beaten earth on which the crop is strewn to be trodden by a team of oxen. Here the team is shown under the control of a boy who urges them forward with a two-thonged whip, singing to encourage them: 'Strike [i.e. thresh] for yourselves, strike for yourselves, oxen, strike for yourselves, strike for yourselves! Chaff to eat (for yourselves) and barley for your masters. Don't let your hearts grow weary! It is cool.' The rhythm of the song, apparent in the Egyptian, even though the true sound escapes us, was here, no doubt, the stimulus as with all good working songs or shanties. Meanwhile another labourer supervises the threshing, forking the heads of barley under the feet of the oxen, and clearing away the trodden heads after the grain is extracted, the waste being piled up in heaps around the threshing floor. The winnowing of the trodden grain comes next in the sequence. Four men, their heads bound in cloths to keep the chaff out of their hair, toss the grain and chaff into the air with specially shaped scoops, one in each hand. In the corresponding scene in the tomb of

Menna, which is painted not carved, the falling chaff is shown separated from the falling grain; and in the same scene there are other labourers who further clean the grain by fanning away the residual chaff.

Finally, the grain is measured and stored. Two men gather the grain in measuring vessels; they are shown so close together that their figures barely overlap. The measuring vessels are probably made of wood and bound with leather, reckoned to be of certain fixed capacities, some multiple of the *hekat*-measure (about 4.5 litres). An inaccurate measuring vessel could be used distinctly to the advantage of its owner; an over-large measure might be used when the harvest was checked for tax purposes, or when a debt was recovered or a payment received; a measure of less than proper size would, on the other hand, be useful for the payment of taxes, or of a debt to another. It might always be to a man's advantage to use his own measure, for he would know its true capacity. In discussing the collection of certain rents to be paid for in grain, the farmer Hekanakhte says: 'Now see! I have got them to bring the corn-measure in which it is to be measured; it is decked with black hide.' In another document from the same man's papers various quantities of grain are listed as being with certain individuals, and qualified as 'what is to be measured in the big measure which is in Nebeseyet'.[31] Use your own measure, specify your own measure for transactions, and you will know where you stand. Use another man's measure, and you will probably suffer a loss. The vessels in the scene in Paheri's tomb are not identified, but as the scene is timeless and for the

after-life it may be supposed that no tricks are being played. In any case the grain is from Paheri's own estate, and as the local administrator he would not need to practise deception on himself. A scribe squatting on a pile of grain is described as 'the scribe of counting grain, Djehutnufe'; he notes down a record of the measuring on his palette, while another man, possibly some kind of supervisor, appears to be keeping a less formal tally of filled measures on a winnowing scoop. It was certainly a difficult matter to keep an accurate check on what was measured, and the two men noting the count probably represented the separate bureaucratic and domestic sides of the operation. Two pairs of labourers carry away the measured grain in sacks raised on their shoulders. They walk towards an enclosure surrounded by a crenellated wall within which there are four piles of grain and a growing tree. Inside the enclosure one man empties his sack while another walks out through the doorway carrying two empty sacks. One of the piles seems to consist of some commodity other than grain; it might be flax seed,[32] although the represented texture seems to be too coarse (*Fig. 11*).

The storing of grain and other agricultural produce in the open air presented little risk in a country where rain at harvest-time was rare. In general, however, produce so stored was usually not for local use, but intended for shipment elsewhere, for the settlement of taxes, for example. You will recall, from earlier in our discussion of these scenes, that Paheri was shown, having apparently walked through the fields at ploughing time, standing and watching the loading of barges. His text says explicitly: 'The mayor, Paheri, justified, proceeds to load the

Fig. 11 Measuring the barley and storing it.

barges in the meadow. He says to the field-workers: "Hurry up, the fields are cleared(?), and the inundation is very great." ' In the part-register below his feet three boats are setting off, with men holding sounding-poles in their bows, while two members of the crew lean over the side of one boat, one of whom lowers a jar to take up water from the river. Four other boats in echelon are moored for loading and four men carry sacks of grain up a gang-plank to empty them into the hold. Eleven lines of hieroglyphs above this sub-scene describe (*Fig. 12*):

> Loading barges with barley and emmer. They say: 'Are we to spend all day carrying barley and white emmer?[33] The granaries are full, the heaps overflowing their mouths; the barges are heavily loaded, with grain bursting out. Yet we are made to go even faster. Are our hearts of copper?'

The small touches of asperity in the remarks given to the workers on Paheri's estates provide only a hint of what might have been said in actuality during the ploughing and reaping of crops. They suggest, nevertheless, that the ideal considered suitable for depiction in the tomb of the mayor of Nekheb was not based on a reality wholly idyllic. Even in Egypt, that specially favoured land, agriculture was hard work. When the back-breaking task of land rehabilitation after the annual flood is added to the regular duties of ploughing and reaping, some measure of the hard lot of the ancient Egyptian field-worker can be made. In all aspects of life the Egyptian recognized the merit of just action and fair treatment, especially for those who could not protect themselves. But in the execution of laborious agricultural duties the good intentions of a noble like Paheri—a man of declared benevolence (if we can truly believe him)—might commonly be nullified by the excessive devotion to duty of a foreman or scribal overseer. In the end it was the peasant, the field-worker, who bore the brunt of ill-directed enthusiasm or plain malicious zeal. A grim picture emerges from the words of a scribe writing to his lord. He starts by assuring his master that he is devoted and energetic:[34]

7 (*above*) *Fine hieroglyphs on a granite block at El-Tod. The names in the cartouches are those of King Sesostris I of the Twelfth Dynasty.*
(*below*) *Part of Papyrus Sallier, one of the scribal* Miscellanies (*BM 10185*), *written in a good literary hand of the Nineteenth Dynasty.*

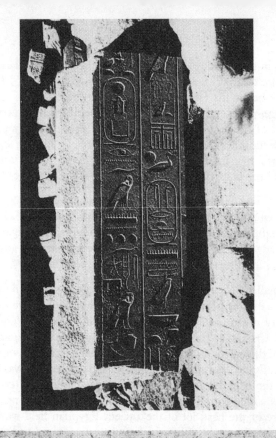

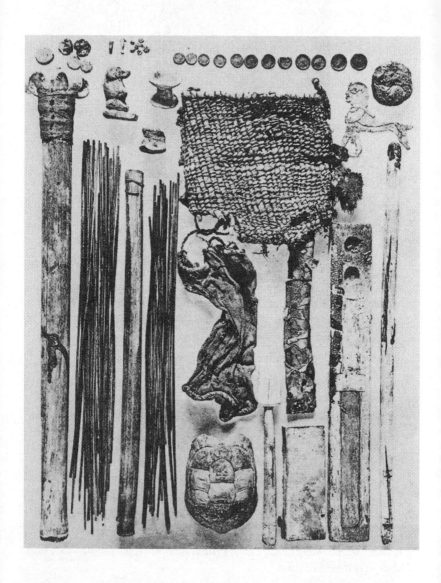

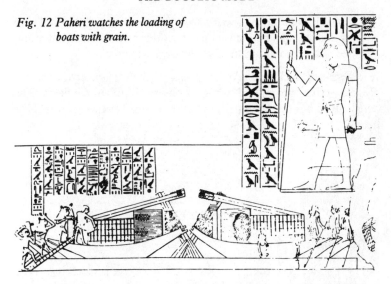

Fig. 12 Paheri watches the loading of boats with grain.

> I am carrying out every order given me by my lord with excellent attention and the hardness of copper. I shall not let my lord be dissatisfied with me.

He then sets out a catalogue of his lord's property, declaring each part to be well, all due, of course, to his own good management:

> The harvest of the crown lands of Pharaoh—may he live, be prosperous and healthy—which are under my lord's control, is being reaped with excellent attention and good care. I note down the ass-loads of barley which are cut daily with the sickle, and arrange for their removal (from the fields). The threshing floor is set out, and I shall arrange for a level area to be set out for 400 ass-loads. And at midday, when the barley is hot, I put all the people who are cutting with sickles on to gleaning, with the exception of the scribes and weavers who take away their daily measure (of grain) from the gleanings of yesterday.

Having stated what he gives the people who work on the harvest, he ends in self-justification:

8 A scribe's equipment found by Howard Carter in a tomb at Thebes.

There is none among them who will denounce me to my lord over rations or unguent. I am controlling them with excellent attention. See! This communication is to let my lord know.

It is a chilling document. And how closely can we associate what this diligent scribe reports with what we observed in Paheri's fields. The details need not be elaborated; but there is small chance of rural bliss here.

NOTES

1 Genesis, 42, 2.

2 Genesis, 12, 10.

3 Probably not a true report, but it reflects contemporary circumstances. It occurs in British Museum Papyrus 10245 (Anastasi Papyrus VI); see A. H. Gardiner, *Late-Egyptian Miscellanies*, 76, ll. 12 ff. Tjeku was the VIIIth Lower Egyptian nome, the region of the Wadi Tumilat.

4 Part of British Museum Papyrus 10470; see E. A. W. Budge, *The Book of the Dead* (London, 1898), 170 f.

5 From Chapter 125 of *The Book of the Dead*; see, for example, Budge, op. cit., 188 ff.

6 From British Museum Papyrus 10243 (Anastasi Papyrus II); see Gardiner, *Late-Egyptian Miscellanies*, 16, ll.9 f.

7 From British Museum Papyrus 9994 (Lansing Papyrus); see Gardiner, op. cit., 104, ll, 10 ff.

8 See p. 85 above.

9 Davies, *Rekh-mi-Rē'*, pl. XL, 2.

10 E.g. in N. de G. Davies, *The Mastaba of Ptahhetep and Akhethetep II* (London, 1901), pl. XX.

11 The tomb scenes are fully published in J. J. Tylor and F. Ll. Griffith, *The Tomb of Paheri*, published in one volume with É. Naville, *Ahnas el Medineh* (London, 1894).

12 Tylor and Griffith, op. cit., pl. III.

13 A good example is shown in the tomb of Sennedjem (Theban Tomb no. 1), well illustrated in A. Mekhitarian, *Egyptian Painting*, 149.

14 See H. Kees, *Ancient Egypt* (London, 1961), 52 ff; also H. Schneider, *Shabtis*, 1 (Leiden, 1977), 9 ff.

15 P. E. Newberry, *Beni Hasan* I (London, 1893), pl. VIII, ll.19 ff.

16 The letter is published in T. G. H. James, *The Hekanakhte Papers*, 31 ff.

17 For this passage, see J. Vandier, *Mo'alla* (Cairo, 1950), 220 (text iv, 15–18).

18 See J. Vandier, *La famine dans l'Égypte ancienne* (Cairo, 1936), 23 ff. For the period of the Middle Kingdom and earlier, see two articles by B. Bell in *American Journal of Archaeology* 75 (New York, 1971), 1 ff., and 79 (1975), 223 ff.

19 F. Ll. Griffiths, *The Inscriptions of Siût and Dêr Rîfeh* (London, 1889), pl. 15, ll. 3–6. On the matter of low and high Niles, their effects, and their control, see K. Butzer, *Early Hydraulic Civilization in Egypt* (Chicago, 1976), 51 ff.

20 I.e. by not allowing people to be thirsty.

21 This matter is well illustrated in the Nauri Decree of King Sethos I, see n.12 to Chapter 3.

22 Generally, H. Schneider, *Shabtis*, I (Leiden, 1977).

23 Schneider's version IVD, op. cit., 102.

24 See W. C. Hayes, *A Papyrus of the Late Middle Kingdom in the Brooklyn Museum*. (Brooklyn, 1955), 47 f.

25 So Hayes, op. cit., 130 f.

26 T. G. H. James, *The Hekanakhte Papers*, text II, ll.29–31.

27 For the tomb of Menna, see n.18 to Chapter Three. The scene here described is best illustrated in Nina Davies, *Ancient Egyptian Painting* (Chicago, 1936), I, pls. 50, 51.

28 The processes of harvesting and preparing flax are discussed in A. Lucas, *Ancient Egyptian Materials and Industries*, 143.

29 Lucas, op. cit., 333.

30 T. G. H. James, *The Hekanakhte Papers*, text I, ll. 3–4.

31 The use of this special measuring vessel is discussed more fully in Chapter 9; see p. 246 below.

32 So described by Tylor and Griffith, *The Tomb of Paheri*, 15.

33 The Egyptian word translated 'emmer' or 'emmer-wheat' may have a wider connotation, as several kinds are mentioned in Egyptian texts, like the 'white emmer' here; see A. H. Gardiner, *Ancient Egyptian Onomastica*, II, 221* f.

34 From British Museum Papyrus 10185 (Papyrus Sallier I); see A. H. Gardiner, *Late Egyptian Miscellanies*, 80.

5

LITERACY AND STATUS
— 'BE A SCRIBE!'

A scene in the great temple of Abydos in Middle Egypt shows the Prince Ramesse standing beside his father, King Sethos I, holding a partly unrolled papyrus in his hands.[1] The prince, who was later to succeed his father and become one of the longest reigning kings of Egypt—Ramesses II, 'the Great', the Ozymandias of Shelley's sonnet—is described as 'reading out praises'. To the right of Ramesse and Sethos a tabulation occupies the wall; it contains, in chronological order, the names of the kings of Egypt from Menes, the founder of the Kingdom of Upper and Lower Egypt at the beginning of the First Dynasty, down to Sethos himself—a conspectus of royalty over about eighteen hundred years. The list is by no means complete; it contains only the names of those kings thought worthy of remembrance at that time, and it omits from the relatively recent past the Queen Hatshepsut, and the kings of the Atenist heresy, Akhenaten, Smenkhkare, Tutankhamun and Ay. According to the superscription, these named kings of Upper and Lower Egypt receive offerings from Sethos.

From this scene and its pendant tabulation of royal names, several reasonable conclusions may be drawn about the literacy of the ancient Egyptians, and their attitude to the written word. To begin with, it is implicit in the scene that the Prince Ramesse can read what is written on the document he holds in his hands. It is perhaps also implicit that the king, his father, does not himself read from the document, not because he cannot read, but because it is more proper for the reading to be done for him. The ceremony of recitation of praises on behalf of the ancestor kings of Egypt may have been one of the most important rituals performed in this slightly unusual temple of Abydos. Its actuality in the lifetime of King Sethos, whether performed by the king and his son themselves, or by priests fulfilling the royal roles, was rendered enduring, if not eternal, by being carved in stone and labelled with the proper descriptive texts. In the scene Ramesse reads out from his papyrus the praises of the ancestor kings; it may be assumed that the papyrus also contained the tabulation of the kings' names. But it was enough to have it all written up in the 'words of the god', as hieroglyphs were sometimes called, to ensure perpetuity. That enduring aspect of a written text could be at once eliminated by the wilful destruction of its signs. Such was the power of the written word to the ancient Egyptians. On the other hand, the omission of the names of certain kings, while denying these kings the advantages offered, in this case by the recitation of praises by Ramesse, did not eliminate them wholly from the historical parade of Egyptian kings. Other lists, notably the papyrus list now preserved in the Egyptian Museum in Turin, of approximately the same date as the Abydos list, contain kings not included at Abydos. Perhaps the only omission from the Abydos list which represents a real attempt at posthumous oblivion was that of the Atenist kings. Even the supposedly loathed Hyksos find their places in the Turin list. [2]

Throughout the written records of Egypt from at least the time of the Old Kingdom, the power of the written word for personal, religious and political purposes is emphasized. The writing of a man's name could perpetuate his memory; its subsequent destruction produced the contrary result. The right spells written on the walls of the royal tomb, or on the papyrus deposited in a private person's burial, would ensure a safe passage to the desired existence in the after-life. The proclamation of success in war, or in the political activities of a king or regional governor, in an inscription in a temple or tomb was a statement of achievement. All these uses of the written word, invested with their own peculiar magic, were secondary to the main purpose of writing, but they surely demonstrated its implicit power.

Almost all the earliest surviving texts from Egypt, dating from the First and Second Dynasties, represent simple acts of recording. Jars and boxes were marked with their contents—the name of a commodity and, perhaps, a number or a quantity. Seals were used to record the ownership or source of the contents of containers; their legends were brief and to the point. In these short labels can be seen the beginnings of writing in Egypt. The hieroglyphic script, that uniquely Egyptian form of writing, sprang, it would seem, almost from nothing. The signs used in the most carefully written texts of this early period were well formed and exactly executed according to the standards of the script in the best texts of the Old and Middle Kingdoms. But the repertoire of recorded signs is small, and the script at that time was not yet sufficiently developed to allow the writing of more than the simplest of ideas. It is still not known whether the notion of recording ideas that went beyond the most elementary picturing of an object, followed perhaps by one or more strokes to represent numbers, developed independently in Egypt, or was introduced from Western Asia or elsewhere.[3] What is particularly interesting about the beginnings of writing in Egypt is that from the outset the need for a cursive, simple form of the hieroglyphic script was appreciated.

The proper execution of a text in the hieroglyphic script was a laborious process. Each sign had its distinctive form capable of great elaboration in the very best examples. The recognizable outline of a sign was, in most cases, all that was needed for its proper reading, but in well-produced texts internal detail was lovingly added so that almost every sign became a small work of art. In general, such care and attention to detail could only be practised when haste was not a factor, and when the medium of the writing allowed elaboration to be employed. The best hieroglyphic texts, in consequence, are those which are carefully carved on stone or wood, and those painted on plaster. Most commonly, the carefully carved texts are also painted.

In its most elaborate forms the hieroglyphic script was decorative, formal, and in many ways unpractical. Not only were the signs in well-produced texts carefully formed individually; they were also carefully laid out so that the general disposition of the writing was neat and economical of space. Tidy arrangement, the choice of suitable signs (where differing choices were available), and the omission of signs not vitally necessary for proper understanding, characterized the full-blown lapidary style of writing; it demonstrated a quadratic tightness in which ease of understanding was marginally sacrificed to beauty of appearance. Monumental texts, however, can support some degree of abbreviation or concision. These attributes are commonly to be observed in funerary inscriptions, as anyone who has spent some time among the gravestones of an English churchyard will know. But abbreviations only work if they are understood, and the kind of shorthand found in the commemorative inscriptions of the dead are, generally speaking, inappropriate to writings of other kinds. Monumental texts in Egypt, whether funerary inscriptions or royal pronouncements on temple walls, were not intended for general or casual reading; the formality of their writing, therefore, might be thought of relative unimportance in the broad consideration of writing in ancient Egypt. Yet the hieroglyphic script, this laborious but decorative way of writing, was the basis of all Egyptian writing, and remained so from the beginning of the First Dynasty until the time when the Greek alphabet was adopted, and enlarged, for the writing of Egyptian in the third century AD.[4] Even then, hieroglyphs were still used for texts inscribed in the temples of Egypt, and the latest known dated hieroglyphic inscription was set up in AD 394, in the reign of the Roman emperor Theodosius. Such a late text, however, scarcely represented the continuance of a lively tradition, and it may be supposed that very few Egyptians could have read what the text proclaimed.

While the hieroglyphic script was the fundamental Egyptian method of writing, it was not, in general, used for most of what was written in Egypt in the day-to-day activities that required some form of written communication. As early as the First Dynasty, in fact contemporaneously with the emergence of the hieroglyphic script itself, scribes found that it was difficult to draw careful, detailed hieroglyphic signs with their principal writing instrument, the rush brush. When they scribbled on the pots placed in tombs the names of the contents, they summarized the appropriate signs, producing forms recognizable for their hieroglyphic equivalents, but lacking the regularity and detail of the full forms. In this abbreviated way of writing lay the beginnings of the hieratic script, that cursive mode of writing which liberated the Egyptian scribe from the relative rigidity of formal hieroglyphs.

In contemplating writing and the craft of the scribe in ancient Egypt, we are faced with a kind of paradox. The hieroglyphic script was not commonly the form of writing employed by the scribe in most of his written endeavours. From the very beginning of the First Dynasty, when scribes realized the advantages of employing abbreviated forms of hieroglyphic signs, the fully formed hieroglyphic script ceased to have a future as a medium for everyday transactions. What is so surprising is that the true hieroglyphic script continued in use with such robust vitality and elegance for such a long time. Indeed, the standard of excellence in the use of the hieroglyphic script seemed always to reach a high point in those periods when the cursive quality of the hieratic script changed markedly, when scribal practice carried the everyday script a stage further away from its formal, precise source. It may, however, be doubted whether cause and effect should be detected in such conjunctions. The particularly fine, well set out, carefully detailed hieroglyphs of Twelfth-dynasty monumental texts happen to coincide temporally with a rapid development—one might almost say deterioration—of the hieratic script. Here the common cause must be sought in the high level reached by Egyptian civilization and culture at that time. The strong, centralized, régime of the Twelfth Dynasty generated the settled circumstances in which fine work was produced, including handsome sculpture, relief-work, and hieroglyphic inscriptions. The same circumstances produced a development of bureaucracy accompanied by a great increase in written documents. Greater scribal activity meant more scribes; the training of more scribes required more scribal schools, and an attention to scribal practices which had not been needed in earlier times.

A similar cultural and bureaucratic expansion took place in the Eighteenth Dynasty. The official archives mentioned in *The Duties of the Vizir* text in the tomb of Rekhmire contained the records of the legal cases which proliferated in the settled conditions of life in Egypt at this time. There were the written dispatches of foreign emissaries, the accounts of state and temple administrations, and the multifarious reports and memoranda spawned by a flourishing civil service. But apart from the vast quantity of scribal activity carried out in the pursuit of good administration, there was much writing of a less important, or at least less official, kind. What is known of the scribes on the lower ranks of the bureaucratic ladder? Were there, for example, free-lance scribes outside the state system? Were there 'amateurs', who could read and write, able to circumvent the scribal closed shop, if they needed to write something for themselves? In short, what was the state of education in ancient Egypt during the time of Rekhmire?

None of these questions is easy to answer in a fully satisfactory way. There is a fair amount of evidence to show that education was essentially vocational, taking the form of training for particular trades or crafts. It was scarcely more than simple apprenticeship, the learning of skills, the passing on of the tricks of the trade, the techniques of craftsmanship to which the material achievements of the ancient Egyptians owed so much. The process was in no way unique to ancient Egypt; it was practised principally, as the evidence of Egyptian inscriptions abundantly shows, at the family level: the son followed the trade of his father. In this way continuity was achieved in skills, in the protection of craft secrets, and in the special advantages enjoyed by individual families. This education of the young craftsman contained little of the intellectual element which has, in most cultures, been considered essential for sound, rational development. For the kind of training which most closely answers to what might be called education, in traditional terms, we should look at the scribal schools.

Of all the careers available to the young Egyptian, the most clearly advantageous was to become a scribe; with scribal training the ranks of bureaucracy were open to a young man of ambition. To aim to be a scribe was a noble ambition, worth working hard to achieve; being a scribe was a favoured condition, accompanied by many advantages unavailable to the ordinary, unlettered Egyptian. The scribe was not necessarily a simple pen-man or copyist; he was a 'clerk' in the fullest sense of that word in the English language. The most senior officials in ancient Egypt were content to include the title 'scribe' in their long lists of dignities and appointments. It was very respectable to be a scribe.

In the hieroglyphic script the word for 'scribe' was written with the sign 𓏞, which depicted the equipment of the scribe as a writer. The elements of this equipment were the palette with cakes of red and black paint, a bag for powdered pigment (possibly later interpreted as a water pot), and the brush-holder, the rush brush being the ancient Egyptian equivalent of the pen. The same sign was used for the word 'write'. Writing was the special ability of the scribe; it was so, you might say, by definition. But the ancient Egyptian scribe was, or might be, much more by being a person 'of letters'. Writing was the mark of his craft; he used writing in the versatility of its many functions, whether he were a priest, or a civil administrator, a simple secretary, or a keeper of archives. Few jobs of any consequence in the state could satisfactorily be performed without the capabilities of reading and writing. A high official would, it must be granted, have relied on his trained staff to prepare documents, and he may also have had a clerk to read out whatever written material needed to be consulted on occasion. But the high official, if he were worthy of his position and not prepared to be at the mercy of his scribes and lettered assistants, would at least have been able to read. Few identifiably autographic texts have survived from ancient Egypt apart from those attributable to named professional scribes, but there is one document which demonstrates beyond a doubt that high officials were capable of writing on their own account. It contains a record of a favourable reply to a petition addressed to Amon-Re of Karnak by a certain Pemou, son of Harsiese, otherwise unknown, in Year 14 of King Psammetichus I of the Twenty-sixth Dynasty (651 BC).[5] The account of the event is attested by fifty witnesses, all of whom write out the same statement in their own hands. There is no doubting the individuality of the fifty handwritings and they belonged to fifty high officials at Thebes, including Mentuemhat, Mayor of Thebes, Nespekashuty, the southern vizir, Nespamedu, also vizir, and the highest priests of the hierarchies of the gods Montu and Amon-Re. The evidence provided by this document for the literacy of high officials, although very much later in date than the Eighteenth Dynasty, can still be regarded as valid for the earlier period. The ability to read and write seems to have been well established as a necessary qualification for high officialdom from early times, although ample evidence for its practice does not occur before the Middle Kingdom.

The acquisition of literate skills by the children of the privileged classes in Egypt was encouraged as a way by which the virtuous achievements of earlier ages, and the exemplary accomplishments of notable predecessors, could be studied and followed. 'Emulate your fathers who were before you . . . See! their words are made lasting in writing';[6] this proposition occurs in a 'treatise' on kingship of the early Middle Kingdom but preserved on a papyrus written during the middle of the Eighteenth Dynasty, possibly during the reign of King Tuthmosis III.[7] This 'treatise', although ostensibly written for a prince, contains like most Egyptian didactic writings a series of high-minded pieces of general advice which could be read by all with profit. The advice is presented in a literary form, designed to be read individually or to be read out to an audience. Literacy is more than implied; it is distinctly alluded to in one admonition:[8] 'Do not slay a man whose talent you know, with whom you at one time sang writings.' Here the writer can be alluding only to someone who had shared the experience of learning by singing out, or reciting, together with his fellow-students in class—a common way of committing lessons to memory. Much might be learned by rote, but the training of a young man to a level adequate to enable him to enter the bureaucracy needed more detailed and advanced instruction. By reciting in unison the sayings of the wise men of earlier ages, the basis of an intellectual education might be laid; but only through practical, individual application could the skills of writing (and with them, the skills of calculating and accounting) be acquired.

In the surviving literary compositions from ancient Egypt, omitting religious texts and quasi-scientific writings from consideration, the scribe understandably is presented in a particularly good light. This probably unbalanced prejudice is easily explained. In many cases these compositions were the essays, at least ostensibly so, of scribes or of literate officials who were proud to call themselves scribes; they were written out, often as school exercises, by scribes, and were designed both to instruct by their content and to exercise by their inherent lexicographical and scribal difficulties. Much of the literature of ancient Egypt was either directed towards, or the result of, scribal education; its tone was both didactic and complacent. The implicit argument was professionally incestuous: go to school, listen to your teacher, work hard, become a scribe, because scribes were so much better considered, and enjoyed so much better a life, than most Egyptians. The scribe belonged to an élite, a kind of loose club through which advancement might come, and outside which lay the discomforts and exploitations experienced by most people. In comparison with the life of the farmer, as we have already seen, the scribe's life was indeed fortunate: 'Be a scribe! It saves you from hard work, and preserves you from every kind of labour.'[9] How might the blessed scribal state be achieved?

Many texts among the series of compositions called *Miscellanies*,[10] which were used as scribal exercises, deal with the trade and training of the scribe, but none includes an account of the latter sufficiently complete to enable a fair picture to be built up of the educational establishments to which aspiring scribes might go. It is reasonably supposed that the principal offices of state ran their own schools, taking in promising candidates who could be trained in the practices and procedures of the individual offices. The same methods of recruitment and training would have been followed in provincial administrative centres, and also in the temples of the land. In the case of temple schools, however, the range of instruction would be greatly extended to include theological dogma, liturgical practices, and the particular problems of estate management required for the efficient control of the temple estates which might be scattered through the length of Egypt from the Delta to the First Cataract at Elephantine.[11]

Instruction for the very young was organized on a somewhat less formal basis, if any conclusion can be drawn from words included in a composition called *The Maxims of Ani*, the most complete version of which occurs on a papyrus in the Cairo Museum, dated on the basis of the handwriting to about 1000 BC, but probably composed, or put in order from sayings in common currency, at least as early as the Nineteenth Dynasty, perhaps three hundred years before. Among the various pieces of advice offered to his son the scribe Ani reminds him of the debt he owes to his mother, and of his obligation to look after her in consideration of the selfless way in which she saw to her child's needs even before he was born. For three years she suckled him; she showed no revulsion at tidying up his messes; further, 'she put you to school when you were ready to be instructed in letters, while daily she waited for you with bread and beer in her house'.[12] This first schooling took place when the boy could scarcely have been of any great age, and certainly before he might have been expected to assume a little responsibility. The words used for 'school' in this passage are, more precisely, translated as 'room' or 'department of teaching'; they are found so used as early as the Tenth Dynasty (c. 2050 BC).[13] It is not likely that they were intended to describe any particular kind of school: the 'room of teaching' was precisely what the words say—a place where teaching took place.

In the case of the young son of the scribe Ani, his school can have been little more than a kindergarten, and yet he was to begin learning about writing, or at least 'written things', there. The conclusion that a small boy might expect to begin his serious education at an early age ought not, however, to be drawn from this reported experience of Ani's son. The passages dealing with the training and experiences of student scribes in the *Miscellanies* and elsewhere suggest that the pupils were probably in their teens by the time they were subjected to the rigours of intensive training, and the bullying of tyrannical instructors.

> I have put you to school with the children of high officials, to teach and instruct you in this office which will lead to power and authority. See! I tell you the manner of the scribe in his (saying) 'Prompt in your place! Write in front of your fellows. Put your hand to your clothes; see to your sandals.' You bring your papyrus-roll daily with good intention. Don't be lazy! . . . Write with your hand; recite with your mouth; accept advice. Let yourself not be tired; and pass no day in laziness; or (it will be) misery to your body. Enter into the ways of your teacher, and obey his instructions. Be a scribe![14]

To act as a scribe, if you were already 'qualified' as a scribe, was all-important. That a young man put to school to become a scribe could be idle was incomprehensible to the teacher, and worthy of severe reproach and heavy punishment. 'Pass no day in laziness,' says the scribe Amenemope, 'or you will be beaten. The ear of a lad happens to be on his back. He listens when he is beaten. Attend to what I say!'[15] Sarcasm might help. The scribe Mahu berates his pupil: 'Do not be a silly fellow, with no learning. The night is spent training you, and the day teaching you; but you do not listen to any instruction, but go your own way. The ape understands words, and it is brought from Kush (Nubia). Lions can be trained, and horses broken, but beyond you there is no one of your kind in the whole inhabited land. Consider that!'[16] But the incorrigible pupil defeated the exasperated teacher. In despair Amenemope writes to Pentaur: 'I am fed up with offering advice . . . Should I give you one hundred strokes, and you will brush them all away. For me you are a beaten donkey who recovers in the day . . . I will make you a man, you bad boy! Consider that!'[17]

To the established scribe the way to success and salvation lay, understandably, in hard work:

> Don't be sluggish! Don't be sluggish! You will be checked forthwith. Do not give yourself over to pleasures or you will be a failure. Write with your hand, recite with your mouth, be advised by those who know more than you . . . Stick at working daily . . . Do not pass the day lazily, or you will be beaten . . . Stick at taking advice. Don't slack! Write! Don't show repugnance![18]

If a young man persisted in his studies, and became a fully-fledged scribe, he would, again according to the self-interested writings of the *Miscellanies*, occupy a place in society invested with many advantages. A scrutiny of the stated advantages shows that most accrue from the avoidance of disagreeable duties, or of unpleasant impositions. How much better it is to be a scribe than a soldier who is taken for training as a child and subjected to all manner of hardships in barracks and on active service: 'His food and his water are upon his shoulders like a donkey's load.'[19] Moreover, when troops are levied, the scribe will escape the call-up; that in itself is good enough reason to 'exercise this high official calling. Your palette and your roll of papyrus are delightful, and bring prosperity.'[20] Disagreeable physical labour of the kind suffered by the farmer is also avoided by the scribe. He does not have to row, or to look after horses; even the priest has to perform services at awkward times, and get himself wet in the regular ablutions of his office. A terrible fate awaits the baker. When he puts his bread to the fire, 'his head is right in the oven, his son hanging on to his feet; should it happen that his son's hand let go, then he slips down into the heart of the oven.'[21] But the scribe, in the opinion of the smug writer of this last comparison, 'he beats all tasks which are in this land'; and in saying this he means that nobody has an easier job than a scribe.

A more positive advantage enjoyed by the scribe, and offered as an inducement to the student in return for his hard work, is the power brought by the exercise of authority as an important official. Thoth, the god of writing, was invoked to come to the help of the aspiring scribe:

> Come to me that you may direct me, and make me accomplished in your craft. Your craft is better than all crafts; it promotes people. He who is accomplished in it is found suitable to be an official.[22]

The scribe might also expect to rub shoulders with the great and famous by being on duty on important occasions. He could become indispensable, and charged with carrying out duties of high responsibility. His training, in fact, is aimed ultimately to make him a trusted servant of the king:

> so that you can open treasuries and granaries, and receive (the cargo) from the boat at the door of the granary; and dispense offerings on feast days . . . A country-house is built (for you) in your city, and you possess a powerful position by the gift of the king to you.[23]

One matter in which the scribe may have enjoyed special advantage was taxation. The plight of the farmer has already been compared with the easy life of the scribe. Exposed to constant and unremitting toil throughout his life, the farmer suffers additionally from the changes of the weather and the depredations of natural pests and calamities. But a particular depredation, which was increased rather than diminished by rare prosperity, was the extraction of taxes. In this disagreeable process the scribe played a central role, in which his petty authority could be exercised with little restraint:

> The scribe is moored at the river's bank and is about to register the harvest-tax, while the attendants carry rods, and the Nubians bear palm switches. They say, 'Hand over grain!'—There is none.

They beat him without holding back . . . But the scribe is master of everyone. There is no tax levied on him who works in writing; he has no levies (to settle).[24]

This immunity from taxation should not, however, be overestimated. The scribe paid no dues of this kind because he had no produce worth taxing. His supposed advantage, therefore, was to some extent illusory. His authority, as the representative of local or central government, was not illusory, and from the frequent tomb scenes in which wretched farmers are shown being beaten for failure to pay up what they owed, it would appear that this authority was frequently exercised. The legal principles which determined action, and the moral principles which guided the springs of action, might favour impartial charity in the treatment of those who might fall foul of the law. In its interpretation by the small-minded officer of the Egyptian civil service, justice and equity were sacrificed to gratify the self-importance of the complacent scribe.

In the written expressions of praise for the scribe's profession (mostly, as we have already noted, written by scribes for student scribes, and to be written out as part of the scribe's training), a somewhat disagreeable picture of the successful scribe develops. The satisfaction to be derived from the practice of being a scribe is set out in a thoroughly selfish manner. Once he had survived the severe training and qualified, the scribe might enjoy a blissful career, avoiding all physical discomfort, exercising authority, and participating in government to some extent. The unctuous satisfaction informing all that Nebmarenakhte says to Unemdiamun is not very commendable:

> Be a scribe that your limbs may be sleek, and your hand may become (easily) wearied, that you may not be extinguished like a lamp, like him whose limbs are soft, for you have no men's bones in you. You are tall and fine-limbed. If you should take up a load to carry it, you would sink down, your feet trailing exceedingly, for you are miserably weak, all your limbs are wretched, and your body puny. Set your mind to being a scribe, an excellent trade, well fit for you. When you call one, one thousand answer. You will walk unhindered on the road, and not become an ox to be handed over. You will be at the head of others.[25]

Most of the ancient evidence quoted above concerning the training, prospects, and fortunate state of the scribe is drawn from the *Mis-*

cellanies, so called because they are made up of short compositions of miscellaneous kinds, apparently composed specially for the training of student scribes, and gathered together in random groupings on rolls of papyrus. Their function in the field of scribal education has never been satisfactorily established. The surviving rolls may represent fair copies written out for the edification of and copying by students; they may, in some cases at least, be the work of scribes still undergoing training. Corrections are noted, and examples of well-formed 'specimen' signs, or groups of signs, are occasionally inserted into the blank areas; but these apparent corrections are not usually particularly better than the writings within the bodies of the texts. It is also unlikely, in terms of general consideration, that so many substantial 'fair copies' of similar kind and similar date should have survived.[26]

By the strange chance that has overseen the discovery of the majority of papyri in modern times, nothing is known of the find-places of these *Miscellanies* papyri. They emerged from illicit excavations, or were found by chance. What information might have emerged if the circumstances of the discovery of just some of these rolls had been properly recorded? Were they from tombs, or from the remains of secular buildings? From temple or town areas? In boxes, in jars, or loosely in the ground? If a secular building, or a building in the precincts of a temple, was it possibly a school-room, or an archive? So many questions without answers are vexing. One conclusion of significance can be deduced from the fact that the *Miscellanies* are written on substantial rolls of papyrus.[27] This material was not easy to come by in sizeable rolls, and it is therefore highly unlikely that inexperienced scribes would have been provided with more than small pieces on which to exercise their skills. As we shall shortly see, the most common materials used for scribes' exercises were limestone flakes and pottery fragments which, when written upon, are usually called ostraca.

Rather more can be discovered from a consideration of the contents of the *Miscellanies* papyri. They consist to a very great extent of pieces composed in the form of letters or addresses directed by one scribe to another; frequently, as we have seen, from a master or senior scribe to a student or cadet scribe. They are, from a compositional point of view, mostly contemporaneous with their being inscribed on the papyrus-rolls. This fact is made certain both by the content of the pieces — a great many are concerned with life and practices in the bureaucracy and metropolitan society of the Nineteenth Dynasty—and by the language in which they are written—a form of Egyptian developed in the New Kingdom. They represent, therefore, in matter and language, the sorts of composition which would be produced by scribes of the higher ranks of officialdom when fully trained and exercising responsibility. They are, in consequence, very testing pieces, full of unusual vocabulary, lists of exotic products, technical terms, difficult computations—in brief, the essays employed in the final stages of training.

In the early stages of scribal training, the matter used by students to try out their budding skills was drawn mostly from literary compositions dating from earlier times, the stories and works of wisdom considered as the classics of Egyptian literature during the New Kingdom. In formal teaching, instruction was apparently carried out principally by rote, recitation in concert with fellow-students, and by receiving dictation from a teacher. Passages for copying were taken from tales like the *Story of Sinuhe*, or didactic treatises like the *Instruction of King Ammenemes I to his son Sesostris*, or the very popular *Satire of Trades*, particularly the last which ridiculed most trades and professions, to the advantage of that of the scribe. These texts, and others like them, were composed in the language of the Twelfth Dynasty, which in ancient Egypt (as indeed by Egyptologists today) was considered as the classic stage of the Egyptian language.[28] It was the form generally used for religious compositions and royal monumental texts right down to the Ptolemaic Period. This Middle Egyptian served as the favoured medium for teaching scribes, probably because it offered a stable base for training, and because of the existence of a substantial body of well-written Middle Egyptian compositions which could be used as examples to be copied and recopied—the 'set books' prescribed by tradition.

In formal classes, perhaps in those organized by the principal offices of state and the great temples, it may be supposed that the scribes in training used writing boards to take down dictation, and to practise their copying. These boards, sometimes as big as 53 cm. by 38 cm., were made of sycomore and covered with a thin layer of fine, hard plaster, often called gesso.[29] Well prepared to take writing, these boards have been considered easy to wipe clean, and so to use repeatedly, rather like the old-fashioned school slate. Many examples have survived with traces of old texts faintly visible beneath later texts. The way in which an old text might be erased has never been satisfactorily established, and it may be supposed that cleaning was not as easy as claimed, or indeed very efficient. Probably the first cleaning was reasonably successful, but subsequent cleanings almost certainly destroyed the smooth surface of the board. It would, however, have been a simple matter to resurface the board with a fresh skin of plaster, rendering it as good as new.

Most scribal training appears to have been undertaken on the disposable ostraca, already mentioned. In areas where limestone was the prevailing stone, these flakes were used very commonly, both by students and by practising scribes; they represented the ancient equivalent of the scrap-pad or memo-pad. They could be picked up in quantity wherever quarrying or tomb excavation took place in the limestone hills, as at Thebes where the limestone possessed the quality of splitting easily into convenient pieces, the surfaces of which needed no preparation or treatment before they could be used for writing. Where limestone was not to be found, then pottery sherds were used for the same purpose. It is noticeable that at Thebes in particular, limestone ostraca have survived in greatest numbers from those periods when tomb excavation in the necropolis was extensive. At other times, especially in the early Christian Period, pottery ostraca were chiefly used. Suitable flakes of limestone were undoubtedly retrieved from the spoil heaps resulting from the cutting of tombs, especially royal tombs, and it can easily be seen how the workman employed on these tombs might have carried back to his village a useful stock of pieces to be used either by himself, or his children. The royal workmen's village at Thebes was a hive of scribal activity, and has yielded, through modern excavation, many thousands of inscribed ostraca dating from the New Kingdom.

The texts on these limestone ostraca in particular cover the whole range of casual written record, from accounts of local disputes to simple notes of expenditure and of working activities. Vast numbers, however, fall into the category which concerns us especially in this chapter, the copies of portions of famous literary compositions produced by student scribes, and probably also by talented artisans who sought to become literate. These copies are written in the conventional hieratic script of the appropriate period, but with care being taken in the formation of signs, and with the general avoidance of the extremes of cursive writing found in workaday texts. The literary passages are quite clearly attempts at fair copies, where the writing is at least as important as the content. There is no sure way of deciding whether they were copied from some other written example, or taken down from dictation; but there is good reason to believe that many were copied out from memory. We may imagine the eager student going off by himself to a quiet corner in the Theban hills with ink, brush, water and ostraca, to practise his hand without interruption.

One text which occurs on many hundreds of limestone ostraca from Thebes suggests something quite special. It is composed in the form of a letter, which, after a long introduction consisting of elaborate greetings, contains a series of statements, aphorisms and injunctions aimed, once again, at exalting the scribe's profession. The epistolary framework of this composition was a literary device much employed by the ancient Egyptians; indeed, many of the individual sections of the *Miscellanies* are cast as letters. They are perhaps the earliest 'open' letters, directed at no single correspondent, but at a class of persons, possibly even the reading public in general. The message is certainly general, but the form is intimate, and therefore perhaps more persuasive than a simple composition addressed to nobody in particular. The letters in the *Miscellanies* are not distinguished by special names, unless they might be characterized by their writers. There is no reason to think that they were identified in this way in antiquity, except that a teacher might instruct his students to write out as an exercise, for example, the letter of Nebmarenakhte, and identify the piece in this way.

The formal letter mentioned above, which was so much copied, and is of special interest to us, is not identified from its contents by any name, but it can be given a name from a quotation in the almost equally popular *Satire of Trades*. At the beginning of this latter work, the writer, the scribe Achthoes, who is about to place his son Pepi in a scribal school, tells the boy: 'Read then at the end of *Kemyt*; you will find this sentence, saying, "As for the scribe, no matter what position he finds himself in the (royal) Residence, he will not be uncomfortable in it." ' This quotation comes almost verbatim from the much used model letter, which can therefore be identified as the work named *Kemyt*, an Egyptian word meaning 'what completes, completion', or even 'what is completed'.[30] The *Satire of Trades* was composed early in the Twelfth Dynasty (*c.* 1950 BC), so *Kemyt* must predate it—a conclusion which is supported by the epistolary greetings found at the beginning of the 'letter'. These greetings are characteristic of proper letters dated to the late Eleventh Dynasty (*c.* 2000 BC).[31] *Kemyt*, as the name of a famous composition, occurs in one other literary text, dated without doubt to the Nineteenth Dynasty, and originating from Thebes.[32] This second mention of *Kemyt*, allusive and unspecific, is followed by references to Achthoes, who can, in the context, only be the author of the *Satire of Trades*. The two mentions of *Kemyt*, therefore, are closely associated with the *Satire*, and it can scarcely be surprising to find that both 'books' were popular school texts in the New Kingdom. Indeed, the evidence of *Kemyt*'s mention in the *Satire* suggests that it was already a standard text in the Twelfth Dynasty.

In the principal publication of ostraca of the New Kingdom that bear literary texts, in which the whole continuous narrative (if it can so be called) of *Kemyt* is established, it is pointed out that more ostraca with portions of *Kemyt* have survived than those bearing parts of any other literary text.[33] Why this should be the case is scarcely to be comprehended, because it cannot be claimed that *Kemyt* is a specially interesting text either in content or in quality of language. Its attraction is possibly to be found, initially, in its simplicity and seeming lack of difficulties for the young scribe. It may, in fact, have been the primer for scribal beginners, the first reader from which the student learned to handle the hieratic script both in reading and writing. This view of *Kemyt* is reinforced by the unusual fact that all copies are written out in a manner quite removed from the practices of the New Kingdom orthography. Writing in the New Kingdom was regularly laid out in horizontal lines written from right to left. Copies of *Kemyt* are written in vertical columns divided by spacing lines in red paint. The hieratic signs are not formed in the New Kingdom manner, but they possess an old-fashioned appearance which may not, however, be precisely described as characteristic of early Middle-kingdom date. Literary texts and letters (and most other writings in hieratic) were regularly written in vertical columns up to the time of the early Middle Kingdom. *Kemyt*, therefore, should originally have been written in vertical columns, and so it survived into the New Kingdom presumably because it was thought in this way to be suited for the initial training of scribes. The banality of the content of *Kemyt* scarcely mattered. It was written distinctively, its writing in columns avoiding the difficult groupings of signs, and ligatures of signs, which were common in well-written texts of the New Kingdom set out in horizontal lines. It was full of formulae and well-tried expressions, easy to learn and hard to forget; in short, an ideal text for instruction.

The frequency of *Kemyt's* occurrences on ostraca from Thebes is hardly surprising, and examples found at El-Amarna,[34] the site of King Akhenaten's model city of Akhetaten, show that it was still used by student scribes even during a time when so much of Egyptian life was turned upside down. Many of the surviving copies of *Kemyt* are probably the exercises of beginner scribes before they graduated to writing in horizontal lines, and to texts of a more advanced kind, like the *Satire of Trades*, or the compositions specially prepared in the scribal schools of the New Kingdom, and preserved in the *Miscellanies*. It may also be supposed that some of the *Kemyt* copies were written, perhaps nostalgically, by Egyptians who had begun the scribal training, but never completed it. Certainly, the abundance of *Kemyt* copies suggests popularity; its uncomplicated form was easy to teach and to learn; its simple script ideal for beginners.

A word of caution should, however, be voiced at this point—one which may apply not only in the discussion of scribal training in ancient Egypt, but also in many other investigations where general conclusions are drawn from what may be unrepresentative evidence. The surviving record is unbalanced, and there exists always the chance that what may appear to be clearly established by this record, should apply only for the places, periods, and social level represented in the record. In the case of the various sources used in this discussion, some facts of significance can be brought forward to help test the general validity of the conclusions, at least as far as the New Kingdom is concerned.

The greatest number of limestone ostraca used to write out portions of the standard texts for training scribes comes from the Theban area. Of these the overwhelming majority have been excavated from within and around the village occupied by the workmen employed on the royal tombs. The texts represented on the ostraca from this village cover the whole range of compositions which can be thought of as forming the standard academic pabulum of the scribal schools, including most of the stories known from the time of the Middle Kingdom, the so-called wisdom texts—the semi-philosophical 'instructions' of famous sages—and even those shorter pieces of the kind found in the *Miscellanies*. The evidence is therefore rich for one, rather select, part of the Theban district.[35] Can reliable generalizations be drawn from it? The commonest text is, as we have already noticed, the book of *Kemyt*, which has its origins in the epistolary forms of the Eleventh Dynasty, as practised in the Theban area. But a few examples of *Kemyt* ostraca have been found at El-Amarna, which in itself is not surprising, for most of those in positions of authority in that new city probably came from Thebes. Their other probable source was Memphis, the northern capital and seat of the northern vizir, where education may well have been organized along the same lines as at Thebes. Some of the papyri containing the *Miscellanies* originated, in all probability, in the Memphite region, although the evidence for this provenance is largely circumstantial.[36] Nevertheless, many of the individual pieces which these papyri contain were ostensibly written, or composed, in Memphis, or in Lower Egypt, while others are apparently Theban. It seems reasonably certain, therefore, that the form and content of scribal education at Thebes and at Memphis had much in common with each other.

This conclusion is scarcely surprising. It should be expected that the two great metropolitan regions in Egypt during the New Kingdom should produce the best evidence of scribal training. And of the two, the primacy of Thebes, from the point of view of surviving evidence, is due principally to the greater use of limestone ostraca in the region of the southern capital. In addition, conditions were more favourable at Thebes for the preservation, and recovery, of ephemeral material than at Memphis. As for the rest of the country, what conclusions may be drawn? Very little positive evidence of student-scribe activity has been found in the principal provincial centres, although it must be assumed that scribes were trained there for the local administrations and for service in the great provincial religious establishments. Provincial schools may well have been influenced by the practices of Thebes and Memphis during the New Kingdom, but there is no evidence to suggest that the metropolitan academies provided the teachers for the whole country. Nevertheless, there is plenty of evidence to show that there was a substantial level of literacy throughout Egypt. The large temples, lavishly decorated with texts and scenes, and private tombs, equally well embellished, required for their construction and maintenance the services of considerable numbers of people trained in writing, and in using writing freely. Further, the whole of Egyptian life was controlled by a bureaucracy whose activities were carried forward by documentation. In Egypt, therefore, where so much depended on the written word, not only was literacy highly valued, it was also exploited daily in the transaction of business at many levels of society; it was by no means restricted to the ranks of the court and to the superior officers of state. Something has been said in the preceding pages about this high level of literacy. Much, however, remains to be said of how the scribe functioned away from school, and outside the great offices and temples. Important men in Egypt were content to be called scribes because the appellation indicated education and an honourable status. But most scribes, employed in the lower echelons of administration and in the remoter areas of the land, probably knew little of the claims of superiority made on their behalf in the pompous passages of the *Miscellanies*. Their modest superiority must be measured against the lot of the peasants and labourers among whom they mostly exercised their scribal duties. Better off they were certainly, but not quite in the élite state envisaged by the prejudiced scribal instructor. After school comes the adverse experience of life.

NOTES

1 The texts are given in K. A. Kitchen, *Ramesside Inscriptions*, I (Oxford, 1975), 177 ff.

2 The Turin list is best published by A. H. Gardiner, *The Royal Canon of Turin* (Oxford, 1959).

3 See I. E. S. Edwards in *Cambridge Ancient History*, I, 3 ed., Pt. 2 (Cambridge, 1971), 43.

4 An excellent account of the script and of the language is given in A. H. Gardiner, *Egyptian Grammar*, 3 ed. (Oxford, 1957).

5 Brooklyn Papyrus 47.218.3, published in R. A. Parker, *A Saïte Oracle Papyrus from Thebes* (Providence, 1962).

6 From *The Instruction for Merikare*; see n. 1 to Chapter One.

7 Accounts on the verso are probably of the reign of Amenophis II; see D. Redford in *Journal of Egyptian Archaeology* 51 (London, 1965), 107 ff.

8 *Merikare*, ll.50-51.

9 See p. 103 above.

10 The texts of these compilations are published in A. H. Gardiner, *Late-Egyptian Miscellanies*, and translated with full commentaries in R. A. Caminos, *Late-Egyptian Miscellanies* (Oxford, 1954).

11 On Egyptian education in general, see H. Brunner, *Altägyptische Erziehung* (Wiesbaden, 1957).

12 *Maxims of Ani*, 7,20–8,1. A bibliography and a translation of the whole are given in M. Lichtheim, *Ancient Egyptian Literature*, II, 135 ff.

13 F. Ll. Griffith, *The Inscriptions of Siût and Dêr Rîfeh* (London, 1889), pl. 14.

14 A. H. Gardiner, *Late-Egyptian Miscellanies*, 68, ll. 16 ff.

15 Ibid. 24, ll. 4 f.

16 Ibid. 3, ll. 13 ff.

17 Ibid. 85, ll. 8 ff.

18 Ibid. 59, ll. 9 ff.

19 Ibid. 26, l. 10.

20 Ibid. 61, ll. 6 f.

21 Ibid. 17, ll. 6 ff.

22 Ibid. 60, ll. 5 ff.

23 Ibid. 107, ll. 7 ff.

24 Ibid. 64, ll. 16 ff. A similar passage has already been quoted in Chapter 4, p. 103 above.

25 Ibid. 106, ll. 6 ff.

26 About one dozen substantial rolls, and a further half-dozen fragmentary rolls.

27 Two in the British Museum are the longest: 10244 (Anastasi Papyrus V) approximately 7 m. long, 10184 (Sallier Papyrus IV) 7.6 m. long. The latter, however, bears its *Miscellany* text on its verso, the recto being occupied by a Calendar of Lucky and Unlucky Days.

28 Translations of these texts can be found in M. Lichtheim, *Ancient Egyptian Literature*, and in W. K. Simpson (ed.), *The Literature of Ancient Egypt*.

29 More precisely, a whiting plaster, made of whiting and glue, see A. Lucas, *Ancient Egyptian Materials and Industries*, 354.

30 See G. Posener in B. van de Walle, *La transmission des textes littéraires égyptiens* (Brussels, 1948), 48 f.

31 T. G. H. James, *The Hekanakhte Papers*, 120 ff.

32 In British Museum Papyrus 10684, verso 6, 11 (Chester Beatty Papyrus IV).

33 G. Posener, *Catalogue des ostraca hiératiques littéraires de Deir el Médineh*, II (Cairo, 1951–72), v f.

34 J. D. S. Pendlebury, *City of Akhenaten*, III (London, 1951), vol. 2, pl. XCVII, nos. 329, 330.

35 The richness of the documentation on ostraca from the village is made clear in books such as J. Černý, *A Community of Workmen at Thebes in the Ramesside Period*; J. J. Janssen, *Commodity Prices in the Ramessid Period*; M. L. Bierbrier, *The Tomb-Builders of the Pharaohs*.

36 See A. H. Gardiner, *Late-Egyptian Miscellanies*, xiii ff., in the introductions to the individual documents. The problem needs further investigation.

6

THE SCRIBE IN ACTION

When Egyptians first began to communicate by writing at the very start of the Dynastic Period, their purpose was to record in a semi-pictorial manner simple facts and events—the contents of a jar, or the performance of a festival. The record was semi-pictorial because of the nature of the hieroglyphic script, the cursive equivalent of which was still, at that time, so sufficiently pictorial as to allow the reader to recognize what might be written in it, and to understand very broadly the meaning, even if he could not 'read' it in the strictest sense. The jar called *des*, drawn (or written) and followed by the two vertical strokes (∪ǁ), could clearly be understood as '2 jars', even by an unlettered person. This process of understanding was simple, and can scarcely be dignified by the word 'read'. From the beginning, however, the Egyptian scripts were capable of doing much more than simple depiction, and an unlettered person would not have got far even in the determination of the nature of objects and (where appropriate) their contents.

The speedy elaboration of the script enabled the writer to record actions as well as objects, but it was a long time before anything like continuous text with recognizable sentences could be achieved. By the end of the Second Dynasty (*c*. 2650 BC) very great advances had been made, and it may be concluded that by then a proper appreciation of the importance of the written word had developed in Egyptian minds. Certainly the scribe was already established as an important person in the official bureaucracy, and great men were ready to have themselves called scribes and to be shown as scribes in their tombs. Among the earliest surviving mature works of art from this early time are the wooden panels found in the tomb of Hesyre at Saqqara. He served Djoser, the king who had constructed for himself the first great stone building in Egypt, perhaps in the world. His Step Pyramid occupied the prime position on the Saqqara plateau, and his senior officials built large mud-brick mastaba-tombs to the north, about half a mile away. The wooden panels which occupied niches in Hesyre's tomb bear fine, strong, low-relief representations of the great man, and enumerations of his titles executed in very stylish hieroglyphs. One of his principal titles was 'chief of the King's scribes', and his pride in this title was demonstrated by his carrying the traditional scribal equipment, made up of palette, brush-holder and pigment-bag.[1] This equipment, which formed the sign used to indicate 'writing', 'scribe', and related words in the hieroglyphic script, remained unchanged theoretically throughout Egyptian history; but in practical terms, the palette changed markedly as time advanced. By the Middle Kingdom already it had become a container for pigment and brushes combined,[2] and this form persisted throughout the New Kingdom.

Yet the brush-container, separate from the palette, did not wholly disappear. A collection of scribal equipment found together in a box in Tutankhamun's tomb included two long palettes fitted with rush brushes, and also a very fine brush-container in the form of a cylinder shaped like a column with a palm-leaf capital.[3] This was the traditional form of the brush-container, although no ordinary scribe would ever have possessed one made of gilded wood inlaid with semi-precious stones and coloured glass. The royal palette which presumably went with the container was similarly gilded, and it carried a short text naming the king with his early name, Tutankhaten, and describing him as 'beloved of Thoth, lord of god's words'. This epithet was here specially significant because Thoth was the god of writing and the scribe of the gods. Another implement which was found with these scribal tools was made of ivory; its head was wedge-shaped and its handle in the form of a column with lily-capital. Howard Carter, describing the piece, noted that the head was fitted with a gold cap, and he thought that it was intended to burnish papyrus before use. Here, then, was Tutankhamun's personal writing outfit, certainly to be used in his after-life, even if it had never been touched during his earthly life. Such grand equipments were in a sense the toys of royalty, although there is no special reason to believe that a king like Tutankhamun would not have been able to write. For the equipment of a working scribe, we may turn to another discovery of Howard Carter.

In the years just before the First World War he was excavating for the Earl of Carnarvon in a part of the Theban necropolis lying to the east of Hatshepsut's mortuary temple at Deir el-Bahri. Here were tombs of the

Late Middle Kingdom and Second Intermediate Period, some of which had been used again for burials in later times. The largest of these, found by Carter in 1911, contained no inscriptions or wall-decorations which would have provided good evidence for the date of its first use. The antiquities recovered from it, however, showed that it had accommodated burials from the Late Middle Kingdom down to the early Eighteenth Dynasty (c. 1750–1550 BC), a span of about two hundred years. Among the litter of objects surviving from the many modest burials deposited here was a well-preserved rush basket with a lid which contained a substantial collection of objects, many identifiable as scribe's implements.[4] It was a true working scribe's outfit, deposited no doubt for use in the hereafter, but quite certainly not specially made for funerary purposes. In the illustration showing some of the objects from this basket, the following items, specifically scribal, can be seen: a brush-container made from a hollow reed with a decorated top of wood bound in place with a strip of linen, containing twenty-six rushes; a similar, but smaller, brush-container, without a decorated top, containing fifteen rushes; a rough wooden palette with two depressions for red and black paint, and a slot to hold rushes when in use; a small mallet-shaped implement, possibly the common equivalent of the fancy ivory burnisher found in Tutankhamun's scribal outfit; a linen bag with a draw-string, possibly for extra pigment; a small leather roll, perhaps to be used as a writing surface; a tortoise-shell, which could have been used as a water-container or a mixing bowl; a small clay figure of a baboon, the sacred animal of Thoth, the scribal god. Similar baboon figures are commonly shown in vignettes of *The Book of the Dead* depicting the judgement of the dead. Thoth, the ibis-headed, writes down the results of the examination of the candidate for entry to the realm of Osiris, while Thoth, the baboon, sits on the bar of the scales in which the dead man's heart is balanced against Truth. In this humble scribe's outfit the figure of Thoth as baboon might be waiting to fulfil the second role, for the outfit also contained a stick notched at both ends and pierced in the middle, which could have been used as the bar of a simple pair of scales. To clinch the idea, there were a number of small discs of various materials and sizes which could be weights. Here then Carter had found what may well have been the working equipment of a scribe engaged in everyday commercial activities, rather than in the high affairs of state, or even simple local secretarial work.

The prime writing material of the scribe in the full exercise of his profession was papyrus, a medium for the reception of the written word unparalleled in the ancient world, with a history of continuous use lasting almost four thousand years. It was peculiarly a product of Egypt, and was in later times exported in large quantities to the Near-Eastern and Mediterranean worlds. Its manufacture is thought to have been a royal monopoly, the name 'papyrus', which has been transmitted to us by Greek writers, possibly finding its etymology in the Egyptian words *pa-per-ao*, 'that of Pharaoh'.[5] Felicitous though this explanation is, the words have never been found in any ancient Egyptian source, and its validity must therefore be seriously questioned. Yet it is possible that the monopoly control was exercised only over the export of papyrus, and that within Egypt it was readily available for use without official restriction, although it is unlikely that it was ever in lavish supply.[6] Unfortunately, questions concerning availability and control of distribution are not easy to answer. But one thing is certain: scribes in general were encouraged to use papyrus, both in sheet and in roll, more than once, and very many surviving documents are written over earlier texts, many traces of which can be distinguished, and even read.

Papyrus, the writing material, was made from papyrus, the plant (botanically, *Cyperus papyrus* L.), which grew widely in the Nile Valley in antiquity where suitable marshy conditions obtained. It may even have been cultivated, although the evidence for this is slight. Today it has disappeared from the intensively farmed land of Egypt, but it can still be found in abundance in the upper reaches of the Nile in the Sudan. The papyrus stem is triangular in section, and within an outer rind is a spongy pith which provides the raw material for papyrus paper. Modern attempts at manufacturing papyrus have achieved variable results. Essentially, strips of pith are laid side by side, and a second series of strips laid on top at right angles. Beaten with a mallet between cloths on a flat surface, the strips fuse together without the addition of any further substance, yielding a sheet of tough, flexible 'paper' with a distinct texture which appears to be woven. The surface, if rough or uneven, can be rubbed smooth with a pebble, or a specially made smoothing implement. It is then fit for use, and it readily receives ink or paint applied with a brush. This method of manufacture, tried successfully many times in the British Museum with papyrus obtained from Kew Gardens or from one of the university botanical gardens, is simple and demands no elaborate tools. The trouble about most modern papyrus, however, is that it tends to be marred by brown spots, imperfections which cannot be seen on good ancient papyrus. Experiments conducted in Italy have greatly improved the colour by techniques of washing.[7] It is clear that modern methods of manufacture, based on classical accounts, do not necessarily reproduce the techniques employed in the days of finest papyrus-making of the Middle and New Kingdoms. The papyrus-makers of ancient Egypt had a vast amount of experience and knowledge to draw on. It may be supposed, for example, that they preferred to cut and make their writing material at specific seasons. It is also possible that the quality of the ground in which the plant grew, and the very water of the Nile, provided adventitiously the ideal conditions for the production of fine unblemished paper. Furthermore, the strong sun of Egypt might have successfully bleached the newly-made sheets when they were laid out to dry. New papyrus was white, but it soon turned yellow away from the sunlight through oxidization. In a sense, therefore, yellow was the regular colour of papyrus as is shown by the yellow ground used on the walls of tombs on which religious texts were inscribed; the walls were, in a magical sense, papered with enlarged open rolls of papyrus bearing the required texts.

It is evident that there was no difficulty in making papyrus; the only

Fig. 13 *The harvesting of papyrus. On the right a man strips the rind from a stem in preparation perhaps for paper making.*

restriction which might have affected the supply of writing material was a shortage of the papyrus plant itself. The modern experiments have shown that freshly cut stems are essential for the manufacture of the writing material, and the best results are achieved with new growth of substantial size. If papyrus plants were not specially cultivated in antiquity, the supply coming directly from the wild, untended growths in marshy districts, then in all probability it was cropped seasonally, and not all the year round. Manufacture of the writing material would then have been more or less contemporaneous with cropping, and it is not at all unlikely that there would have been seasonal shortages in the weeks before the new crop was ready. Unfortunately, ancient records provide no information on this matter; there are tomb scenes showing the gathering of papyrus, but the activity occurs most commonly in association with the making of papyrus-boats and matting; and the scenes are unplaced seasonally in the cycle of the year (*Fig. 13*).[8]

While there may have been in Pharaonic times no royal monopoly in the manufacture and sale of papyrus writing material, the bulk of the new material was surely produced by specialized papyrus-makers who may or may not have operated under licence. Anyone who had access to a supply of the fresh papyrus plant, provided that he had some knowledge and manual dexterity, could have made small quantities of

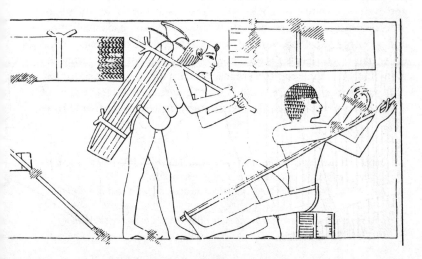

paper; but manufacture on a substantial scale, with reliable uniformity of the product, required adequate equipment, a well-trained team of craftsmen, and responsible control. If surviving papyri may be taken as a guide to the principal uses of the material in antiquity, it is abundantly clear that during the New Kingdom new papyrus was available, almost without restriction, for private funerary purposes. What has actually survived from the period can represent only a tiny proportion of what was used, and of that small quantity, perhaps as much as one half consists of copies of *The Book of the Dead*, the most popular funerary compilation of the time, and of other religious texts. And almost all these texts owe their survival to the fact that they were deposited in dry subterranean tombs of the Theban necropolis. Yet the economics of the business of burial, and the provision of an adequate equipment for the after-life, are puzzling. A fairly simple burial will contain a long and finely executed copy of *The Book of the Dead*. Among the many copies in the British Museum are two which may serve as instructive examples: the roll prepared for Nu is only a few centimetres short of twenty metres, while that found with the burial of Ani is over twenty-three metres long.[9] The text written out for Nu is generally considered the best, the most error-free, of all surviving copies of *The Book of the Dead*; Ani's copy, although full of mistakes, contains the most beautiful illustrations of all known copies. Yet Nu was simply a 'steward of the chief treasurer', and Ani a 'king's scribe'. Neither of these officials is known from sources independent of their few surviving grave-goods, and even their tombs are not known. Presumably the nobles and senior officials, the occupants of the highest ranks of society, had equally fine, and probably finer, copies of the essential funerary texts. Kings, on the other hand, required texts of a more esoteric content, and during the New Kingdom their copies were inscribed on the walls of their tombs. No papyrus rolls were found in the virtually intact tomb of Tutankhamun; in his case the texts were presented on the four shrines

9 *(above) Casual entries on the* verso *of Papyrus Sallier IV (BM 10184): a grid of dots, perhaps for calculation, and a drawing of a bull.*

(bottom left) A letter from the Hekanakhte archive, folded, tied and sealed for delivery.

(bottom right) The letter sent by the mayor Mentuhotpe to the scribe Ahmose (BM 10102).

which surrounded his coffin, from the safety of which he could conveniently consult the appropriate texts as his spirit wished and as the stages of his posthumous journey required.

The lavish use of papyrus for funerary purposes suggests a well-organized, regular trade; but it is not known whether the trade was officially, even royally, sanctioned. During the New Kingdom the quality of copies of *The Book of the Dead* varies immensely, and their lengths appear to be determined by expense. Some copies were undoubtedly written to the order of the prospective owner, some were ready prepared, the mark of the latter being the clearly subsequent insertion of the name of the owner into blank spaces left in the various sections of the text. It is possible that official permission might have been required for the obtaining of a personal funerary papyrus, but the buyer—the prospective owner—appears to have had considerable freedom over the size and quality of what he acquired. How else could the rare and expensive use of gold leaf be explained on the vignettes of *The Book of the Dead* of Neferronpe in the British Museum?[10] He again was a person of no high rank, but his title, 'chief of the makers of gold leaf (literally, "thin gold")', indicates the way in which he could have secured such unusual decoration for his posthumous pleasure. New papyrus was generally used for these mortuary compositions, probably for practical purposes as much as for reasons of propriety: large rolls of papyrus, already covered with texts, were unlikely to be available for re-use; while the removal of old writing was a laborious process, and generally only partially successful. Traces of another document, for example the account of legal proceedings, might surely be considered an adulteration of a religious text which itself would be of truly vital importance to a dead person. Copies of *The Book of the Dead* were also commonly written on one side of the papyrus only.

No similar indulgence in the use of new papyrus can be found in the secular writings of the ancient Egyptians, except in the preparation of important state documents, for which the best material was, most properly, employed. It is not at all uncommon to find quite long texts written on papyrus from which earlier writing has been expunged. The

10 (*above*) *Modern tinkers at work on the river-bank at Luxor.*

   (*below*) *Negroes bring gold rings and rough nuggets from Nubia; a scene from the tomb of Sobkhotpe (BM 921).*

word 'palimpsest' is used for such documents, although its meaning 'scraped again' more properly belongs to the field of documents written on vellum. The removal of a text from papyrus by abrasion, and possibly by water, was rarely a wholly successful operation; many first texts remain in substantial traces beneath and around their replacements, presenting tantalizing hints of what was originally written. Again, few papyri were allowed to remain blank on their reverse sides, and the supplementary texts added on the back may have no connection whatsoever with the texts on the front. Sometimes a papyrus has been so exploited that the determination of the relationship of the various texts on its front and back becomes a kind of archaeological activity, similar to the interpretation of a confused site under excavation. A good example is Papyrus Sallier IV in the British Museum which is 7.6 m. long.[11] The side commonly called the front, or recto, is occupied by a calendar of lucky and unlucky days, in which days, and parts of days, are characterized as being good or bad. This text, however, is written over the traces of an earlier text, which presumably was the first text to be written on the papyrus. It is likely, therefore, that the calendar was written later than those texts on the reverse, or verso, of this papyrus.[12] The verso texts are of different kinds: about one fifth of the space is filled by one of those miscellaneous compilations of scribal exercises discussed in the last chapter; there is a letter, possibly the copy of a true missive, about the delivery of poor grain; there are several texts about grain collection and threshing, some odd jottings and memoranda, and a few other short texts. The contents of this reverse side of Sallier IV form a strange mixture of genuine notes and scribal exercises, as if the roll, after it had been used on its recto for a text (or texts) which had lost its importance, was then employed for occasional writings. In its use as a kind of scrap-book it apparently received pretty rough treatment, for when someone decided to wipe out the text on the recto, and to replace it with the calendar of lucky and unlucky days, the roll had to be strengthened with patches of papyrus stuck on the verso, and obscuring parts of the verso texts. No doubt the frequent unrolling of the papyrus for the addition of new texts, and for the reading of the old, had led to the tearing and cracking; and this damage would no doubt have increased greatly with the frequent consulting of the calendar for guidance in day-to-day matters.

Papyrus Sallier IV provides a good example in the economical use of papyrus paper. A date in one of the verso texts fixes that entry to Year

56 of Ramesses II of the Nineteenth Dynasty (*c.* 1234 BC), and in consideration of the long earlier and later texts written on the recto, it is not impossible that the roll was in active use for several decades. Papyrus is a resilient, hard-wearing material, capable of withstanding much handling and re-use. Even if it was not particularly expensive to purchase new, it may frequently have been difficult to obtain. Its use, therefore, for private purposes was probably always limited, and tended to be restricted to those occasions when other means of communication were inappropriate for one reason or another. In a community like that of the workmen of the royal necropolis at Deir el-Medina, most casual documents were written on limestone or pottery ostraca, about which something has already been said in this book. Those somewhat cumbersome objects could easily be passed from hand to hand within the small compass of the social scene of Western Thebes; they could, inconveniently, be stored if necessary, but for the most part, in accord with their transient application, they were discarded; many were thrown, perhaps deliberately, into great pits, kinds of waste-paper baskets for out-of-date personal documents. Written material which had more than a temporary importance was best put down on papyrus. Documents on papyrus were easily stored, easily retrieved—as we have noticed in the administration of justice by the vizir—and easily consulted.

For similar reasons of convenience, documents which were sent some distance were better consigned to papyrus. They were more portable than ostraca, more private, and could be sealed. If the document were official as likely as not it would be written on new papyrus. If it were private, in all probability it would be a palimpsest, written over the traces of an old text. Of private documents in general, few are more private than personal letters addressed by one individual to another. Writing, as we have seen, was invented, or developed, principally as a means of recording; but by recording the writer is also communicating. To communicate privately with someone by writing is by no means a primitive activity; it demonstrates the appreciation of the independent status of the written word, which can be read and understood far away from the place where the word was written. By writing a letter the writer confirms his confidence in the belief that the writing will convey his meaning with accuracy when it is read at its destination.

In spite of the robust nature of papyrus, not very many casual documents have survived from antiquity. Yet there is much evidence that personal correspondence was common from at least the Middle Kingdom; while the sending of official dispatches and reports was certainly organized on a regular basis. The writing of such documents undoubtedly represented the principal work of the professional scribe. On the floor of rooms in the fortress of Uronarti in Nubia, an outpost of Egyptian power at the southern end of the Second Cataract of the Nile in the Sudan, over four thousand five hundred mud seals from letters and dispatches were found in excavations, all dated by their discoverer to the Thirteenth Dynasty (c. 1750 BC).[13] In the exceptionally dry conditions of this area, large quantities of papyrus fragments were found, but in such a destroyed state that no substantial documents could be reconstructed. Here was evidence of massive correspondence at a time when Egyptian power was already losing control in the southern empire. Again, in the excavation of the Palace of Amenophis III in Western Thebes, over eleven hundred seals from papyrus documents were collected.[14] The size and nature of these tiny pieces of mud make it highly probable that very many more were overlooked or destroyed in the course of excavation. No associated papyrus fragments were, it seems, discovered here, but there can be no doubt that the seals provide ample testimony of active correspondence. In Uronarti Fort and in the Palace of Amenophis III, remains of correspondence should cause little surprise, but most of it would have been of an official character—instructions in and reports out; indeed, remains of dispatches from the fort of Semna, only a few miles to the south of Uronarti, have survived, and provide fascinating shreds of evidence of the duties and responsibilities of the garrisons of Nubian fortresses in the Twelfth Dynasty.[15]

To be able to correspond on private and family matters by sending a written communication was appreciated in all its aspects by the literate Egyptian. Provided that the sender and the recipient could both read and write, or have the services of a scribe to perform these functions for them, the letter was quite the best way of passing a message or sending news. The earliest comprehensible letter on papyrus which has survived is more official than private, but its content is personal, and its tone sharp and to the point. A military commander writes from Tura, the site of the finest limestone quarries in Egypt, which lie a few miles to the south of Cairo. He refers to a letter he had received from the vizir instructing him to bring his men across the river to Saqqara to receive the clothes they require from the vizir there, and he grumbles at the inconvenience involved in such a journey. The commander hints that the clothes could be sent to Tura, perhaps in a stone-barge with the letter-carrier, and he goes on, referring to himself in the polite Egyptian manner as 'this servant':

> Now this servant has (in the past) spent as much as six days with this detachment at the Residence before it was clothed, which was an interference with the work in the control of this servant. Only one day should be wasted for clothing this detachment. That's what this servant says. Let the letter-carrier know (the answer).

This letter was found at Saqqara, torn up, and it is thought, not improbably, that the recipient's answer to the complaint may be deduced from the way the letter was treated.[16] Written in the late Sixth Dynasty, this letter shows that by about 2200 BC the written message was already taking the place of the verbal message. It is a very simple missive, lacking the greetings and phrases of politeness which commonly occupied a large part of any formal letter of later times. But it is carefully dated to 'Regnal year 11, first month of summer, day 23'. Dates were later not generally included in letters, although they were used to introduce other private documents for which an element of precision might be required for legal reasons.

Many of the practices of the ancient Egyptians would have remained unknown, or only partially known, but for chance finds. In the history of letter-writing between private persons, a discovery made in 1922 by an expedition of the Metropolitan Museum of Art, New York, revealed the extent to which a person of fairly ordinary status was prepared, and able, to commit his thoughts as well as his instructions to a letter, as early as 2000 BC. The find consisted of a number of letters and accounts, all written on papyri, the business papers of the family of a farmer called Hekanakhte; they had probably been thrown away by a member of this family, probably a son of Hekanakhte. In addition to being a farmer, Hekanakhte performed a mortuary function; he was the *ka*-servant of the vizir Ipi who had served King Mentuhotpe II of the Eleventh Dynasty (*c.* 2061–2010 BC). As a *ka*-servant his duties were to ensure that the necessary daily offerings needed by Ipi for his posthumous survival were provided, in return for which Hekanakhte had probably received a small grant of land. From time to time, Hekanakhte was obliged to travel away from the Theban region and he sent a deputy to perform his duties at the tomb, which lay in the cliffs at Deir el-Bahri in the Theban necropolis. It was undoubtedly the deputy—probably his eldest son—who had discarded the letters and accounts presumably because they were finished with. He had, like someone today undertaking some duty which takes him from home, brought his unfinished business papers with him to work on in whatever time might be available to him after he had completed his official duties. The letters written by Hekanakhte to this deputy, as appears to have been the case, are wholly devoted to personal matters—the management of his farms and the behaviour of his family and retainers.[17] Although they are in their entirety fascinating documents, only a few short quotations from them can be included here, because they belong to a period much earlier than that which is the principal concern of this book. But as very early examples of private letters, they do reveal in a quite remarkable way how quickly the Egyptian correspondent learnt how to exploit the epistolary medium. There is practical instruction about the detailed distribution of rations.[18] There is concern, even indulgence, for the young members of the family:

> Now any possession of Anpu's which you have, give it back to him; whatever is lost, make it up to him. Don't make me write about it another time. See! I have written to you twice about it. And if Snofru wants to be in charge of those bulls, you should put him in charge of them. Now he did not want to be with you cultivating, going up and down; nor did he want to come hither with me. Whatever else he wants, you should let him enjoy what he wants.[19]

And there is scandal. In one letter Hekanakhte writes:

> Now have the housemaid Senen turned out of my house—take great care!—on the very day when Sihathor reaches you. See! If she spends a single night (more) in my house, watch out! (?); it is you who let her do evil to my concubine.[20]

But the trouble seems to be greater than he thought. In the next letter he is even more angry:

> (I swear) he who shall commit any act upon the person of my concubine, he is against me and I am against him. See! This is my concubine, and it is known what should be done for a man's concubine . . . Indeed, would anyone of you be patient if his wife had been denounced to him? Then shall I be patient? How can I be

in the same establishment with you? No! You will not respect my concubine for my sake.[21]

The two long letters written to the family, from which the extracts given above come, were written with great informality by the same scribe, almost certainly not Hekanakhte himself, who makes no claim to literacy. A third letter, of a more formal character, was written by another scribe, who revealed in his writing the partiality for flamboyance which characterized the scripts of many professional scribes throughout Egyptian history. It was addressed to Hrunufe, described as 'Overseer of the Delta', a person who, from his title, should have been of considerable official standing in the bureaucracy. What is odd about this letter in the context of the rest of the discarded documents is that it was never sent. It was found folded and sealed with string and a mud sealing impressed with a device which was probably made by Hekanakhte's personal seal.[22] Its alien presence among the domestic papyri thrown away by Hekanakhte's deputy suggests failure on the part of that deputy (it might be thought) to send it on to its proper recipient. Plenty of reasons could be adduced to explain this failure, apart from simple forgetfulness, but for us the interest in having the letter preserved precisely in the form in which it was prepared for dispatch far outweighs any vexation which the lack of its receipt in antiquity might have occasioned.

From the physical evidence provided by these early private letters of Hekanakhte, and by others of the same and later dates, it is clear that most letters of this kind were palimpsests, written on papyri already used once and washed clean. Where did this papyrus come from? There is again no ready answer. Rarely can more than a few consecutive signs of an old, washed-out text be distinguished. One Twentieth-dynasty letter in the Cairo Museum bears sufficient traces of its first text to show that this first text also was a letter. It has, chiefly it would seem on the basis of this example, been suggested that palimpsest letters were often written on old, washed-out letters.[23] This conclusion, however, is not very likely, because old letters which had passed through the post, as it might be said, provided poor material for re-use, the letter having been rolled and folded flat into a tight, small packet. The folds would not have made the sheet easy to wash clean and to write upon again. The Cairo letter does not provide a real exception; the traces of the earlier text show that it was written by the same correspondent as the second letter. It must, therefore, have been either an unsent letter, never rolled and folded, or a copy of a letter previously sent. Generally speaking, it would have been unlikely that a scribe (the writer of the Cairo letter was such) would have old, dispatched letters of his own to hand which he could wash out for re-use. Nevertheless, writing material was available to the scribe who might write letters for others and, except when new papyrus was used, it must have been in the form of documents which for one reason or another had lost their importance. We have already seen that both official and private documents were preserved in state or temple archives; they might be records of criminal proceedings, census lists, land records, and legal instruments which might be needed for consultation or invoked in disputes occurring many years subsequent to their compilation and deposit in the archives.

Although the Egyptians through the stable character of their civilization possessed a strong sense of continuity, an aspect of which was the preparation and preservation of records, they yet were not conservationists beyond the practical requirements of life. A title to a plot of land was worth preserving, but other documents of temporary interest could be disposed of after a suitable time. Lists of people, commodities, rents, tribute, and so on, ceased to have significance after a relatively short period of time. Such documents might be kept for historical reasons, but there is little evidence to suggest that the Egyptians were much inspired by a sense of history as were the Greeks. It may reasonably be supposed that archives were weeded out from time to time, and the documents thought to be no longer needed passed for recycling to scriptoria. Such superfluous documents might even have been wiped clean before being put back to service. Here possibly lay the source of supply for the scribe who had a private letter-writing practice. Sadly the evidence which would confirm the ways and means of papyrus-supply, outside the official and religious circles, is lacking. No doubt there were more ways than one by which a scribe might secure the material for his trade; it is not at all unlikely that stocks of official papyrus were diminished by civil servants and diverted to private uses with, or without, some reciprocal payment by the receiver. But the existence of so many palimpsest pages, especially among surviving letters, suggests that new papyrus was not commonly used for private correspondence.[24]

When someone writes a letter today, he takes a sheet of writing paper, writes on one side, turns the sheet horizontally, and continues writing on the back; on both sides the top lines of writing coincide. If there is more to write, a second sheet is taken, and the letter continued on that, and on as many further sheets as may be necessary. Such was not the case in ancient Egypt. Suppose a letter is to be written to a colleague or an official, in which some degree of formality is required, the scribe who will write out the letter is approached, and engaged, presumably according to some general tariff of charges. As there is no standard size for a sheet of letter papyrus, the scribe will want to know roughly how long the letter is to be. He may even ask his client to recite the gist of what is to be said. This central core, the message, of the letter will be incorporated into the formal framework of the standard letter. Commonly, a letter begins with a statement naming the sender and the recipient, followed by a series of salutations invoking particular deities; then comes the message, and the letter concludes with greetings to others and a final salutation.[25] The scribe will put the letter into order, and provide the proper wording for the standard elements, varying them only in so far as the sender (his client) may wish to invoke specific deities in addition to, or instead of, those regularly named at a particular place. If the message is to be short, then the scribe might be able to re-use a sheet which he may judge to be of sufficient size. Otherwise he will take his current roll of papyrus, new or (more probably) washed clean, which could be of standard full width, half width, or even a quarter width. In the Eighteenth Dynasty, the full roll width was approximately 36 cm., the half and quarter widths being 18 and 9 cm. For the later New Kingdom, the corresponding measurements are 42, 21 and 10 or 11 cm.[26] Full-width rolls were mostly used for important official documents, and for copies of *The Book of the Dead*, so the commonest available roll would almost certainly be the half roll of 18–20 cm.

From his preliminary discussions with his client the scribe will have a fair idea of how much papyrus he will need to transcribe the letter, using both sides of the papyrus, leaving on the back enough room for the writing of the address after the letter has been rolled, folded and sealed. Until the time of the Middle Kingdom scribes wrote in vertical columns down the papyrus from top to bottom, the columns proceeding from right to left. The papyrus, therefore, lay on the scribe's kilt, which was stretched tight to serve as a rest, with the open end to the right, and the unrolled portion to the left. In writing a letter the scribe could proceed in transcribing the agreed text until he judged that he had written more than half. He could then cut the papyrus at that point, and turn over the piece on which he had already written to finish the letter on the back. Sometimes, in turning the papyrus, he also reversed the sheet, so that the text on the back was upside down in relation to that on the front.[27] During the Twelfth Dynasty scribes abandoned writing in vertical columns and thereafter for most texts, other than certain religious compilations like *The Book of the Dead*, they wrote in horizontal lines from right to left. The change was probably made for practical reasons, which may have included the requirements of calligraphy, the wish to follow the use of horizontal lines in the principal parts of hieroglyphic inscriptions, and even the need to avoid smudging what was already written. The scribe still held his papyrus as before, resting it on his stretched skirt, unless the requirements of the text to be written demanded a page-size greater than the space offered by a stretched kilt. On the flat open part of the roll he wrote his first page, in horizontal lines, each line being of approximately the same length. Among papyri of the New Kingdom, page widths vary considerably: in BM Papyrus 10247 (Anastasi I), a literary text, the pages vary from 23 to 30 cm. in width; in BM 10244 (Anastasi V), a miscellany, they are about 24 cm.; in BM 10682, another literary text, about 22 cm.; in the Great Harris Papyrus (BM 9999), an official text of great calligraphic splendour, the pages range between 46 and 64 cm.

In the New Kingdom, when a scribe started to write out a letter, he seems in many cases to have adopted a procedure different from his common practice. As he might not be able to judge the length of papyrus needed, and as no letter was written in pages, it was simpler for him to turn the papyrus through ninety degrees, placing it with the beginning of the roll away from himself, and the unrolled part next to his body. Our putative scribe, therefore, having completed his preliminary discussion of the letter needed by his client, takes his roll and, with it open on his skirt, as just described, writes in horizontal lines down the length of the papyrus, the writing being at right angles to the longitudinal axis of the papyrus. Then, when he judges that he has written more than half of the text, he cuts off the used part and turns it over, usually in the direction away from himself; in this way the continuation of the text on the back is upside down in relation to the writing on the front. When the letter is finished, it is folded, or more probably rolled up, flattened and folded in two, yielding a small package about 2 cm. wide, on one side of which the name of the sender is written, and on the other, the name of the recipient. Tied and sealed, the letter is now ready for dispatch. How is it to be delivered? In many cases it is stated specifically that a letter is brought 'by the hand of so-and-so'; it is thought that private correspondence was generally conveyed and delivered by casual travellers, friends or servants who might be going in the right direction.[28]

The delivery of official correspondence, on the other hand, was better organized. From the existence of significant titles it seems that the centres of administration throughout Egypt were linked to the capital cities, Thebes and Memphis, and, from the Nineteenth Dynasty, the Delta royal Residence of Piramesse, by a system of couriers. They also serviced the outposts of Egyptian power in Nubia and Asia, as circumstances required. There is no evidence to show how the system worked, or even to indicate whether it was organized on a regular basis. Officers called 'dispatch-carriers' performed the duties, and there is some evidence to show that registers were compiled, recording the delivery of dispatches. One of the *Miscellanies* contains extracts from a Nineteenth-dynasty register recording items sent to Palestine and Syria:[29]

> Regnal Year 3, first month of summer, day 15. Going up [i.e. journey] by the attendant Baalry, son of Djaper of Gaza. What he carried [lit. what was in his hand] to Syria: 2 dispatches; namely:
> The garrison-commander Khay—one dispatch
> The prince of Tyre, Baaltermeg—one dispatch

Later in the same piece:

> Regnal Year 3, first month of summer, day 22. Arrival by the attendant Djehuty, son of Tjerkerma of Gaza, by Metjedet, son of Shemabaal of the same place, and by Setmose, son of Aperdeger of the same place. What he carried to the place where the King is (from) the garrison-commander Khay: presents and one dispatch.

If one were fortunate enough to have access to the services of an official dispatch-carrier, and his route suited one's needs, then he could be used as a postman for one's private letters. The military officer Penamun writes to a colleague of similar rank, Paheripedjet, thanking him for his letter and congratulating him on his promotion to a position previously held by his father. 'Your letter has reached me and I am wholly delighted . . . And write [lit. send] to me about your own condition and your father's, by the way of the dispatch-carriers who come here from you.'[30] It is not likely, however, that the privilege of using the dispatch-carrier's pouch—the ancient Egyptian diplomatic bag—was available to many people; and indeed the internal system of routes would not necessarily have suited the requirements of private persons except in a limited way. Private letters were probably only written when the certainty of delivery was sure, or thought to be sure. If it were known that someone happened to be travelling to a place where a friend or relation lived, the opportunity for sending a letter might be seized. A letter written on such an occasion might be little more than a greeting, a gesture of contact, a remembrance of past association, or a sign of continuing affection. A good example of such a newsless letter runs as follows:[31]

> Hori greets his lord, Ahmose, in life, prosperity and health, in the favour of Amon-Re, King of the Gods, of Ptah, South-of-his-wall, of Thoth, Lord of the god's word, and of all the gods and goddesses who are in Karnak(?); may they give you favour, love and cleverness wherever you are (or in whatever you do). Further, how are you? How are you? Are you in good shape? See! I am in good shape.

The reverse side of the scrap of papyrus which carries this letter bears the simple address: 'Hori to the scribe Ahmose of Peniaty, his lord'. This Ahmose is comparatively well known for a modestly placed official. He was at some stage in his career the deputy of the overseer of works, Peniaty, and for this reason was sometimes called Ahmose of Peniaty. This Peniaty was an official of much greater consequence, who was engaged on royal business under five kings of the first half of the Eighteenth Dynasty (Amenophis I to Tuthmosis III), and may have been partly responsible for the construction of Hatshepsut's funerary temple at Deir el-Bahri.[32] Ahmose himself cannot be so precisely tied to particular monuments, although claims have been made that a shrine at Gebel es-Silsila in Upper Egypt, well south of Thebes, was made for him, and that two personal objects in the British Museum (a *shabti* or 'deputy'-figure, and an eye-paint vessel) were his.[33] Unfortunately the name Ahmose was exceptionally common during the Eighteenth Dynasty, and to identify as the same person two or three Ahmoses named on different objects on the basis of a title of common occurrence does not constitute a convincing proof of identity. To establish identity between persons of the same name exceptional concidences of titles, or additional family relationships, are required. In the case of our Ahmose, the clinching detail is that he was Peniaty's man; for nowhere, as far as his known records are concerned, are his parents or wife named. Not often were Egyptians particularized by the naming of their superiors or masters; it is most unlikely, therefore, that any other Ahmose would have named himself 'of Peniaty'. This Ahmose, then, is known especially from six private letters, four in the British Museum and two in the Louvre in Paris, all of which were probably found at the same time, and divided into the two groups subsequently.[34] He is in addition known from a scribe's palette, also in the Louvre, which carries invocations of Amon-Re and Thoth on Ahmose's behalf. It is from the inscriptions on this palette that Ahmose's appellative is fully made clear; in the invocation of Amon-Re he is named 'the scribe, Ahmose, deputy of the overseer of works of Southern On [Armant, just south of Thebes], Peniaty'.

Of the six letters, four are addressed to Ahmose by different correspondents, and two are drafts or copies of letters written by Ahmose himself. They form together a miniature archive, the collected correspondence of a small, although perhaps not an insignificant, official of the mid-Eighteenth Dynasty. As none of the documents is dated, there is no way of judging whether the letters cover a short or a long period. The evidence provided by family archives of later periods shows without any doubt that important documents of family interest were kept together in jars, and they sometimes covered many years.[35] Ahmose's letters, while dealing in most cases with business matters, do not constitute legal documents in the ordinary Egyptian sense, although they might have been produced as evidence in the case of a dispute. Consequently it should not perhaps be suggested that they represent much more than a group of letters of approximately the same date, kept together for temporary reference, and preserved for posterity by some exceptional chance. As the circumstances of their discovery are unfortunately not known, little more can be hazarded in explanation; it would also be a mistake to believe that the six letters were all that were found in the early nineteenth century. It is known that papyri were sometimes burnt by their modern discoverers, unaware of their interest, and (more important) of their monetary value, because they liked their smell in conflagration. And documents in fragments were also thought nothing of, although the techniques of reconstruction were very early developed in those museums where papyri were collected and their contents appreciated. So Ahmose's letters can be considered only as a minor archive of six pieces, and not as possibly the remnant of some larger collection.

And yet these six letters provide a good conspectus of the formalities and informalities found within the Egyptian letter-writing tradition, and a range of topics thought worthy of initiating a correspondence. We have already read the brief letter of polite greeting sent by Hori to Ahmose, a missive of no content, but full of greetings and good wishes, formally presented. The first five lines of a letter written by Ahmose to the chief steward of the king, Wadjetrenput, preserves nothing beyond formal greetings. It is of interest principally for two reasons. Firstly, because it seems to be a draft or copy kept by Ahmose for reference, and used on the back for an account; secondly, because Wadjetrenput is known from other small records of mid-Eighteenth-dynasty date, including an ink text on a pottery ostracon in which he is mentioned along with the great major-domo of Hatshepsut, Senenmut. They are named as being part of a reception committee on the river-bank at Thebes,[36] possibly awaiting the arrival of the sacred barque of Amon-Re, bringing the image of the god on a visit to the necropolis region from Karnak. Ahmose did not belong to this illustrious company of the highest officials, but he appears to have been on its periphery—a useful fellow, reliable and competent, ready and willing to transact business for his superiors, and worthy of their trust.

Of all the letters, the best preserved shows Ahmose being used in the capacity of a local agent by a person called Mentuhotpe, an official bearing a title commonly translated 'mayor' in New Kingdom texts.[37] It is a reasonably formal letter:

> The mayor Mentuhotpe greets the scribe Ahmose, he of Penit,[38] in life, prosperity and health, and in the favour of Amon-Re, King of the Gods, of Atum, Lord of Heliopolis, Re-Horakhty, Thoth, Lord of god's words, Seshat(?), Lady of writing, and your noble god who loves you; may they give you favour, love and cleverness wherever you are [or in whatever you do]. Further: you should have installed the matting and beams of the store-rooms together with the back part of the house, the wall being six cubits in height. And allow for the doors of the store-rooms to be five cubits in height, and allow for the doors of the sitting room to be six cubits in height. And you should instruct the builder, Amenmose, so that

he does it just so, and hastens the building of the house. See to it! What a good thing my brother is with you. It is on you that I place my trust.
Further: I shall send you the height of the house, and its width also. Further: get a protection made out of some of the matting, and have it given to Benia. Further: cause the value [i.e. price] of the house-plot be given to its owner, and let him be pleased. See to it! Take care that when I arrive he doesn't have words with me.

As ever with an isolated letter, there are many matters raised in this document which puzzle us, and which will probably never be resolved without further discoveries of correspondence to or from Ahmose. The loss, however, is not particularly sad, because the subject of the letter is but a trivial piece of business to be transacted on Mentuhotpe's behalf by Ahmose. It shows Ahmose as a trusted agent, but one for whom instructions have to be set out in detail, the various elements interspersed with exhortations and veiled threats. It is no rare thing to find letters from superiors to inferiors interlarded with similarly forceful calls to action. The medium of contact, the letter, probably seemed so unlikely to carry the force of instruction required by the writer, that a hectoring manner was frequently adopted. We must, nevertheless, not conclude that the peremptory tone, characteristic of so many private letters, was held to be anything other than normal by the Egyptian who received a communication from a superior.

A rather different attitude is found in another letter sent to Ahmose by his brother Teti.[39] Politeness and respect establish the flavour here; but there is also affection: 'See! My wish very especially is to see you. Further, I am cultivating a lot of barley for you . . . And I shall not let you be in need(?) of anything in respect of whatever I do, while I live.' Some remarks about a house being built by Ahmose—not that mentioned in Mentuhotpe's letter quoted above—follow these considerate declarations, and the end of the letter is lost. Although written between brothers, this letter includes formal greetings of the kind we have already met. The remaining two letters of the archive, however, are much more concerned with business, and greetings in one are cut to a minimum, and wholly omitted from the other. Troubles over servant-girls prompt both letters. From the contexts it is reasonably clear that the girls were closely tied in service to their masters, and considered virtually as chattels; they were in effect slaves, although in a very different category from those whose servitude arose from military actions abroad.[40] The first letter was sent to Ahmose for information:[41]

> Ptahu greets the scribe Ahmose in life and prosperity, and in the favour of Amon-Re. A note to let you know about the business of the servant-girl who is in the care of the mayor Tetimose. The chief of slaves Abui was sent to him to say: 'Come, you should settle the matter with him.' He (that is) Mini does not answer what the overseer of field-workers Ramose said. See! As for the servant-girl of the mayor Mini, the sailor, he does not listen to me over settling the matter with me in the court of magistrates.

Without proper knowledge of the background, it is very difficult to understand what is the true problem in this case. Ahmose does not himself appear to be involved in any way, and Ptahu writes to him apparently just to let off steam in an excess of exasperation. Of greater personal interest is the case of another servant-girl which prompts Ahmose to write in great vexation to Ty, who seems to have been his social and official superior. There are no epistolary niceties here; and it could be thought that the letter was actually penned by Ahmose himself:[42]

> What Ahmose of Peniaty says to his lord, the treasurer, Ty: What is the reason for the carrying off of the servant-girl who was with me, now given to another? Am I not your servant, obeying your orders by night as well as by day? Let her value, as far as I am concerned, be taken, for she is indeed young and does not (yet) know work. Let my lord order to have her work carried out like that of any servant-girl of my lord's; for her mother sent a message to me, saying: 'You have let my child be taken away while she was there with you. But I did not protest to my lord as she was with you as a child.' So she said to me in protest.

As ever the lack of context makes much of this last letter obscure, and the obscurity is not helped by the apparent loss of the end of the letter. Nevertheless, it again provides a good illustration of the kind of topic which might drive an Egyptian to put pen to paper—or brush to papyrus, to be more precise. It is not surprising to find that the day-to-day problems which bothered the ancient Egyptian, were little different from those which disturb us today, but it is not a little unexpected to see the medium of the letter being used so readily to ventilate these problems. Practical business was one important stimulation of correspondence, but matters of private concern might equally inspire a letter. In this last letter Ahmose seems mostly to be bothered by the fate of the young girl over whom he had apparently exercised some kind of wardship. She seems hardly to have been a slave in the modern sense, but a girl willingly handed over into his care, perhaps to be trained in his household for domestic service. Her status can only have been lowly, yet he represents himself as vulnerable to the complaints of the girl's mother. If the reference to value implies some kind of indenture fee, paid perhaps to Ahmose in expectation of a course of training, or conversely a sum paid by Ahmose to the girl's mother for allowing her to enter service, then there is an element of business in the letter. But Ahmose refers only incidentally to this 'value'—which may even not be a 'monetary' value[43]—and seems inspired by concern for the girl. This interpretation, if it is correct, reveals an admirable sentiment which, furthermore, is here expressed in a private document between two people; it is not a public statement in which grand expressions of morality might be expected. In letters like these we can come closest to the ancient Egyptian; far more so than in the arcane expressions of religious belief, the pompous declarations of royalty in monumental inscriptions, or the studied compositions which make up the corpus of Egyptian literature.

The writing of letters was undoubtedly a prime occupation for many scribes, especially those who failed to find employment in the ranks of the various bureaucracies that managed the civil and religious affairs of ancient Egypt. What they wrote for their clients, although commonly contained within a standardized framework of greetings and invocations, was usually expressed in a vernacular speech much less contrived than the language of literature or religion.[44] The message or core of a letter was written for the recipient to understand; it was full of ellipses, allusive and consequently, for us, elusive. But such messages reflect, often with startling vividness, the realities of ancient Egyptian life. The sad thought is that so few private letters have survived; from the Eighteenth Dynasty rather less than a dozen written on papyrus,[45] of which the Ahmose correspondence forms more than a half. But in them true passion burns, and unrehearsed thoughts are expressed. In a sense a letter sent by one person to another in a private context, properly comprehended only by these two, represents a great achievement socially and culturally. It also marks a triumph of literacy for which the scribe by his training and ability is largely responsible. Let us end this tribute to his skills with another of these rare Eighteenth-dynasty letters. It is written by a mayor of Thebes, Sennefer, to a farmer who has not fulfilled his quota of produce. The tone is distinctly *de haut en bas*, and it is surprising that a mayor of Thebes felt able to write to a man of fairly humble station. It brings us close to two named individuals, but it also brings home to us how inadequate is our knowledge of so much in ancient Egyptian life. Yet, how precious are Sennefer's final remarks to this farmer for whom he had scant regard:[46]

> The mayor of the Southern City [i.e. Thebes] says to the farmer Baki, son of Kysen:[47] This letter is sent to you to inform you that I shall reach you after mooring at Hut-sekhem[48] in three days. Don't let me catch you out in your position. Don't let it be lacking in very good order. And gather for me many plants, lotus blooms, flowers and . . . (?), ready to be used as offerings. And cut 5,000 pieces of wood *seb* and 200 pieces of wood *merhenen*. Then the boat which will bring me will take them away. For you have cut no wood this year. Look out! You should not be lazy. If you are not allowed to cut you should take the matter to Woser, mayor of Hut-(sekhem). See! The herdsman of Gasy,[49] and the herdsmen of the cattle, who come under my authority, fetch them to yourself to cut wood together with the workmen already with you. And instruct the herdsmen to get milk ready anew in jars in advance of my coming. Look out! You should not be lazy; for I am well aware that you are lackadaisical, and like eating in bed.

NOTES

1 Well illustrated in K. Lange and M. Hirmer, *Egypt*, 4 ed. (London, 1968), pls. 18, 19.

2 Good examples for the early Twelfth Dynasty in N. de G. Davies, *The Tomb of Antefoker* (London, 1920), pl. XIII.

3 All illustrated in H. Carter, The Tomb of *Tut·Ankh·Amen*, III (London, 1933), pl. XXII.

4 The excavation is published in The Earl of Carnarvon and H. Carter, *Five Years' Exploration at Thebes* (London, 1912). The basket and its contents are described on p. 75 f. and illustrated on pl. LXVI. See also Pl. 8.

5 J. Černý, *Paper and Books in Ancient Egypt* (London, 1952), 4. This account remains one of the most authoritative expositions of the use and exploitation of papyrus.

6 Janssen, *Commodity Prices from the Ramessid Period*, 447 f., demonstrates that the few records of papyrus prices in the New Kingdom show that it was not exorbitantly expensive.

7 Carried out by Dr Corrado Basile in the Tecnico Istituto del Papiro in Syracuse.

8 For a discussion and illustrations, see J. Vandier, *Manuel d'archéologie égyptienne*, V (Paris, 1969), 447 ff.

9 British Museum Papyri 10477 (Nu) and 10470 (Ani).

10 British Museum Papyrus 9940; see *Journal of Egyptian Archaeology* 51 (London, 1965), 51.

11 British Museum no. 10184. The papyrus takes its name from François Sallier of Aix-en-Provence to whose collection it belonged. It was purchased after his death by the British Museum in 1839.

12 Traditionally the terms recto and verso are used for the front and back of a papyrus when it is used in the regular manner. The recto surface shows the upper layer of papyrus fibres lying in the horizontal direction; on the verso the fibres are vertical. This distinction has now been challenged, particularly by papyrologists who study the texts of the Graeco-Roman Period. The objections to the traditional terminology are set out by E. G. Turner, *The terms recto and verso. The anatomy of the papyrus roll* (Brussels, 1978). The terms 'front' and 'back' are there preferred. Egyptologists in general adhere to the use of recto and verso.

13 See G. A. Reisner in *Kush* 3 (Khartoum, 1955), 26 ff.

14 Described by W. C. Hayes in *Journal of Near Eastern Studies* 10 (Chicago, 1951), 165 ff.

15 British Museum Papyrus 10752, found at Thebes; translated and discussed by P. C. Smither in *Journal of Egyptian Archaeology* 31 (1945), 3 ff.

16 B. Gunn in *Annales du Service des Antiquités de l'Égypte* 25 (Cairo, 1925), 242 ff.; also A. H. Gardiner in *Journal of Egyptian Archaeology* 13 (London, 1927), 75 ff.

17 Published in T. G. H. James, *The Hekanakhte Papers*.

18 Letter II, ll.7–23.

19 Letter II, ll.34–36.

20 Letter I, verso ll.13–14. In this context the word translated 'concubine' means perhaps a woman taken by a man after his wife had died, who does not quite have marital status, possibly for reasons of inheritance.

21 Letter II, ll.41–44.

22 Illustrated in James, op. cit.; pl. 9. See also Pl. 9 (*bottom left*).

23 J. Černý, *Late Ramesside Letters* (Brussels, 1939), xx.

24 Of the 52 letters published by Černý in *Late Ramesside Letters*, 11 are identified as not palimpsest; of the remainder, 21 are palimpsest, 2 probable, and 18 unidentified as palimpsest or not palimpsest.

25 In earlier times the formality was greater than in the New Kingdom, see T. G. H. James, *The Hekanakhte Papers*, 119; A. M. Bakir, *Egyptian Epistolography* (Cairo, 1970), 31 f.

26 There are, however, many variations, see J. Černý, *Paper and Books in Ancient Egypt*, 14 ff.

27 The Hekanakhte letters, written on what seem to have been full-height papyri of the time (26–28 cm.), show no consistency in the relationship of the recto and verso texts.

28 See A. M. Bakir, *Egyptian Epistolography*, 29 ff.

29 A. H. Gardiner, *Late-Egyptian Miscellanies*, 31, ll.7 ff. The reign is that of King Merneptah.

30 Gardiner, op. cit.; 62, ll.9–13.

31 British Museum Papyrus 10103; see S. R. K. Glanville in *Journal of Egyptian Archaeology* 14 (London, 1928), 303. In this letter, note the use of 'lord' as the respectful way of addressing the recipient of a letter. In the epithet of the god Thoth, 'god's words' means 'writing'.

32 The name Peniaty occurs in an ink graffito on a limestone fragment found in the neighbourhood of Deir el-Bahri (now British Museum no. 52883, see H. R. H. Hall, *Hieroglyphic Texts . . . in the British Museum*, V (London, 1914), pl. 27).

33 Glanville in *Journal of Egyptian Archaeology* 14, 296 f.

34 The British Museum papyri are published by S. R. K. Glanville in *Journal of Egyptian Archaeology* 14, 294 ff; those in the Louvre by T. E. Peet in *Journal of Egyptian Archaeology* 12 (London, 1926), 70 ff.

35 Two Theban archives were found in pots, see G. Botti, *L'archivio demotico da Deir el-Medineh* (Florence, 1967), 1; and Mustafa el-Amir, *A Family Archive from Thebes* (Cairo, 1959), Part II, 21. The second of these archives, containing 32 documents, spans one hundred years, from 317 BC to 217 BC.

36 Published by W. C. Hayes in *Journal of Egyptian Archaeology* 46 (London, 1960), 36.

37 British Museum Papyrus 10102.

38 I.e. 'of Peniaty'. Mentuhotpe or his scribe made a poor attempt at spelling this name.

39 Louvre Papyrus 3230a.

40 On slavery in general, see A. M. Bakir, *Slavery in Pharaonic Egypt* (Cairo, 1952).

41 British Museum Papyrus 10107.

42 Louvre Papyrus 3230b.

43 There was no money as such in ancient Egypt; all transactions were carried out in terms of commodities. See Chapter Nine below.

44 Monumental texts were nearly always couched in a stylized Egyptian based on the classical Egyptian of the Middle Kingdom.

45 Almost a complete list is in A. M. Bakir, *Egyptian Epistolography*, 9.

46 Papyrus Berlin 10463; see R. A. Caminos in *Journal of Egyptian Archaeology* 49 (London, 1963), 29 ff.

47 Or, possibly, 'Kysen's man'.

48 Modern Hu, a place about 70 miles downstream from Thebes.

49 Modern Qus, about 20 miles downstream from Thebes.

7

CRAFTSMEN IN METAL AND WOOD

It sometimes happens, when a tourist boat lies up in front of the great temple of Amenophis III at Luxor, that the tinkers come down to the river bank to overhaul the great cooking vessels from the boat's galleys. Some of the copper pots may need retinning; others will have holes to be repaired, or bulges to be beaten out. A makeshift workshop is set up under a ragged awning; a charcoal fire contained by a primitive hearth of small stones is lit, and work soon gets under way. To generate sufficient heat the tinkers use a simple bellows made from a goat's skin. A metal nozzle at one end is directed into the fire; the other, open end is fastened to two battens which close the mouth very efficiently when they are held tight together. The assistant or apprentice tinker with regular and dextrous movements opens the mouth to fill the bag with air, then snaps it shut and presses downwards to drive the trapped air through the nozzle into the fire. The equipment is simple, the technique efficient, the results perfectly adequate. But it is hot and dirty work, and the tinkers are not encouraged to come on board.

> I have seen the coppersmith at his work at the mouth of his furnace; his fingers like crocodile's (scales?).[1] He stinks more than fish eggs.

In this dismissive way spoke the ancient scribe whose main aim was to convince his son of the superiority of the scribe's calling.[2] We may suppose that he looked no further for his example of the disgusting coppersmith than the small workshop in the back alleys of the Theban capital, or even the booth of an itinerant smith like the riverside tinker of the present day in Luxor. If he had looked a little further and inspected the workshops attached to the Temple of Amun he might have found something rather more estimable. His judgement, partial and prejudiced, was based on the worst available example, just as the modern tourist, in no matter what country he is travelling, will paint his retrospective picture of life abroad on the basis of his own partial and prejudiced memories of unrepresentative experiences.

The simple skills of the riverside tinker are quite adequate for the tasks he is required to perform. He cannot, however, be expected to do much in the way of creative metalwork. For that the modern tourist will have to look elsewhere, perhaps in the workshops which turn out the objects of 'native craftsmanship' sold in the better bazaars of Cairo and the large provincial towns. In antiquity the scornful scribe could have accompanied the vizir Rekhmire on his visit of inspection to the work-shops of the craftsmen of Amun, one of the vizir's fields of responsi-bility. On the eastern half of the south wall of the passage in Rekhmire's tomb the upper registers of scenes show various craftsmen at work.[3] Standing to the right of these scenes, Rekhmire is described as 'Seeing all the crafts[4] [practised in the workshops of the Temple of Amun]; letting every man know his responsibilities in the execution of every occupation; by the vizir . . . Rekhmire'. The crafts depicted are metalworking, carpentry, leather-working, stone-vase making, and the jeweller's trade. Most of the objects on which the craftsmen are shown working were undoubtedly intended for royal or temple purposes, and we may suppose that these workshops were among the best in the land. But the craftsmen are credited in the scenes with no special status, and there is little reason to believe that they were considered to be much more than workmen especially good at their respective crafts. The very best would be employed in the best workshops; they would derive some benefit of protection from the excessive zeal of government officials and from the needs of the *corvée*, perhaps; their accommodation might have been privileged, like that enjoyed by the workmen in the Place of Truth. They were not, however, artist-craftsmen in the modern sense, or even to the extent found in the Graeco-Roman world. In the exercise of their skills they were anonymous. The continuation of any modest good fortune they enjoyed depended on the successful practising of whatever special skills they possessed.

Strict supervision and the absence of security in employment surely acted as strong incentives to hard work, but they would have done little to turn a good workman into a first-class craftsman. Skill combined with a true feeling for the craft concerned, and a sympathy with the materials employed in the craft, were all necessary for the making of well-designed, finely decorated, and superbly finished objects of the kinds which have survived in surprising quantities from antiquity. Very specially has the Eighteenth Dynasty left a remarkable legacy of what are now, unfortunately, called 'the minor arts', a term from which we cannot wholly shrug off the derogatory tone. The particular concentration of tombs of important people at Thebes, in conditions of environment peculiarly favourable for the good survival of perishable materials like wood, cloth and metals destroyed by corrosion, and mostly belonging to a period when Egypt's status and wealth were at their highest, created a remarkable kind of reservoir of fine antiquities. The yield of metalwork, jewellery and fine furniture from Thebes, and dating from this period, has fully supported the evidence of achievement in crafts provided by scenes in contemporary tombs. The contents of the tomb of Tutankhamun in themselves form the ultimate testimony of this achievement; but if that tomb had never been discovered the ascendancy of craftsmanship during the Eighteenth Dynasty would still have been amply exemplified by the many choice pieces preserved in collections throughout the world. Let us consider now, through the scenes in Rekhmire's tomb, the metal-workers and the wood-workers (*Figs. 14–21*).

It is generally maintained that the Egyptians were by no means as skilled in working metals as other ancient peoples of the Near East. In matters of pure technology this claim may well be true, but on behalf of the Egyptians it can be amply demonstrated that they were apt in acquiring skills developed elsewhere, and that their craftsmen were without equals in matters of design and decoration. The scenes of metal-working in Rekhmire's tomb deal with precious metals and with bronze.[5] On the right side stands a scribe supervising the handing out of gold and silver, 'supplying the goldsmiths [of the temple of Amun . . .?] to carry out every task of the Residence according to their daily custom, their numbers being millions and hundreds of thousands,[6] in the presence of the mayor of Thebes, the vizir . . . Rekhmire'. The scribe records how much gold and silver is issued, and it may surely be concluded that his record will be eventually used to check the weight of the finished work. All metal was in a sense precious in antiquity because of the difficulties of mining, extraction and smelting; even with bronze, a strict check was kept on the weight of bronze tools issued to the workmen of the royal tombs, to reduce the theft of metal.[7] In the workshops of the goldsmiths of Amun, the gold and silver is issued in the form of rings. A basket in front of the scribe holds four gold rings (coloured yellow) and three silver rings (coloured white), and further rings are weighed carefully on a balance, presided over by an assistant who steadies the plumb-bob with one hand and checks the beam of the balance with the other. Five gold rings in one pan of the balance are weighed against two weights in the other pan, one of which is dome-shaped, the other in the form of an ox-head. Additional weights, including one shaped like a hippopotamus, lie in a basket under the balance. This introductory section of the metal-working sequence of scenes includes representations of finished examples of the craftsmen's work. In a subsidiary register above, gold and silver stands and bowls are shown, two of the latter reproducing the shapes of lotus flowers. A group of three men, possibly supervisors, leads forward a craftsman with long hair, probably a master, who holds a large spouted vessel of silver (*Fig. 14*).

Gold in particular occupied an important position in Egyptian life. Economically it was more important in the exercise of international diplomacy than in the estimation of the prosperity of the country from the domestic point of view. Gold was always more common than silver because it could be obtained with relatively simple technical equipment

Fig. 14 Weighing and issuing precious metals.

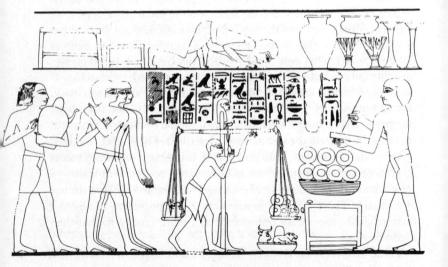

from the mines of the Eastern Desert and from Nubia, and there remain to this day substantial traces of gold working, including mining, the crushing of ore and of washing.[8] The imperishable quality of gold, together with the ease with which it could be worked, made it exceptionally desirable in antiquity, but it was not easy for people outside the ambit of the Court to obtain supplies for personal use except by theft or fraud. We have seen how the tomb-robbers of Thebes acquired gold in the late New Kingdom;[9] a more subtle method was by adulterating the gold by the addition of copper.[10] It may readily be supposed that in all workshops where gold was handled there were opportunities for fraud and theft.

Silver, on the other hand, was up to the time of the Middle Kingdom considerably rarer than gold in Egypt, due to the absence of easily worked deposits in any of the territories open to Egyptian power. Silver also required a better command of technology than gold for its extraction. In consequence, silver remained almost as valuable as gold until the New Kingdom, when supplies could be obtained relatively freely from Asiatic lands dominated by Egyptian arms, or accessible through trade. Its value then dropped dramatically in comparison with gold, achieving a standard ratio of two to one throughout the New Kingdom.[11] Nevertheless, silver was never apparently as plentiful as gold in Egypt, and it was certainly not as appreciated.

Much of the industrial preparation of gold was carried out in the regions of the gold mines, and the metal was imported into Egypt, if we may trust the evidence of the tomb-paintings again, in the form either of rings, or of roughly shaped nuggets. A painting from the tomb of Sobkhotpe at Thebes now in the British Museum shows negro porters bringing gold in both of these forms as tribute to the Egyptian king.[12] Sobkhotpe was an important official, though not of the highest rank, during the reign of Tuthmosis IV (c. 1413–1403 BC). The rings hang like paper-chains from the negroes' arms, similar to those weighed out for the goldsmiths in the scene already described. The nuggets are piled on trays; they represent, in all probability, the ragged, unformed pieces of gold produced when molten gold is slowly poured into water—a convenient way of making small, manageable, nuggets without the use of a mould. These nuggets, in appearance like pop-corn, provided a form of gold more easily transported and more readily melted than ingots or rings.

Trade in silver is far less well documented in Egyptian records than the gold trade. Most of the sources mentioned lie in Asiatic lands,[13] and it is likely that silver was a commodity which played an important part in trade between Egypt and Asia. There is good evidence to suggest that much silver was imported into Egypt in the form of scrap. A treasure dating from the reign of Ammenemes II of the Twelfth Dynasty (*c.* 1929–1897 BC) found in the temple of El-Tod in Upper Egypt, contained ingots of gold and silver, and one hundred and fifty-three silver cups, all but ten of which had been flattened and folded small, presumably to allow them to be packed more tightly. The whole treasure of El-Tod represents perhaps part of a consignment of tribute or of a gift from a foreign potentate to the Egyptian king; the cups, deliberately damaged, were treated as bullion, not as carefully worked pieces to be valued at a higher price than if they were scrap-metal. The design of the cups suggests an Aegean or Syrian origin.[14] An even clearer case of silver 'waste' imported for use in Egypt either by native Egyptian craftsmen or by foreigners settled in Egypt, was excavated at Akhenaten's town, El-Amarna (Akhetaten), in 1930. A small jar was found in the courtyard of a house or estate. The excavators describe what happened: 'With a certain amount of unwillingness to perform what they knew by experience to be a fruitless and troublesome task, the workmen prised off the lid and shook the earth to loosen it. A bar of gold dropped out. Then came twenty-two bars of gold, much silver and a figurine of a Hittite god in silver with a gold cap.'[15] The silver included many pieces of jewellery, armlets, bangles, rings, mostly twisted into small size, and fragments of vessels folded up into tiny parcels of metal. The excavators concluded that this hoard had been buried by a thief perhaps at the time of the abandonment of the city in about 1350 BC. It is more likely, however, that the contents of this jar represented the surviving metal stock from a jeweller's workshop, consisting of gold and silver ingots (roughly cast in channels drawn in the sand with a stick or even a finger), and second-hand jewellery and metal vessels. The jewellery is not Egyptian in style, and the so-called Hittite god, although surely not Hittite, is equally not Egyptian. Again an Asiatic source is suggested, although this source cannot be precisely determined.

So, of the gold and silver rings signed out by the scribe to the goldsmiths of Amun, the former probably came from Nubia, newly mined and processed, perhaps from small water-cast nuggets, and the latter from Asia, cast into rings from scrap silver vessels and jewellery.

The craftsmen at work on the gold and silver occupy two small registers, and their efforts are devoted entirely to the making of vessels. They are not jewellers or workers in gold and silver leaf and foil. Two pairs of craftsmen work at raising vessels from sheet metal by hammering it on anvils; these are made of bent sticks anchored to the ground by supports which seem designed to take differently shaped anvils, to be changed as the work progresses. The hammering is carried out with rounded pounders, probably stones covered with cloth or leather to temper the rough effect which uncovered stones would produce on the metal (*Fig. 15*).

A similar pounder is used by the very first workman on the right of the scene; he pounds his disc of gold on a low block, possibly of wood, on top of which is placed some kind of cushion. The technique of beating out the metal shown here is one found in Egyptian tomb scenes from the time of the Old Kingdom, and it has been compared closely with the modern technique used from at least mediaeval times for the beating of gold into leaf. The Egyptians used gold beaten into thin sheet or foil for the embellishment of important wooden objects, the metal being applied and beaten over any decoration carved on the wood. They also used gold leaf, appreciating at an early date that gilding with leaf was not only more economical than gilding with foil, but also more

Fig. 15 The making of metal vessels and gold beating (right).

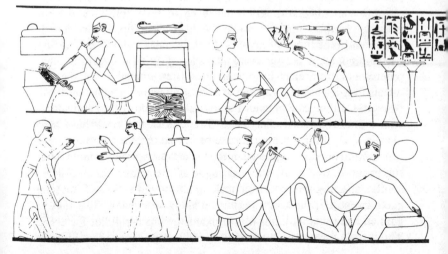

effective from the point of view of pure craftsmanship. Yet foil was generally preferred to leaf for royal objects, presumably because it was conspicuously more opulent. The gold-beater in Rekhmire's tomb can, in the context of the whole series of gold scenes, only be engaged in reducing the disc of gold to a thickness suitable for the vase-makers to employ for the raising of vessels. The skill of the gold craftsmen in raising sheet gold by the techniques shown here is best exemplified by the gold mask of Tutankhamun, the face of which is raised by beating from a single sheet of gold.

Other techniques involved in the production of gold and silver vessels are also shown in the same series of scenes. Behind the gold-beater sits a man chasing a design or an inscription on a tall, graceful vessel with a high-domed stopper. Such vessels, often used for religious libations, were frequently inscribed on the shoulder (as here) with a short dedicatory text naming the honoured god and, possibly, the person for whom the vessel was made. The craftsman uses a pointed tool, probably of bronze, to chase or punch (but not engrave, which involves cutting a fine channel in the metal) the signs into the gold. Two small charcoal furnaces are also available for the goldsmiths. The fires are built in pottery containers, and their heat is intensified by blowpipes made of reed fitted with pottery nozzles. These furnaces are to be used to braze together parts of a vessel when, for example, a handle or a spout is added. One of the furnaces stands ready for use, the fire flaming gently; the two craftsmen working beside it have made three silver offering stands—one is just being given its final polish—and from existing examples it is known that the dish-shaped upper part in each case would probably be brazed on to the slender stand. This brazing was commonly carried out with a filler alloy of the basic metal and some other metal of lower melting point, in this case possibly tin, the two metals forming a solder capable of making a secure union between the two parts. In the case of gold, the solder was made of gold and silver, with copper also added sometimes.[16] In addition a flux would have been needed to de-oxidize the surfaces to be brazed together; it might have been natron or even burnt wine-lees. A short inscription accompanying this group of workmen, but referring to all the goldsmiths and silver-smiths, specifies their work as 'making all sorts of vessels of (for) the god's limbs [i.e. the king's person], making very many ritual jugs in gold and silver in all kinds of workmanship which will last for ever'. The second furnace is in use with a workman placing a piece of work into the coals with bronze tongs, while he intensifies the heat with his blowpipe. The operation of brazing required great skill and dexterity in the use of very simple equipment, for the bronze tongs themselves would melt at a temperature (about 1030°C) lower than that of gold (1063°C), and not much above that of silver (960.5°C). Speed and accuracy were essential in bringing the work to and away from the fire. In the making of very fine work, like jewellery, another form of brazing, known as diffusion bonding, a colloidal hard soldering, was almost certainly used. Its advantage lay in the fact that work so soldered could be brought time and again to the fire without the separation of joins already made. The contemplation of jewellery made up of inlays set in fine gold cloisons, soldered to gold base-plates, and of fine granulation and filigree work, can only increase dramatically our admiration for the technical prowess of Egyptian goldsmiths and jewellers.[17]

Jeweller goldsmiths occupied no doubt the top end of the social scale of metalworkers in ancient Egypt, where the bottom place was filled by the horny-handed tinker of the *Satire of Trades*. In between came the metal-vessel craftsmen whom we have already discussed, and the copper- and bronze-smiths, some of whom are shown at work to the left of the gold- and silversmiths. They are engaged in the casting of bronze doors, a truly monumental operation, requiring large quantities of metal and a considerable body of workmen to service the furnaces. Three men bring up the raw metal, one carrying a large ingot and two with baskets of smaller ingots. The inscription above them reads: 'Bringing the Asiatic copper[18] which His Majesty took in his victory over the land of Retjenu,[19] to cast the two doors of the temple of Amun in Luxor, their surfaces overlaid with gold in the likeness of the horizon of heaven. It is the mayor of Thebes and vizir Rekhmire who [arranged?] this.' The workshop bustles with activity, several stages in the casting of the doors being shown simultaneously. Four furnaces are in operation: one is being stoked with charcoal taken from a pile shown above, and its fire is coaxed to great heat by two men on bellows; another is shown with a pottery crucible just lifted off the fire by means of flexible rods; a crucible is about to be placed on the third; while the fire of the fourth is blown up to heat while its crucible is probably the one being emptied into the pottery door-mould on the right (*Figs. 16, 17*).

The artist has here attempted to convey some idea of the complexity

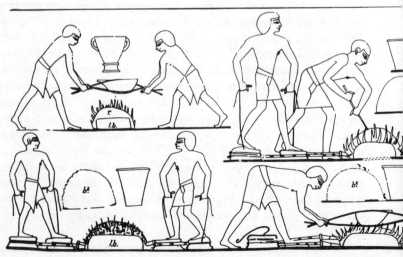

of operations involved in making a bronze door by casting. It has been
suggested that it would not have been possible to cast a bronze door
using the simple techniques available to the Egyptians; perhaps only
the top pivot and bottom angle-piece and pivot are being cast.[20] No
great bronze doors have ever been found. But we cannot avoid interpreting the evidence of the scene in Rekhmire's tomb as showing and
describing the casting of bronze doors. And bronze doors for temples
are mentioned elsewhere. In the Great Harris Papyrus in the British
Museum, in which are listed the pious benefactions of King Ramesses
III of the Twentieth Dynasty (c. 1193–1162 BC), when the king
enumerates his acts of generosity to Ptah and the other gods of
Memphis, he describes the new temple he built for Ptah: 'I made for
you a temple anew in your court, the place of your delight wherever you
appear . . . founded with granite, bedded with limestone, its great
door-posts carrying a lintel of Elephantine stone [Aswan granite], the
doors upon them being of copper in a proportion of six.'[21] It may be said
that what is being referred to here, and indeed what is being shown in

Fig. 16 Bringing the raw material for the casting of gilded bronze doors.

*Fig. 17 Casting gilded bronze doors. Metal is melted in crucibles heated on fires
intensified by foot-operated bellows. The mould is filled and the completed
doors shown (right).*

Rekhmire's tomb, is not a pair of bronze doors, but a pair of wooden doors overlaid with bronze. But even doors of this kind on a large scale have never been found in Egypt, and the texts refer specifically to metal doors.

In the tomb scene, one crucible of metal is shown being drained into a long rectangular mould of pottery (it is coloured red) at the top of which is a series of funnels to receive the molten metal. The successful making of a cast-metal object of large size depended on the swift filling of the mould with the metal; otherwise it would be impossible to achieve an even result. So in advance of the casting the master smith would calculate the amount of molten metal needed and arrange to have enough furnaces and crucibles available to ensure a total filling of the mould without a significant break in the pouring. In consequence, all has been prepared, and the four furnaces shown represent the many more needed. The bellows used for these furnaces are in the same tradition as those seen with the Luxor tinker today, but they are more elaborate, and designed to produce a more efficient result. Every furnace has two men at the bellows, which are worked by hands and feet moving together left and right. Each bellows-man works two bellows made of leather and fitted with an air outlet made of hollow reed ending in a pottery nozzle, like the blowpipes used by the goldsmiths in the adjacent scene. The bellows-man stands on his bellows and raises his feet in turn, pulling up the top of each bellows by means of a cord attached to its surface. Presumably, a vent in the top lets in the air as the bellows is raised, but it is unlikely that there was some kind of valve to prevent the air escaping again as the man trod down, except through the proper outlet into the fire. By marching on the spot the operator pumped the pair of bellows and effectively intensified the heat. The weak point in this simple piece of equipment was the reed pipe which would quickly be ruined by the heat. But replacements involved no difficulty, provided that a good supply had been arranged in advance.

11 (above) Silver scrap and a crude ingot, part of a hoard found in a jar at
    El-Amarna (BM 68503).

   (centre) Small wooden box embellished with ebony veneer and inlays of plain and
    pink-stained ivory and blue glazed composition (BM 5897).

   (below) Tutu's toilet box (BM 24708), containing the cosmetic equipment of the
    wife of the scribe Ani.

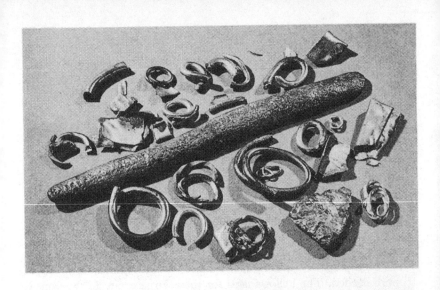

Here three men are seen hurrying up with spares, and with tongs to help them make the running repairs. The logistics of the operation in the ideal conditions depicted in the tomb were evidently successful, for two completed metal doors are shown to the right of the mould above the figure of one of the less skilled men involved, who empties out a basket of charcoal.

The placid, well-organized activity represented in this tomb scene can scarcely reproduce the actuality of feverish pandemonium which surely prevailed when such a great casting of bronze doors was carried out. And we may doubt that the craftsmen had the time or the inclination to sing out the words of praise recorded for them in six short lines of text between the fitters who hurry up with the spare parts, and the upper furnace being actively stoked: 'They say [according to the text] "O King, beautiful of monuments, Menkheperre [Tuthmosis III], given life eternally! He will endure as long as they [the monuments] endure, for ever. He [Amon-Re] gives him [the King] a return for them [the monuments] in life and dominion while he [the King] continues to set up monuments in the house of his father [Amon-Re]."' The implausibility of this paean of praise as uttered in the course of the frenzied activity of the bronze-founders' workshop suitably reminds us that tomb scenes like these in Rekhmire's tomb were not intended to picture precisely the circumstances and conditions obtaining in the actual performance of the various works and activities represented. In showing himself visiting the groups of craftsmen and artists at work for Amun and the king, Rekhmire provides himself with the *mise-en-scène* for one part of his after-life; as in any stage-setting, the illusion alone of reality is created. We may hope to accept the general impression of the detail of what is shown, both because the products of the craftsmen are often physically available for inspection, and because the techniques by which they were produced can be checked against the experience and knowledge of craftsmen of subsequent ages. But the scene presents a pale travesty of the reality of workshops in ancient Egypt, even those in the domain of Amon-Re, King of the Gods. The heat, dust, noise,

12 (above) Successive levels of human habitation revealed by modern excavation at Elephantine.

(below) Looking westwards along the temple axis at El-Tod. The buildings of the modern town lie at a much higher level.

smell, are all lacking; the linear presentation of activities, in the lay-out of horizontal registers on the tomb walls, gives space and movement where there can only have been constriction, with room scarcely sufficient to swing an implement. There seems no reason to believe that the craftsmen of antiquity chose to work (whether with or without option) in workshops any more spacious than those found in the old districts of modern Egyptian towns, including the bazaars. 'Health and safety' are in such places today of no more concern than they would have been in the workshops of the New Kingdom.

Unfortunately, the few excavated 'industrial' areas of ancient Egyptian towns provide poor evidence of spatial arrangements. For the most part, the traces of industrial activity have been obliterated by destruction and subsequent building. In El-Amarna, the abandoned city of Akhenaten, where surviving traces of buildings are generally less disturbed than elsewhere, the remains of workshops on large and small scale have been found; some operated presumably for the temple and the palace, others seem to have been small and privately owned.[22] More is known of the arrangements of industrial workings, the activities appropriate to which belonged to the more primitive processes which yielded raw materials to be used eventually in the crafts depicted in tomb scenes. The smelting of copper and the extraction of gold by ore crushing and washing, took place close to the sites where the raw materials were mined;[23] we have already learned something of the expeditions to the turquoise mines of Sinai, enterprises which belong to the same category.[24] These 'heavy' industrial activities were carried out by squads of labourers, supervised by expedition leaders along quasi-military lines, and the processes were crude and only moderately efficient in comparison with the precision and craftsmanship of the work carried out in the urban workshops.

Equally crude were the living conditions suffered by the expedition-ary workmen, who endured immense discomfort in Nubia and Sinai. The goldsmith or coppersmith working in Thebes, perhaps in the temple workshops of Amon-Re, could expect much better. In status he might be equal to men of other crafts and even of other non-manual professions; his house might be in a quarter of the city occupied by other craftsmen; and by scribes and by relatively highly placed officials. A papyrus in the British Museum[25] contains as a supplementary text on the back 'The town-roll of the West of Thebes beginning from the Temple of King Menmaatre [the funerary temple of Sethos I] and ending at the settlement Maiunehes', dated to Year 12 of an unnamed king who has been plausibly identified as Ramesses XI of the Twentieth Dynasty (c. 1110–1080 BC).[26] In all 182 houses identified by their owners are listed. The area covered by the roll stretches along the edge of the cultivation following the line of royal funerary temples which extends from that of Sethos I of the Nineteenth Dynasty in the north to that of Ramesses III in the south. The settlement of Maiunehes is not known, but it has been identified as the workmen's village of Deir el-Medina occupied by the makers of the royal tombs of the Valley of the Kings,[27] and also as the township which grew up in and around the temple complex of Ramesses III at Medinet Habu.[28] It is just as possible that Maiunehes lay to the south of Medinet Habu in the direction of the abandoned palace of Amenophis III.

The precise identification of the site of this settlement does not seriously concern us here. What is of interest in the list is the analysis of professions of the householders together with the status of these house-holders in the society of the community on the western side of the Nile at Thebes. It cannot seriously be thought that these 182 households represented the whole of the settled population in this part of Western Thebes—a narrow region stretching over about two miles. The houses, named by their owners, are specially mentioned, either because of their size and the status of their owners, or because the owners are sufficiently prosperous to pay taxes in respect of the land they may hold, locally or elsewhere. The owners surely are of some importance. They include the mayor of Western Thebes, a chief of police, a number of administrative officials, twelve scribes, and forty-nine priests. There are many representatives of trades and crafts: a doctor, stablemen, gardeners, herdsmen, brewers, sandal-makers, incense-roasters, fishermen; there are nine coppersmiths and one goldsmith. These humble workers, so despised by the writer of the *Satire of Trades*, appear in this society of Western Thebes in the late Twentieth Dynasty to be not so humble. They qualify for inclusion in the town-roll along with scribes and important bureaucrats, and the dispositions of their houses within the roll do not reveal any segregation by trade or profession. The coppersmith Peteh's house lies between those of a fisherman and a retainer; the goldsmith Nesiptah lives between a priest and a storeman (?); the coppersmith Wenennekhu, who is also a priest, has priests as neighbours on both sides; a series of five houses are occupied by a gardener, a coppersmith, a priest, a coppersmith, and a district overseer.

A trade not represented among the named householders of this settlement is that of carpenter or joiner. Yet woodworking was always important in ancient Egypt, and the skills of the carpenter and the cabinet-maker are amply revealed in the many wooden objects which have survived from antiquity in the favourable conditions of the Theban necropolis. Inlay, overlay, painted decoration, carved decoration, marquetry and veneering were all practised in the making of elegant furniture and fine boxes.[29] One notable example of high craftsmanship from among the many outstanding pieces found in the funerary equipment in Tutankhamun's tomb is a chest made of soft wood, transformed by the application of strips of ivory and ebony veneer, and marquetry panels of tiny pieces of ivory and ebony arranged in a herring-bone pattern; gold studs cover the pegs holding the cross-members together. Howard Carter's unpublished notes contain an estimate of 33,000 marquetry pieces.[30] Work of this quality and intricacy would not be produced by the oaf of a carpenter, described in the *Satire of Trades* as if he were a rough forester:

> Any carpenter[31] who takes up the adze becomes more tired than the worker on the land. His field is the wood, and his hoe is the adze. There is no limit to his work; he labours beyond what his arms can do; by night he lights up (to go on working).[32]

Carpenters and joiners—a distinction of profession possibly not made by the ancient Egyptians—certainly belonged to the community of honoured workmen whose labour might be dignified as craftsmanship. The workshop of those who served the Temple of Amun in Thebes is among the places visited by Rekhmire in the course of his 'letting every man know his responsibilities in the execution of every occupation'.[33] Here work of the finest quality is produced, and the painted scenes provide splendid evidence of techniques and the use of tools. As will be seen shortly, many carpenter's tools have survived from the time of the Eighteenth Dynasty (and from much earlier periods also), and from them and from the representations of similar tools in use in tomb scenes a fairly full picture of ancient Egyptian carpentry and cabinet-making can be built up. In the register and sub-registers allotted to woodworking in Rekhmire's tomb, the right-hand representations show, as in the case of the metal-working scenes, some of the craftsmen's products: in the upper sub-register, a fan-handle, a head-rest, a plain table, and a chest with a lid shaped like a shrine top; below, a statue of a king, presumably of Tuthmosis III

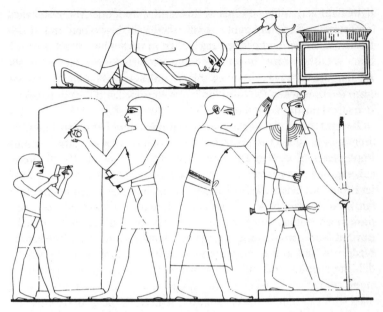

Fig. 18 The products of the wood-worker's craft.

himself. The upper objects are all of fairly commonplace kinds, although made in these workshops to a high standard for important owners, even the king, possibly as part of his funerary equipment. The statue is almost certainly destined for the royal tomb. Stone statues of the king, the making of colossal examples of which is depicted else-where in Rekhmire's tomb, would be used for temple decoration, both in cult temples and in the royal mortuary temple; wooden statues on the other hand, of the kind shown here, were intended for the tomb. It is almost life-size, and is painted black (for the exposed flesh) and yellow (for gilded accoutrements), very similar in style and conception to the two guardian statues found watching over the sealed entrance to the burial chamber in Tutankhamun's tomb (*Fig. 18*).

To the left of the wooden statue and its presenter, a tall shrine-shaped chest receives its decoration from the hands of a painter and a carver or engraver. The former marks out the designs on the side of the shrine, while the latter strikes his carving tool with a piece of stone used as a light hammer. Many shrines of this kind were found in the so-called Treasury in Tutankhamun's tomb; they held blackened and gilded figures of deities and of the king shown in particular roles.[34] It is not likely that the shrine shown here being completed was intended for the royal figure we have already examined, unless it was for simple storage until the time when the royal tomb was equipped and the figure placed in its final position of guardianship.

Beyond the group working on the shrine, a number of workmen are seen busy at tasks that illustrate the uses of tools that were the common implements of ancient Egyptian carpenters and joiners. In the lower sub-register, the first man works on a plank of wood with a small adze, levelling the surface, where a modern carpenter would use a plane. The small hand adze, of which some actual, and many 'model', examples have been found, consisted of a suitably shaped handle with a flat upright face, almost at right angles to the shaft, along which the bronze blade was laid and tightly bound with leather thongs. Designed for delicate shaping and smoothing, it was used in conjunction with the stone rubber or polisher for finishing surfaces. A much larger adze, used with two handles, was employed at an earlier stage in the preparation of wood for carpentry, for trimming side branches from tree trunks, for the removal of bark and for rough shaping. No example of the larger adze is shown in this series of scenes in Rekhmire's tomb, but it can be seen elsewhere wielded in energetic manner in scenes where the carpenter's work is less fine, as in boat-building. The adze-worker in the present scene sits on a neat three-legged stool of a kind often used by craftsmen when they are not standing or squatting on the ground. He rests his work on a wooden block from which a distinctive notch has been cut, designed possibly as a stop to prevent work from slipping. He does not use it as such, any more than his colleague in the upper sub-register, a little further to the left, who has just put down his adze in order to check the regularity of his work with a straight-edge. There is a nice touch in the way the artist has shown the adze casually, but handily, stuck into the top of the craftsman's block. Other tools are shown ready for use nearby, a square with a ridge to allow its being held tight against the work, and a block or flat implement, also with a ridge, containing a cut-out making an angle of about 110°, perhaps to be used in marking out dovetails or something similar. This second, well-equipped, carpenter sits on a block-like seat with a coved top, and just to his front is a chest with painted or veneered panels and a lid eccentrically hunched like the top of the shrine we have already examined (*Fig. 19*).

Chests of this kind, and others of less elaborate workmanship and decoration, were used for the storage of goods in Egyptian houses where capacious pieces of furniture were not to be found. The idea of the drawer contained within the bulk of a chest was not wholly unknown; gaming-boxes, for example, were frequently fitted with long drawers to hold gaming-pieces, as in that gem of the ancient joiner's craft, the ebony-mounted gaming-box on a stand and sledge from Tutankhamun's tomb. The principle of the drawer, however, was never applied on a larger scale, and the Egyptians were content to use chests to protect their personal belongings.[35] Simple flap-lids of chests might, in especially fine examples, be hinged, but most chest lids were completely removable, and were held in place when closed by simple devices like projecting pegs that fitted into recesses cut in the corresponding side of the chest, or a flange on the underside of the lid that connected with a slot cut in the inner side of the chest. Security of a kind was achieved by winding a string around two knobs, one on the top of

Fig. 19 Carpenters working with adze, saw and straight-edge, and applying some material with a brush, possibly gesso-plaster.

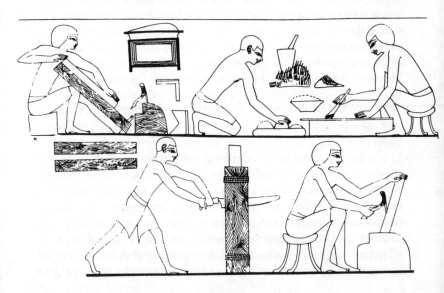

the lid at the end away from the hinge or other fitting device, the other on the side of the chest. When this string was sealed, in the same way as a letter was sealed, the contents of the chest were protected from casual pilfering at least, though not from the determined attention of a thief.

Three chests which can be taken as good examples of the kinds of pieces used in the Egyptian's daily life belonged to Tutu, who lived at about the end of the Eighteenth Dynasty, and to Ramose and Hatnufe, the parents of Senenmut. All these chests were used in the funerary furniture of tombs, but none shows any sign of having been made specially for the tomb, and none is embellished with funerary texts. Tutu's box, now in the British Museum,[36] was used for her personal cosmetic equipment and fitted with compartments to hold jars of ointment, her eye-paint tubes and mixing palette (in bronze), her pink-stained leather sandals, an ivory comb, and a piece of pumice for scrubbing the body. The box stands on short legs braced with lattice-work; it is simply but sturdily constructed, fitted with a flat lid held in position by wooden lugs. When it was found it was apparently still fastened with a cord around its two knobs, sealed with a mud sealing. The only non-functional decoration is a simple beading of alternating soft- and hard-wood inlays on the edges of the internal partitions. The two chests from the tomb of Ramose and Hatnufe, in the Metropolitan Museum of Art, New York, are very simply designed, and are made of sycomore wood, painted white inside and out; one is no more than a box with a flat lid, raised off the ground by two battens; the other has a gabled lid and four short legs.[37] The former is about 76 cm. long and 48 cm. high, the latter 70 cm. long and 44 cm. high. Yet between them they contained fifty-five pieces of linen, ranging in length from 4.25 m. to 16.50 cm., each piece neatly folded small, forming as a whole a stock of household linen stored in its proper chests, ready for use in the after-life as it was undoubtedly used during the lifetime of Senenmut's parents.

The accuracy and craftsmanship of the makers of their household chests, aided by the favourable conditions prevailing in the tombs of the Theban necropolis, have secured the survival of their products in almost perfect state. The joints hold firm, the boards, cut certainly from properly seasoned timber, are unwarped, the lids fit tight. It is not impossible that they were made by the carpenters in one of the great official or religious workshops of Thebes, for much of the linen in the two chests of Ramose and Hatnufe bears the marks of official and temple stores. The craftsmen employed in these great workshops could scarcely have been employed continuously on the production of objects for royal burials, or even for the royal palaces; but a large cadre of craftsmen and apprentices needed to be maintained to meet the emergencies of those occasions, such as an unexpected royal death, when large quantities of funerary material might be required in a short period. The long reign of Tuthmosis III (over thirty years after the death or dislodging of Hatshepsut) provided ample time for the output of the metropolitan workshops to be exploited for non-royal persons.

The craftsmen shown in Rekhmire's tomb are, as should be expected, working on royal commissions, but many are engaged in simple activities that are not seen to be concerned necessarily with the manufacture of specifically royal objects. In the group of carpenters we have been examining, all are so engaged. The two already described work with adzes, shaping planks. A third, in the lower sub-register, cuts planks, using a very primitive kind of vice to hold the timber while it is being cut. A thick upright post, set firmly in the ground, acts as the essential element to which the wood to be cut is fastened by rope in two places. The method of cutting employed with this apparently inefficient vice is made clear by a close examination of tomb scenes and of models from Middle Kingdom tombs showing carpenters at work.[38] To begin, the wood for cutting is bound near the bottom and some way below its top. As the cut progresses downwards, the wood is moved higher up the post and the rope-ties adjusted. The act of setting the wood in a new position is illustrated in the same series of Rekhmire scenes, further to the left, where the first stage of cutting is just completed. In the first example of the sawyer at work, he cuts further down, and the cut lies between the two ties. It must be presumed that the saw was prevented from binding in the cut by the insertion of wedges to keep the cut open.[39] No clear examples of wedges used in this way are known, but it is manifestly certain that without a wedge the cut would be held tight by the rope-ties. The action of the sawyer in this representation and in others elsewhere demonstrates that the saw, which in the New Kingdom would be made of bronze, was used by pulling, and not by pushing, as is the case with the modern saw. The sawyer pulls at his saw with both hands, putting the whole weight of his body into the action which rips the wood.[40] Actual examples of saws now in museums show that the teeth are not of very even size, and they are not set in alternate directions as in saws today; unset saws would be more inclined to bind than set saws. Two planks already cut and neatly finished are placed in the field behind the craftsman's back. We shall see smaller hand-saws in use later in this same range of scenes.

In the upper sub-register two men face each other, engaged in activities that are probably connected. Between them in the field is a small fire heating up a vessel from which protrudes what may be a brush. This may be a glue-pot for the heating up of solidified glue extracted from animal products.[41] The craftsman on the right, sitting on a low three-legged stool, appears to be applying glue with a brush to a thin piece of material, which might possibly be a strip of wood veneer to be stuck to the plain wood carcase of a box. His colleague, kneeling on the ground opposite him, grinds a white substance with a stone grinder on a flat surface. The most plausible suggestion is that he is grinding material for the making of fine plaster.[42] Such plaster, commonly called gesso by archaeologists—not wholly incorrectly[43]— was manufactured from ground whiting (chalk) mixed with glue. It was used to mask wooden objects made of inferior material; it could be carved, gilded or painted; it might serve simply as a ground for painting; it might be applied over a linen base, itself stuck with glue to the foundation surface; it might itself be treated with glue before gold foil was applied. From these diverse uses of glue and gesso in the ornamentation of furniture, the difficulty of determining precisely what the two craftsmen are doing becomes evident. One seems certainly to be grinding whiting, and the other certainly applies something with a brush to some object. It is possible that the bowl set in the field just below the fire contains ground whiting ready to be mixed with glue for the making of gesso. It is also possible that the painter is actually applying gesso to a board. No kind of certainty about their tasks can be achieved.

The techniques employed by the carpenter in the workshops of Amun are further demonstrated and extended in the scenes to the left of those already described. At the higher level sawing with a small hand-saw is shown. The carpenter squats on a three-legged stool, holding the piece of wood to be cut in front of him; its bottom end anchored against his foot. By pushing the top end of the wood away from him he holds it braced, while the angle so achieved allows him to saw with a horizontal stroke that in practical terms reproduces the oblique downward stroke used by sawyers employing the two-handed saw and post method. To the left of this sawyer, three men put the finishing touches to a wooden lotus-bud column which is laid on its side. The three have finished shaping it in general terms, and one of their adzes lies beside them on a wooden block. Now they smooth and polish the surface of the column with stone rubbers. Columns of this kind might be used in private houses or in the royal palace itself (*Fig. 20*).[44]

At the lower level, on the right, two carpenters prepare the frame of a bed for the addition of the string mattress woven between the bed-stretchers. They drill holes down each side, using a drill driven by a bow. The drill itself consists of a wooden stock into which a bronze point is fitted. When in use the drill is held upright, and allowed to turn freely in the hand of the operator by a cup of stone, or of a *dôm*-nut shell which fits on the top of the stock. The bow has an eccentric curve, well suited for use with the necessary sawing motion. From examples of bows of this kind preserved from antiquity, as well as from those shown in tomb scenes, as here, it is clear that this shape was standard; it seems highly likely, therefore, that branches of suitable trees were trained by careful cultivation accordingly. Each end of the bow was pierced, or provided with a notch, for the tying of the string, which itself was loosely stretched to allow a turn to be made around the drill-stock. The string might be made of linen, papyrus or rush, all of which are known to have been used for cord in ancient times.[45] Rather more robust cords would be needed for the stringing of the bed. A scene in another

Fig. 20 Carpenters work on a bed-frame and a pillar.

Theban tomb, originally prepared for a contemporary of Rekhmire, but later usurped by someone else in the Nineteenth Dynasty, contains what seems to be a representation of the stringing process, with two men handling long hanks of cord.[46] Surviving beds, with part or the whole of their stringing intact, show a rather open mesh, although the methods and the patterns employed differ markedly from example to example. A close weave was not necessary because a filled mattress was usually laid on top of the stringing. With chairs the weave was much closer.

Two workmen, seated on low three-legged stools to the left of the bed-drilling group, belong properly to the team further to the left, who are busy with an open-work shrine. One of these two uses a small hand-saw on a small plank, cutting it, apparently, into short lengths suitable to be carved into amuletic shapes needed for the decoration of the shrine. An adze, lying on its side, was used for shaping the pieces in a preliminary way; the finished form and detail are achieved with a small hand tool, a kind of chisel with a wooden handle and bronze blade. The man using this tool is just completing the shape ▯, the *djed*-pillar,[47] which was closely associated with the cult of the god Osiris, possessing the magical values of stability and endurance. It is one of the elements used repeatedly in the decoration of the shrine. A general text, which refers to all the wood-working craftsmen, fills the small space above these two carpenters. It reads:

> Making furniture in ivory and ebony, in *sesnedjem*-wood and *meru*-wood, in real cedar from the heights of the terraced hills,[48] by this official who establishes guide-lines and controls the hands of his craftsmen.

Rekhmire is thus made out to be the source and inspiration of the skills of the craftsmen under his control—part of the general fiction which allowed the great, from the king downwards, to claim for themselves all the credit in the achievements more properly belonging to their subordinates.

The shrine, which is the principal object under construction in the carpenter's shop, takes a form well exemplified in the two middle shrines of the four which protected the sarcophagus and body of Tutankhamun, while the open-work decoration upon which the craftsmen are shown working is found on the outermost of Tutankhamun's shrines.[49] Pairs of *djed*-pillars alternate with pairs of ▯, the *tyet*-sign, often known as the 'girdle of Isis'. Both signs possessed powerful amuletic force for the ancient Egyptians, but it is not easy to assign precise values to them, or to provide accurate translations of their meaning. Two craftsmen squatting on very low stools work on the fretted amuletic shapes, one with an adze and the other with a chisel, while two others, standing by the shrine, trim the frame and make final adjustments to the elements already fitted into place. A door with two panels occupies the space above the shrine; it probably represents one of the two doors of the shrine itself. Like most Egyptian doors, it is not to be hung on hinges; its inner vertical runner extends beyond the edges of the door, top and bottom, to be fitted into sockets in the upper and lower door-frames. The lower extension, which will carry most of the weight of the door, is shaped to a rounded point, designed for easy turning (*Fig. 21*).

To the left of the shrine, the register is again divided into two sub-scenes. At the top two craftsmen, seated on solid stools with coved tops, are busily engaged in making chairs. The man on the right puts the finishing touches to a chair leg in the shape of a lion's leg; he rubs away imperfections with a small stone rubber. Three other finished legs lie about, and his small shaping-adze rests on his work-block. The legs have tenons cut at their top ends for fitting into the mortices in the chair seat; at their bottoms are those very characteristic tapering cylinders, often ringed with incised lines, found with animal-shaped legs of beds and chairs in particular, and occasionally of other pieces of furniture standing on legs. The purpose of these cylinders has never been satisfactorily explained; the most plausible explanation is that they were originally designed to protect the animal-paw terminals which might break under irregular pressure.[50] The four legs shown here are probably intended for a chair of the kind depicted on the left, the seat-frame of which is being drilled in preparation for its string- or rush-woven seat. This chair is typical of the Eighteenth Dynasty, although the form was undoubtedly developed during the Middle Kingdom, if not much earlier.[51] It has a sloping back supported by vertical struts, which between them produce the triangular space characteristic of the side view. Many chairs of this kind, including some of the actual examples existing in museum collections, appear to be rather low, like the one shown here. A height of 25–30 cm. is by no means unusual, in comparison with the 45-cm. height which is common for most modern chairs. The low Egyptian chair is, surprisingly, very comfortable to sit on, and its seat is conveniently large if the person sitting on it wishes to draw up his or her legs, as can frequently be seen in tomb scenes and on funerary stelae.

In the lower sub-scene one joiner sits on the piece of wood which he is working on, cutting mortices, it would seem, with a wooden-handled bronze chisel and a mallet with a cone-shaped head, very little different in form from the modern carpenter's mallet. He is probably preparing one of the principal members needed for the shrine which is shown near to completion to his right. The other two men wield axes on similar pieces of wood, perhaps splitting them roughly into shape, which are also to be used for the construction of the shrine. The axes again are in form characteristic of actual examples surviving from the New Kingdom: the hafts are well shaped for comfortable holding, and the bronze blades, fitted into slots cut into the hafts, are held in place by leather thongs bound tightly around the splayed ends of the blades and the hafts. To the left of the axe-men stands the second primitive vice for sawing, which has been mentioned already. The sawyer here has just moved the wood he is cutting higher up the fixed pole, and is tying it firmly in position again. Meanwhile his saw has been left in the cut. This sawyer is shown with long hair, while most of the craftsmen in

Fig. 21 Carpenters make shrines and a chair.

these scenes have close-cropped hair. Long hair is generally taken to be a sign of old age and of modest authority; this sawyer, therefore, is probably an old employee in the royal workshops, perhaps a foreman or supervisor.

The scene of carpenters is completed by a final group of two crafts-men finishing off the surfaces of another shrine mounted on a sledge. In the compass of the space allotted to carpentry and joinery in Rekhmire's tomb, as in the scenes of metal-working described earlier in this chapter, a little only of the work carried out in the royal workshops can be shown. In a sense, the well-organized series of vignettes concerned with a craft or trade should encapsulate both the techniques of work and also the products of the work. The scenes need not be comprehensive, but they should be typical and representative. The raised vessels stand for all raised vessels, the cast door for all castings; the shrines may be viewed as embodying all ritual furniture, the chairs and the bed as all domestic furniture. It is important to show many methods of work and many different tools. In the tomb scenes they are perpetuated for use in eternity, and it is crucial that the artist does his best to demonstrate a technique and reproduce a tool as accurately as possible. From the best tomb scenes, therefore, a very fair idea may be

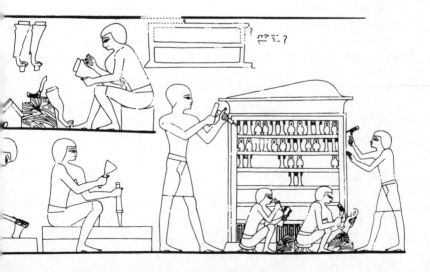

gleaned of ways and means in the crafts of ancient Egypt. This faithful intention provides the evidence which in many cases allows the student of Egyptian technology to elucidate the techniques by which finely made surviving objects were produced. The whole of a process, however, cannot be shown, and the best artist cannot convey the special skill of the artist-craftsman which transforms a well-made piece into a finely wrought object of the highest technical achievement.

Contemplation of some of the finest surviving works of metal-workers and joiners, and a consideration of the tools which have been found in considerable numbers, increase rather than diminish the respect and wonder with which the achievement may be measured. While tomb scenes, by the simple methods of artistic representation that are commonly employed by the Egyptian draughtsman, show each activity individually and arranged in extension along the horizontal registers into which the decorated wall-surfaces are divided, it may be supposed that the reality of a busy workshop was quite otherwise. Some crafts might be practised in the open, or under awnings, or in open-sided sheds; others, because of the precious nature of the materials used, the delicacy of the detail to be worked, or the degree of control required, might be carried on in enclosed workshops without direct sunlight. Individual craftsmen, or small groups, might work in open booths of the kind still found in the bazaars of Cairo and the provincial towns of Egypt. But the great workshops of the royal estates and important temples were surely of large size, crowded, busy, noisy and dusty. In the matter of environment the scribe might be justified in preferring his lot to that of the craftsman; but it cannot be believed that the craftsmen who produced such splendid objects acquired little satisfaction from their achievements, or failed to be appreciated, and indeed honoured, for their skills. Of such success and satisfaction the scribe does not write, and we are obliged to speculate on the condition of the craftsman. His work alone provides the testimony, and it is in itself enough.

NOTES

1 The text in all variants has 'crocodile's things'. Some scholars see the word for 'things' as a corruption of a rare word for 'talons'. Is the comparison between fingers and claws, or between the roughness of the fingers and of crocodile's skin? The latter seems to me the less obvious, and therefore to be preferred.

2 From the *Satire of Trades*, the whole purpose of which seems to have been to poke fun at the manual trades. For the Egyptian text, see W. Helck, *Die Lehre des Dw3-Ḥtjj* (Wiesbaden, 1970); for the quotation, see pp. 36–7.

3 N. de G. Davies, *Paintings from the Tomb of Rekh-mi-Rē' at Thebes* (New York, 1935), pl.XXIII.

4 Or, possibly, 'craftsmen'. The words between square brackets are restored without absolute certainty. The missing signs are lost through deliberate destruction during the reign of Akhenaten, undoubtedly because the name Amun was included among them.

5 Davies, *Tomb of Rekh-mi-Rē'*, pls. LII–LV.

6 An extraordinary example of exaggeration.

7 J. Černý in *Cambridge Ancient History*, II, pt.2, 621.

8 See J. Vercoutter in *Kush* 7 (Khartoum, 1959), 120 ff.

9 P. 44 above; also p. 264 below.

10 A. Lucas, *Ancient Egyptian Materials and Industries*, 229.

11 J. Černý in *Journal of World History* I (Paris, 1954), 904 ff.

12 British Museum no. 921, see Pl. 10 (*below*).

13 Usefully listed in Lucas, op. cit., 247.

14 Published by F. Bisson de la Rocque, *Le trésor de Tôd* (Cairo, 1953). See also É. Drioton and J. Vandier, *L'Égypte*, 4 ed. (Paris, 1962), 256; G. Posener in *Cambridge Ancient History*, I, pt. 2, 543 f.

15 H. Frankfort and J. D. S. Pendlebury, *City of Akhenaten* II (London, 1933), 59. A lively, somewhat dramatized account of the discovery can be read in Mary Chubb, *Nefertiti Lived Here* (London, 1954), 132 ff. See also Pl. 11 (*above*).

16 See P. M. Roberts in *Gold Bulletin* 6, no. 4 (Johannesburg, 1973), 112 ff.

17 Gold-working in jewellery is well treated by A. Wilkinson, *Ancient Egyptian Jewellery* (London, 1971), 1 ff.; and C. Aldred, *Jewels of the Pharaohs* (London, 1971), 70 ff.

18 Possibly a natural alloy of copper and tin, a fortuitous bronze; see J. R. Harris, *Lexicographical Studies in Ancient Egyptian Minerals* (Berlin, 1961), 57.

19 A part of Syria-Palestine; see A. H. Gardiner, *Ancient Egyptian Onomastica* (Oxford, 1949), I, 142*.

20 So N. de G. Davies, *Tomb of Rekh-mi-Rē'*, 53.

21 Presumably six parts of copper to one of tin, making a bronze with about 14% of tin, a rather higher percentage than was common in antiquity; see A. Lucas, *Ancient Egyptian Materials and Industries*, 217, and the analysis 487 ff.

22 See W. M. F. Petrie, *Tell el Amarna* (London, 1894), 25; and the perceptive remarks of B. J. Kemp in P. Ucko, R. Tringham and G. W. Dimbleby (eds.), *Man, Settlement and Urbanism* (London, 1972), 673.

23 The Old-Kingdom copper-smelting settlement at Buhen is yet to be published, but

see W. B. Emery in *Kush* 11 (Khartoum, 1963), 116 ff.; for gold extraction, see J. Vercoutter, *Kush* 7 (1959), 120 ff.

24 See p. 38 ff. above.

25 British Museum Papyrus 10068, verso 2–8; see T. E. Peet, *Great Tomb-Robberies of the XXth Egyptian Dynasty* (Oxford, 1930), 93 ff.

26 Peet, op. cit., 86 f.

27 Peet, op. cit., 84. This suggestion was made before Deir el-Medina was identified as the necropolis workmen's village.

28 B. J. Kemp, op. cit., 666.

29 On wood, Lucas, op. cit., 429 ff.; on furniture and techniques, H. Baker, *Furniture in the Ancient World*; G. Killen, *Ancient Egyptian Furniture*, I (Warminster, 1980).

30 Baker, op. cit., 94 and fig. 116.

31 The word translated 'carpenter' here (*ḥmww*) carries more than a slight suggestion of craftsman.

32 W. Helck, *Die Lehre des Dw3-Ḥtjj* (Wiesbaden, 1970), 39–42.

33 N. de G. Davies, *Tomb of Rekh-mi-Rē'*, pls. LII, LIII, LV.

34 For example, H. Carter, *The Tomb of Tut·Ankh·Amen*, III (London, 1933), pl. XI; C. Desroches-Noblecourt, *Tutankhamen* (London, 1963), figs. 47, 158, 159.

35 A good account of fine and ordinary chests in H. Baker, *Furniture in the Ancient World*, 91 ff. (from Tutankhamun's tomb), 144 ff. (from elsewhere).

36 British Museum no. 24708; see Baker, op. cit., 146, fig. 223. Also Pl. 11 (*below*).

37 Illustrated in Baker, op. cit., 146, figs. 222, 224; for the contents, see W. C. Hayes, *The Scepter of Egypt*, II, 203 f.

38 First properly elucidated by M. Lane in *Ancient Egypt, 1935* (London, 1935), 55 ff.

39 So Davies, *Rekh-mi-Rē'*, 51.

40 The action of the sawyer in the model carpenter's shop from the tomb of Meketre is very explicitly described by H. E. Winlock in *Models of Daily Life in Ancient Egypt* (Cambridge, Mass., 1955), 33 f.

41 See Lucas, *Ancient Egyptian Materials and Industries*, 3 ff.

42 Davies, *Rekh-mi-Rē' I*, 51.

43 Lucas, op. cit., 354.

44 See T. E. Peet and C. L. Woolley, *City of Akhenaten*, I (London, 1923), pl. IV for a restoration of a room in a private house with wooden pillars, here with palm capitals; also H. Frankfort and J. D. S. Pendlebury, *City of Akhenaten*, II (London, 1933), 98, pl. XVI. For earlier times, H. E. Winlock, op. cit., pls. 9, 11.

45 Lucas, op. cit., 134 ff.

46 Nina Davies and N. de G. Davies, *The Tombs of Menkheperrasonb, Amenmose and Another* (London, 1933), pl. XXX, F, and p. 25.

47 Note the fitting of *djeds* and *tjets* in N. de G. Davies, *The Tomb of Two Sculptors at Thebes* (New York, 1925), pl. XI.

48 The Lebanon.

49 C. Desroches-Noblecourt, *Tutankhamen* (London, 1963), 260 and fig. 171.

50 H. Baker, *Furniture in the Ancient World*, 21.

51 H. Baker, op. cit.; 128 f.; for an example from an Early-Dynastic tomb at Naga ed-Deir, see G. Killen, *Ancient Egyptian Furniture*, I, 51; its contemporaneity with the original burial must, however, be questioned.

8

A DESIRABLE RESIDENCE

Where people lived in ancient Egypt was determined by one factor above all others—a factor which has continued to exercise significant control until modern times—namely, the height of the land above the flood-waters of the Nile. No sensible person builds his house where the flood of the summer season will reach it and wash it away. He builds either on the high ground beyond the cultivated area of the Nile valley, as in the villages among the tombs of the Theban necropolis, or on those slight eminences within the cultivated area which will not be covered by the flood-waters in most years. A foot or two of extra height will do and if, very rarely, the flood rises higher than usual, the gods can take the blame, not the lack of prudence. The village eminences of modern Egypt are clearly to be seen if a drive is taken through the flat Delta lands, or within the broad bands of cultivation in parts of Upper Egypt. In picturesque isolation they rise above the level land like islands, as indeed they became every year before the construction of the great High Dam south of Aswan, and the ending of the annual inundation.

Most villages within the cultivation occupy ancient sites, because elevation above the surrounding land could only be achieved by occupation. Over a long period of time an uninhabited eminence of modest height would gradually be overtaken by the slow rise in the level of the cultivated land, due to the annual deposit of Nile silt. The same irrevocable rise in land level was accompanied by a rise in the level of the river bed, so that, in effect, the relationship between land level and the river remained generally constant. In the course of a man's lifetime the rise would be scarcely noticeable, but it would be registered throughout the land of Egypt at those places where the river levels in inundation were recorded, and the gradual rise would be visible in the recorded marks. The fate of gradual submersion suffered by un-inhabited eminences did not befall inhabited sites. They too rose gradually as buildings were renewed from time to time, the new frequently being built on the level rubble of the old, producing the stratifications so clearly observed in the sections cut vertically through an abandoned occupation site.

As the centuries advanced the occupied eminences rose higher and higher, for the rate of increase in height considerably outstripped the slow rise of the surrounding countryside. By late antiquity, therefore, many of the inhabited sites had become quite considerable hills, and those that were deserted in the subsequent centuries remained like stark fortresses overlooking the level land around. A few of these *tells*, as they are called, still remain in the remote parts of the Delta, at Mendes (in part), at Tanis, and at Buto; but the majority have been reduced to the level of the country by local peasants who have used the ancient decayed brickwork as fertilizer on their land. In this way have many city and village sites disappeared, where continuity of occupation has not been maintained since antiquity. Where there has been continuity of occupation, then the ancient levels are to be found deep below the present surface. This phenomenon can graphically be seen in the town of Esna, the very name of which perpetuates an ancient name, Ta-seny or Seny.[1] Landing from a boat, the visitor steps on to the remains of a stone quay probably built in the Graeco-Roman Period; a stiff climb up the steep river-bank brings him to the level of the road running along the Nile, from which at approximately right angles runs another road through the buildings of the modern town to the site of the great temple of Khnum, the existing buildings of which date from no earlier, probably, than the second century BC. When the visitor reaches the modern temple precinct he is amazed to find himself standing on a level with the cornice of the temple pronaos—the only surviving part of what may have been a vast building. The façade of this pronaos is more than fifteen metres high, yet it rises barely above the level of the roads and paths of the adjacent parts of modern Esna.

The same sort of thing can be observed in one of those countryside islands, approached through the fertile cultivation a few miles to the south of Luxor. This relatively low mound carries the village of El-Tod, and it conceals beneath its stratified layers the ancient town of Djarty, a name corrupted to Toout or Taout in late antiquity, and providing the etymology for the modern name.[2] Here was a cult-centre of the god Montu, and when excavations were carried out in the 1930s a deep trench was cut through the mound down to a depth of many metres to reach the level of the Ptolemaic temple and earlier religious buildings. A walk along this trench on the axis of the temple and its approach gives the visitor a vivid demonstration of the succession of occupations. The houses of the modern village in places stand ten metres or more above the temple pavement, which itself now lies at a level below the fields surrounding the village. In its day we may suppose that the temple pavement stood high on the mound of Djarty, well above any possible level of flood-water, even in a year of exceptional inundation. Now there is no annual inundation, but as in most ancient sites within the cultivated area of Egypt, the seepage of sub-soil water, an insidious and destructive hazard, keeps the lowest excavated strata wet and strongly salty—conditions excessively damaging for ancient remains. What a weight of ancient occupation lies locked up in the inhabited sites of Egypt! How inaccessible most of it is! The existence of bustling, flourishing towns and villages, occupying the tops of these sites, effectively prevents the investigation of what lies below.

Throughout Egypt the case is the same, and rarely can an excavating organization afford, as in the case of El-Tod, to buy out the owners of large numbers of buildings in order to excavate what lies below. The very names of places in Egypt today perpetuate those of antiquity, unknown to the present-day inhabitants, and often identified only through detailed philological and phonetic argument. As already mentioned, Esna was Ta-seny, El-Tod was Djarty; Aswan in antiquity was Sunu, and Asyut was Sawty. The town of Damanhur in the Delta conceals in its name the ancient Egyptian Demy-en-Hor, 'Town of Horus'; Ashmunein in Middle Egypt was Khmunu, '(Town) of the Eight', i.e. the eight deities who made up the local (but nationally important) ogdoad, or system of divine creative beings. These names are but a few among hundreds which demonstrate the continuity of land-occupation throughout Egypt; if more ancient names were known, there is no doubt that the number of identified corresponding modern names would be even greater. Very much, therefore, about the character of ancient towns and villages may be learned from an examination of undeveloped towns and villages within the cultivated area of Egypt today. Then, as now, the possible space suitable for habitation was defined by the line of the inundation around the occupied mound. Unless this space could be enlarged by the construction of dykes and the dumping of rubble, there was little possibility for the expansion or improvement of the buildings within the area. Urban and village renewal was, in consequence, grossly constricted, and as the generations succeeded each other, with a normal tendency towards an increase in population, living conditions would tend to deteriorate. From time to time a kind of relief would occur through famine and disease, brought about by the vagaries of the inundation and the lack of hygiene.

In general, however, living conditions tended to become tighter as time went on; and the same trend to overpopulation in towns and villages may be observed in modern Egypt. The prime example is Cairo where the population has increased approximately four times from the 2,350,000 of the 1954 census—a precise figure cannot, for many reasons, be given for the number of inhabitants almost thirty years later. The city has vastly expanded, with new housing-estates marching out into the desert, and eating up the cultivable land lying between the old city and the desert plateau where the Giza pyramids stand. But most of the new inhabitants live within the boundaries of the city as it existed just after the Second World War. Cramped districts have become even more cramped as more and more buildings are squeezed into every available space. In spite of the misery of life in such conditions, most people appear to prefer the close but friendly atmosphere of the crowded slums to the open but impersonal environment of the new developments. This state of affairs is, of course, not unique to Cairo, or to Egypt. It is, however, most common in countries where the strength of the family spirit remains dominant, and where families are large and closely knit.

The village rather than the town in modern Egypt provides the most useful comparison with the town of ancient Egypt. The village often lacks those phenomena of modern towns, like metalled roads, stone buildings, organized services, which do much to establish a kind of uniformity of planning inimical to the organic, undisciplined species of living found in the village. If the ancient Egyptians possessed an idea of how a town should be planned, it may be thought to include some regularity in the lay-out of the principal streets. The hieroglyphic sign representing a town-plan shows a circle crossed by two thin bands at right angles—a circular enclosure with two principal roads dividing the inhabited area into four equal segments ⊗. Something of this principle may be seen in the very few surviving examples of towns and villages which have been excavated sufficiently well for plans to be prepared.[3] Beyond this simple principle there seems to have been very little planning, except perhaps in those towns which had a distinctly military function, such as the fortress towns of Nubia, or in those small settlements specially designed for workmen, where normal urban life would not necessarily be expected.[4]

Most Egyptian villages today have a few relatively wide and straight streets which act as the arteries for the circulation of goods and of traffic generally. For the rest they consist of a tangle of buildings of all kinds, built, seemingly, to no plan and abutting, even encroaching, on each other. Spaces may be filled with temporary structures of wood, reeds, cloth, plastic sheeting erected for occasional purposes, perhaps even to establish in some cases a kind of squatters' right over land of uncertain ownership. To discover precisely who does own a particular property, or the land on which it is built, in a village is difficult. Herein lies one of the greatest obstacles to the excavation of ancient towns still occupied by villages: the legal problems over the ownership of property are too complex, and are usually not capable of resolution by the examination of documentary evidence. Even a palm tree may be owned by several families, the ownership becoming increasingly divided and complicated by inheritance, and by the disputes attending inheritance. In such circumstances the gradual confusing of property ownership and the uncertain determination of property boundaries are easy to understand. The consequent problems only emerge as such when change is demanded by an interested party, and they may need months or years of legal and semi-legal argument to be resolved at headman, district and possibly national levels. The situation was very similar in antiquity, as the case of Mose over the disputed inheritance of land during the New Kingdom amply demonstrates; although, from the discussion in an earlier chapter,[5] it is clear that land was the principal concern, not houses.

From the modern Egyptian village to the ancient Egyptian town may not be as great a step as it might at first appear. Although the evidence for antiquity is not very great, it points clearly to towns being occupied to remarkable density, in which buildings were crammed close together in a jumbled confusion.[6] There was no shortage of land for settlement but it was mostly desert land on the verge of the cultivation, and thought to be too far either from the river, the principal artery of communication in ancient Egypt, or from the lands to be worked by the local peasantry. Where such desert land could be used, as in the establishment of the new city of Akhetaten, founded by King

Akhenaten, it was so used. Now, more than three thousand years later, the cultivation has encroached deeply on the ancient city because of the rise in water and land levels discussed earlier in this chapter. Akhetaten had broad streets, but also—even though it lasted as an occupied city less than twenty years—crowded districts that, already in their first generation of existence, showed the characteristic tendency to crammed buildings and haphazard planning.[7] In this urban tangle can be observed the beginnings of a typical Egyptian town, and it can also be noted that this form of domestic environment appears to result from deliberate choice. For in Akhetaten (modern El-Amarna) there was no shortage of land for expansion, unlike most Egyptian town sites where the Nile flood controlled the limits of building. Also the most important parts of the city were laid out very expansively, providing a pattern to be copied in the less grand suburbs but actually ignored. The view that the most crowded districts of Akhetaten were slums has been challenged, probably rightly;[8] but with very little surviving from houses deliberately plundered of all their most desirable features— stone lintels, wooden doors, pillars, beams—it is difficult to be sure about conclusions reached concerning the status of those who inhabited such districts. It is also not at all established on what basis the inhabitants of Akhetaten owned or leased the land on which their homes were built. Possibly the bulk of the population had no choice over where it was to live. Unfortunately, written evidence on such matters is lacking; perhaps too much has been inferred from the uncertain evidence of archaeology, and from comparisons with con- ditions of later periods substantiated by documents.

The letter written by the mayor Mentuhotpe to the scribe Ahmose concerning a house being built for himself under Ahmose's super- vision, which has been quoted earlier,[9] gives very little information about the size or location of the house; but from mention of the value of the house-plot it may be fair to assume that it was being built in a town, not in the countryside. A far better idea of some of the difficulties facing a person constructing a house in a town can be gained from a contract on papyrus in the British Museum dated to late in 290 BC, Year 16 of Soter I, the first of the Ptolemaic rulers of Egypt.[10] It was made between Taheb, daughter of Pedineferhotep, and Pemerah, son of Djehutirdis, to enable Taheb to construct a house up against one side of Pemerah's house. Incidental to the substance of the contract is the light it sheds on the status of Taheb who, though a woman, can own property and enter into legal obligations quite independently. After the date and pre-amble, the contract begins:

> I am responsible to you if I build my house which forms the western (boundary) of your house, and which is in the northern district of Thebes in The-House-of-the-Cow,[11] its boundaries (as follows): southwards, the courtyard of the house of Pedinefer-hotep . . . to its north, the house of the woman Tedineferhotep, the King's Street lying between them; to its east, your house upon which the walls of my house abut at the south and the north, your wall serving me as a supporting wall, provided that I do not place beams upon it; to its west, the house of Pabimut(?) . . . and the house of . . . Djeho . . . making two houses, the King's Street lying between them. And I shall build my house from my southern wall to my northern wall up to your wall, provided that I do not insert any timber in it, except the timbers of the building which was there before. And it will serve me as a supporting wall provided that I do not insert timber in it. And I shall lay my beams from south to north so that I may roof over the ground floor if I wish to build above, and I shall build on my walls, already mentioned, up to the wall of your house which is to serve me as a supporting wall. And I shall leave the light-well(?) opposite your two windows the distance of a brick from the bricks which are built in front of your house opposite your windows. And I will build south and north of them [the windows] up to your wall; and I will roof them from south to north . . . If I fail to act accordingly to everything aforesaid, I shall pay you 5 silver pieces, that is 25 staters . . . If you obstruct the building of my house, I shall do to you according to everything already mentioned, and I shall build my house without leaving for you a light-well—without penalty.

From the details of this contract much can be learned about the conditions governing the construction of houses in Thebes at a time when it was no longer a great imperial city; and also about the dis-position of houses in a district inhabited by people of moderate, although not very humble, status. The house, or house-plot, of Taheb is closely confined by other houses on two sides and separated from houses on the other two sides by a road called 'the road of Pharaoh', or 'King's Street', presumably a road of some consequence, although it seems not to have been straight if it passes Taheb's plot on two sides.

The new house is to be built right up against the neighbouring house of Pemerah, the west wall of the latter serving as the east wall of the former, except where the existing windows lie; there a light-well is to be left, apparently only one brick in depth, which is not much room. However, direct sunlight within doors is not generally appreciated in Egypt, and most windows in village houses are used for ventilation rather than light. As no beams are to be allowed to be fixed into this wall of Pemerah's house, the new house is in a sense to be quite separate from the old, yet built right up to it. Its roof-beams, running in a north–south direction, will avoid connecting with Pemerah's house and will be, as stated, ready to carry a second storey, if it is ever required. These arrangements have clearly been agreed in principle by preliminary discussion, and are now made legal by the drawing up of a contract, which will in due course be registered officially. It is witnessed by sixteen people.

During the Eighteenth Dynasty, and indeed throughout the New Kingdom, when Thebes was very much the city of empire and the seat of administration of the southern vizir, land for housing in the city area was undoubtedly hard to come by. Conditions were certainly tighter, and the quality of urban life less pleasant than in the early years of the Ptolemaic Period. In a house of any pretension the option to go up by building a second storey or more was surely exercised, and this upward tendency was not one greatly to the liking of Egyptians who had some appreciation for the quality of life. There is good evidence that Egyptians, when the opportunity was available, chose not to live in the crowded city. But opportunity and choice were not usually available, and even Egyptians of some position had to make the best of what the town could offer. In the last chapter mention was made of 'The town-roll of the West of Thebes', in which 182 houses lying between the mortuary temples of Sethos I and Ramesses III, are identified by their owners. The greatest number of the houses lie close together, possibly in and around the temple of Ramesses III at Medinet Habu. This suggested location cannot be established with certainty, but the concentration of houses belonging to people of very different professions, and possibly covering a wide social spectrum, throws interesting light on the apparent lack of zoning in a community either by trade or by wealth. Excavations in the temple precinct of Medinet Habu have revealed for the later New Kingdom and subsequent centuries (c. 1100–900 BC) an extraordinary tangle of streets and houses which had developed above a reasonably carefully planned settlement of the preceding period.[12] Here substantial houses of several rooms with roofs supported by columns and surrounded by courts and outbuildings were replaced by houses of more modest character, but by no means hovels, described by the excavator as being 'laid out arbitrarily without planning. The streets and alleys were at most 1.50 m. wide, often even narrower, and wandered crookedly up hill and down hill, with steps here and there, over existing rubbish heaps. Some groups of dwellings were closed off by gateways built in the streets . . . as in many modern villages of Upper Egypt.'[13] In such a place we can get a little closer to the kind of urban scene with which most ancient Egyptians were familiar.

The excavator's words 'laid out arbitrarily without planning' may even in its unenthusiastic way overestimate the degree of control exercised in the construction and development of such urban warrens. The ease with which additions could be built, using the common building material of unbaked mud-brick, meant that houses could grow organically as needs required, and as opportunities for expansion occurred through the destruction or abandonment of adjacent properties. The process may perhaps be seen in a group of four houses described in some detail, two of which are entered from a winding street, and two from a narrow court opening off this street.[14] One house had a largish antechamber and a main room with two columns, measuring about 5.5 m. by 4 m. Against one wall a platform about 2.5 m. long was built, reached by two steps, and intended, no doubt, for the chairs or stools of the master of the house and his companions—a common feature of the principal room in an ancient Egyptian house. Another house could be entered directly from the first house, and the excavator surmises that the two houses belonged to members of the same family. This explanation may be correct; alternatively, this second house may represent an extension of the first. It contains, for example, features not found in the first house, including two small closets which could have been used as bedrooms, and a small court containing a grain bin. There is no way of deciding which is the correct explanation, and indeed a correct explanation is not needed to reinforce the demonstration of urban organic growth provided by this group of houses.

Town housing of this kind, and even more so the smaller one- and two-roomed houses found jumbled together not so far away in the same settlement at Medinet Habu,[15] may represent what most town-dwelling Egyptians had to put up with. But these conditions were not what an Egyptian of some position readily regarded as ideal. A good idea of the Egyptian 'dream house' may be obtained from examining what sort of house was thought proper to depict in the tomb of a dead person. Many Theban tombs of Eighteenth-dynasty officials of varying status contain scenes in which the deceased is shown standing in front of his house, preparing to make an offering to the gods, and frequently accompanied by his wife. The house is commonly shown standing alone, with trees before and around it, and a garden pool with lotus flowers, water-birds and more trees. Space, water and shade, trees and flowers, seem to have been important elements in the ideal—elements not usually found in the house built in town. It should also be mostly of one storey, although in parts it might rise to two storeys, or have small rooms, storage bins and perhaps even a kitchen on the roof.[16]

A simple, but well-preserved and revealing, example of such a house occurs on the funerary papyrus of Nakhte, a royal scribe and general, who lived towards the end of the Eighteenth Dynasty in Thebes.[17] Nakhte and his wife leave their house to recite a hymn to the sun-god Re. Trees—a fruit-tree and a date-palm—stand before the house, and there is the obligatory pool in the garden. The house is built on a raised platform, the front door reached by a ramp which probably incorporates a stair with shallow treads. This platform possibly served the purpose of raising the house sufficiently high above the surrounding land to preserve it from damp seeping through the floor, and even to protect it from flooding. Such a platform might well be needed for a house built out of town. The house itself is undistinguished. It has a door of substantial proportions, with jambs and a formal lintel designed in the characteristically architectural manner of a temple doorway, these features painted a reddish brown, indicating probably that they are made of wood. Yellow colour is used for the frames and bars of the four windows placed high in the wall, so situated to minimize the amount of direct sunlight entering the rooms within. Window gratings found in houses at Akhetaten are usually made of limestone or a kind of cement, but are often painted reddish brown, no doubt to cut down the glare.[18] The principal doorways of houses at Akhetaten were also sometimes made of stone, but those that have been found are not painted reddish brown.[19] The colour shown on the papyrus picture may, therefore, be deceptive; Nakhte's doors and windows may have been of stone or of wood. Both materials were rather precious, and were used again and again, as they are in villages in modern Egypt. The last visible features of Nakhte's house are two triangular vents on the roof, designed to catch 'the sweet breeze of the north wind', so much beloved and prayed for by the ancient Egyptians. The whole house, apart from the door and the windows, is painted white, representing a whitewash or white-painted plaster applied to the sun-dried mud-brick, which was the common building material for palace and hovel in ancient Egypt. It remains so in the countryside in modern Egypt, the method of brick-making being almost precisely the same as in antiquity. Increasingly, however, the river-bank brickyards of modern Egypt are marked by kilns in which the traditional mud-brick is baked.

Very little of the inside of Nakhte's house can be deduced from the papyrus scene. Much more can be learned from the houses of Djehutnufe depicted in his two Theban tombs, and from the houses at Akhetaten. The former are almost certainly town houses, dating to the middle of the Eighteenth Dynasty, while the latter, although built in a town, are laid out more spaciously, and are about one hundred years later in date. Djehutnufe, a royal scribe and overseer of the treasury, served King Amenophis II, and probably also his predecessor Tuthmosis III. The two tombs he had cut for himself in the Theban necropolis, not much more than two hundred metres apart, may correspond to two stages in his career, one (number 104) being abandoned when his career advanced in the reign of Amenophis II. His second tomb (number 80) is scarcely bigger than the first, perhaps a little better situated, not particularly better or more interestingly decorated. It contains the remains of a scene reminiscent of that found on the papyrus of Nakhte, showing Djehutnufe's house, in form not very unlike Nakhte's. The house is narrow and stands tall, with a large doorway and with one window set high up in what appears to be a kind of structure on the roof; the walls are painted a blue colour to represent plain mud-brick.[20] Certainly no actual house is being pictured here; it is in a sense a token house.

In his other tomb, however, there is a much more informative scene in which his house is shown in section (*Fig. 22*). The interpretation of the section is open to considerable variation. The house appears to have three floors, with additions on the roof, but what is shown may represent not floors but parts of the house which lie on the same level but behind each other. Interpretation is complicated by the selective method used by the artist in showing only certain parts of the house.

Fig. 22 Djehutnufe's house.

Nevertheless, the conclusion which extracts best sense from the scene makes it a house of three storeys,[21] the lowest floor of which is probably a basement or semi-basement in which domestic activities— preparation of bread and making of cloth—take place. This basement is not shown with windows, and it seems possible that it might have been partly open to the street or court. The arrangement of having some of the domestic activities of the household at ground level or even lower was eminently sensible, raising the living quarters of the family high above the street and above possible damp from sub-soil water, or even occasionally a high Nile. The principal floor, which comes next, contains the main reception rooms of the house; on the top floor the house-owner has his office. Bins for the storage of grain stand on the roof, and part of the same area is used apparently for cooking, so that the smells and heat are carried away from the house. The scene is peopled with members of the household engaged in many activities: the spinners and weavers at their spindles and looms, the bakers grinding and sieving grain, servants running upstairs with meat and drink for the kitchens, carrying prepared food to Djehutnufe in his reception room, scribes attending their master in his study, while attendants fan him and offer him refreshment. Incomplete and selective though it is, this representation manages to convey a good idea of the cramped con- ditions and bustle of the town house of a man of some standing in Thebes during the Eighteenth Dynasty. For the details of domestic arrangements absent from tomb scenes we must look to archaeology.

At Akhetaten, a city abandoned before one full generation had lived there, and mostly never built over again, many houses have through excavation revealed their plans. From them much has been learned, even though it must ever be borne in mind that the city was not quite a typical Egyptian settlement. Nevertheless, allowing for the special nature of its foundation and for the lavish use of space in its lay-out, we can find in the design and appointments of the houses, particularly the houses of senior officials, many things that might be expected in the ideal house of the late Eighteenth Dynasty. The essential features

13 (above) The house of the scribe Nakhte, from a vignette in his copy of The Book of the Dead (BM 10471).
  (below) Modest houses at El-Amarna, characterized by the excavators as a 'council' development.

include a large central hall placed in the middle of the house, another hall to the north, possibly a kind of loggia used by the family in hot weather, a small porch and vestibule leading into the second hall, an inner hall for more intimate family gatherings, bedrooms for the family and guests, and a large master's apartment with a bathroom and lavatory adjacent.[22] Such rooms are found not only in the great houses, like that of the vizir Nakhte, which had at least thirty rooms in the main building, but also in the houses built for less important people whose names are not usually known. One of the latter, known by its excavation number V.37.1, had about sixteen rooms.[23] Both houses lay within courtyards, with outhouses for storage and many domestic activities, making use of space in a way which was rarely possible in most ancient towns. Unbaked brick was as usual the main constructional material, but stone was employed for thresholds, door-frames, and the bases of pillars in the larger rooms. The pillars themselves were of wood, either painted or plastered and painted; and wood was also used for roofing beams and for the support of the stairs leading from the central hall to the roof. What exactly happened on the roofs of houses at Akhetaten is not certain, but there is some evidence that a further pillared loggia may in some cases have stood above the main loggia on the ground floor—a place to take the air from the north when the weather was hot and sultry. In the case of the grander houses the stonework of the principal doorways might be carved with inscriptions containing the titles and honours of the house-owners, and in some cases offering texts of a kind more commonly associated with tombs, with the dead rather than with the living.[24] This type of inscription may not be typical of the houses of important Egyptian officials, but may owe its special character to the peculiar circumstances of the Atenist cult under Akhenaten.

Within the houses, the main rooms were brightly and elaborately decorated with painted plaster, the scheme frequently incorporating floral designs; such decorations were not confined to the larger houses. The north loggia in the vizir Nakhte's house was very tastefully

14 (above) Reconstructed wall-painting from a private house at El-Amarna: a
    garland and ducks.
   (below) Two chairs from Thebes, one of simple design (BM 2479), the other with
    lion legs and a back inlaid with ebony and ivory (BM 2480).

decorated. The ceiling, supported by reddish brown columns, was a brilliant blue; the walls, predominantly white, carried near the ceiling a frieze of blue lotus petals on a green ground, above which ran a red band; the floor, made of unbaked tiles, had been painted white originally, and subsequently in a design of bright colours including red and yellow. In house V.37.1 again there were found traces of a frieze of petals, presumably lotus, elaborate pendent swags with flowers and ducks, and shaped and painted plaster in red and white from the roof beams. Sadly the evidence is fragile and very incomplete; but it shows, without the possibility of doubt, that Egyptian house-decoration in the Eighteenth Dynasty was colourful and very lively. It has been pointed out, very properly, that although Akhetaten as a city was unique in its lay-out, in the generosity of its use of space, and in the ethic behind its foundation, yet it is most likely that in decorating their houses the inhabitants of the city were following a tradition well established else-where. In Akhetaten the opportunities were far more considerable, and they were clearly exploited. Happily, enough of the decoration has survived, even if only in a fragmentary state, to provide a convincing taste of its richness and quality.[25]

Not the least interesting information retrieved from Akhetaten concerns the sanitary arrangements found in many houses, and not confined to the greatest. We have already mentioned bathrooms and lavatories. Many houses contain small rooms clearly designed for these purposes, and attached *en suite* to what is usually designated the master bedroom. Archaeological evidence, unfortunately, does not reveal the extent to which these rooms were available for use by members of a household apart from the master, and the possibility of their exclusive use by him and his wife should not be ruled out. The bathroom is identified by a limestone bath-slab, set in a corner with the two adjacent walls lined with thin limestone slabs—splash slabs to protect the mud-brick of the walls.[26] The bath-slab usually has a slight depression to contain the water poured over the bathing person, and a spout at one side to lead the water either into a channel drain running through the wall of the house to the outside, or into a large pot set into the floor of the bathroom. In one house of fairly moderate size the outlet through the wall was filled with a tubular pot with the bottom knocked out, to serve as a conduit.[27] It led to a large pottery vessel containing a small dish which was probably used to bale out the collected water. It is assumed that the person taking a bath stood on the limestone slab and had water poured over him, perhaps from behind a low wall by a servant. The careful collection of the water was, no doubt, arranged to prevent the floor of the bathroom from becoming a muddy and unpleasant marsh.

Close to the bathroom in many houses lies the lavatory, equipped as a dry closet, with fittings of some elaboration.[28] In only a few cases have seats survived, but the arrangement of two brick walls of appropriate height, designed to carry a seat of stone or wood, indicates quite clearly that the advanced lavatory of Akhetaten—and it may be assumed of properly appointed houses of New-kingdom Egypt in general—was of the seated kind, and not of the squatting sort which prevails in many parts of the Eastern world (including Egypt) in present times. A very fine stone seat was found, not in position, in one relatively unimportant house in Akhetaten in 1930. It measures 55 cm. by 45 cm. and the carefully curved depression in the upper surface offers a comfortable seat for the person of moderate size. A hole of keyhole shape completes the design.[29] It is thought that a pottery vessel placed between the brick supports served as the necessary receptacle. In some cases there are small brick-built boxes by the sides of the lavatories, almost certainly containers for sand to be thrown into the pottery vessel after use.

The extent to which the Akhetaten lavatories are representative of ancient Egyptian sanitary arrangements is a matter of great uncertainty. So few houses have survived elsewhere, and even fewer of these in states sufficiently complete to provide adequate and reliable evidence. The generally smaller houses of the workmen who prepared the royal tombs at Thebes, to be considered shortly, have no clearly defined rooms or niches for baths or for lavatories. Yet some idea of Eighteenth-dynasty domestic practice may be drawn from an object found in the burial chamber of Kha, a senior official in the hierarchy of the workmen's community during the middle reigns of the dynasty.[30] It is a low stool of sturdy construction with a hole cut out from the coved seat (*Fig. 23*). It could certainly have been used in conjunction with a pottery vessel as a portable easing-stool, to be placed and used wherever convenient in a house.[31] Another wooden stool with an opening in the top and of very heavy construction, found in the Theban tomb of Khnummose, an agricultural scribe of about the same date as Kha, has been similarly identified.[32] This identification, however, has been challenged on the rather slender grounds that a Theban tomb is just as likely to have contained a birth-stool.[33] Unfortunately the width of the

Fig. 23 The lavatory stool from the tomb of Kha.

opening through which in theory the newly born baby would descend is barely more than 15 cm., scarcely sufficient for a normal-sized baby to pass through.[34]

Portable lavatories of the kind just described would certainly have removed the need for special closet-rooms in small houses, and their general use would also provide an explanation for the absence of extensive surviving evidence. Most Egyptian furniture preserved from antiquity has come from tombs, and what has been found represents only a small fraction of what was buried in ancient times, and an even smaller fraction of what was actually used in Egyptian houses. Much household furniture placed in tomb equipments was not made specially for burial, and undoubtedly came from the houses of the tomb-owners, selected at the time of death. It may be thought probable that the easing-stool was not considered suitable in many cases for inclusion. There can, however, be little doubt that seated lavatories, whether fixed or portable, were not uncommon in Eighteenth-dynasty houses. And there is good evidence to show that the practice went back to the beginning of the Dynastic Period. Some Second-dynasty tombs in North Saqqara, with internal room arrangements apparently designed to reproduce house-plans, contained lavatories with fixed features. They had, it seems, seats, but the excavator has provided no details of their construction.[35] Nevertheless, it would be quite wrong to conclude that the ancient Egyptians, generally speaking, made use of specially built lavatories; most people, no doubt, went into the fields, if they were accessible, or used simple sand or earth trays which could be emptied into one of the refuse dumps which received all household waste.

The Egyptians were practical and, for the most part, tidy in the disposal of what was not wanted. Dig a hole and throw in what had to be thrown away. In Karnak they dug a huge hole in the court just in front of the Seventh Pylon, and filled it with hundreds of pieces of sculpture which had cluttered up the courts and halls of the great temple. At Deir el-Medina a great hole was used as a vast waste-paper basket, into which thousands of inscribed ostraca were thrown. If you lived near the Nile, the river served as a convenient rubbish dump and sewer, as it does still in many parts of Egypt where modern services are not provided.[36] Where the river was too far away, rubbish and household refuse were deposited on open ground, in dumps or in pits which might be specially dug, or be the result of excavations for brick-making and other purposes. The traces of many dumps and pits in and around the various quarters of Akhetaten have been found in the course of excavations,[37] and particularly interesting evidence came to light in the work on the North Suburb.[38] Here it could be shown that in the early stages of building in the north-western quarter rubbish pits were dug in what was probably common ground beyond the line of the first, rather substantial, houses. Subsequently, other lines of houses were added, and the areas between were filled up with smaller houses, described by the excavators (perhaps too dramatically) as 'hovels'. These small houses with insubstantial walls were in many cases built over filled-in rubbish pits, the contents of which later contracted, leading to subsidence and the collapse of house walls. The owner of one house, it was noted, finding it necessary to build his corn-bin over a rubbish pit, set fire to the contents of the pit before building his bin above it. The burning is interpreted as disinfection by the excavators, and it is not uncommonly stated, on the basis of this one case apparently, that rubbish pits were disinfected by burning.[39] Disinfection in Egypt, however, is most generally effected though the heat of the sun. It seems more likely that the burning of the contents of a rubbish pit was designed to reduce its contents to a compact mass, so as to avoid later subsidence when it was built over.

In Akhetaten water was obtained from wells, its ultimate source being the Nile by sub-soil infiltration.[40] Many of the larger estates possessed their own wells; but most houses received their supplies from public wells that were carefully dug and provided with properly constructed well-houses. A stair following the circular contour of the excavation led down to a platform set above the water level, which in general seems to have been at about eight metres below the ground surface. The water was raised possibly by a well-sweep with counterpoise, like the modern Egyptian *shaduf*, but also, no doubt, more laboriously by the hand-filling of jars. Water was not so easily obtained at the workmen's village of Deir el-Medina at Thebes. Set high on a rocky saddle well away from the Nile and the cultivation, it provided no possibility for the digging of wells; all water had to be brought on donkey-back or by human hand from the valley. Water-points were established at places around the main settlement, and great pottery containers provided to hold the precious liquid. From these points water would be distributed to individual houses within the village, or to intermediate water-points within the village area.[41] There is evidence that these arrangements were greatly improved in the reign of Tuthmosis III, who in consequence received special devotion from the inhabitants of the village.[42] Because of the particular character of this village, its restricted nature and isolated location, very careful controls over maintenance and development were apparently exercised, if the evidence of excavation can be trusted.

Bernard Bruyère, who completed the modern clearance of the village, and published a comprehensive account of its buildings and characteristics, was an unusually careful and observant excavator. He noticed that the ground level of the main village, within the walls established at first as early as the reign of Tuthmosis I (*c.* 1500 BC) remained unchanged through centuries of occupation. In this respect the village differed markedly from the typical settlement described earlier in this chapter, where successive generations built upon the crumbled and levelled remains of previous occupations. House tenure was more strictly controlled in the workmen's village than elsewhere; properties tended to pass from father to son, as did their trades and professions. Constrained by the village limits, house-owners were not normally in a position to increase the sizes of their houses, as so often happened elsewhere. With few exceptions, and those mostly in later official extensions of the village, the workmen's houses conformed to a type which is often cited as characteristic of the houses of Egyptians who were not of the humblest categories of society, or of the ranks of officialdom. The peculiar nature of the village of Deir el-Medina may not be ignored, but it may also be considered as representative of a settled community with long-established practices and traditions, in contradistinction to those other surviving ancient Egyptian settlements which were perhaps of less durable purpose.

The inhabitants of this workmen's village were not notably well favoured in the nature of their houses. They formed a homogeneous community of highly skilled craftsmen, protected and provided with most of the necessities for living; but they were still representatives of a modest stratum of society. As such they were nevertheless fortunate in being specially housed, and the complaints which are raised in the many documents surviving from the village are in the main concerned with the failure or the inadequacy of rations and services, but not with housing. By modern Western standards, the workmen's houses were tiny; but not so, perhaps, by the standards of the mediaeval journeyman craftsman, or certainly by those of the inhabitants of many present-day Egyptian villages. Within the walled village space was severely restricted, but the villagers seem rather to have drawn strength and a lively community spirit from their crowded conditions than to have developed claustrophobic tendencies. The plan of most of the houses in the village is long and narrow, one room wide, running back from one of the village streets to the enclosure wall.[43] The largest houses are about 27 m. long and 6 m. wide; the smallest not much more than 13m. long and 4m. wide; while the average might be set at about 20 m. by 4 m. Where the excavation of the houses has been careful and vigilant, it has been noted that, although there were numerous rebuildings during the centuries of the village's occupation, the general plan of individual houses tends to follow the pattern established in the first period of construction during the Eighteenth Dynasty. The walls of the houses, as far as can be established, rose to between three and five metres, and there is no evidence for second storeys; indeed the walls of the houses are mostly too thin to have supported building above (*Fig. 24*).[44]

Entering the house from the street, the visitor descended two or three steps into a room roughly square, with a vent for light and air in the roof. The lower parts of the walls were painted white. In one corner stood a brick structure with something of the nature of a boxed bed with sides sometimes reaching to the roof. Its inner surface stood about seventy-five centimetres above the floor of the room, and a small brick stairway gave access. Its purpose in a room which was essentially one of reception remains undetermined. Bernard Bruyère, who studied the

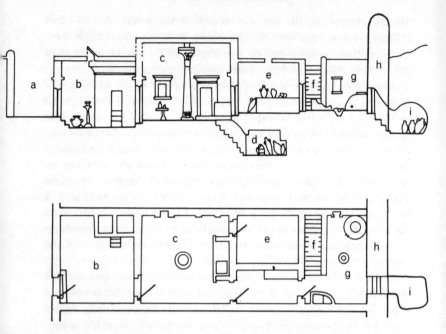

Fig. 24 Plan and section of a typical workman's house at Deir el-Medina: a. street; b. room with boxed bed; c. reception room; d. cellar; e. storeroom/bedroom; f. stair to roof; g. kitchen; h. village wall; i. cellar.

village houses in great detail, came to the conclusion that it had some devotional function, particularly as a few examples retained traces of painting showing representations of the household deity Bes, a leonine dwarf of terrifying appearance but of benevolent purpose.[45] It may also have accommodated a bed used by the house-owner and his wife, or by his wife before labour. Whatever its function, its position of prominence in the room first entered establishes its importance among the fittings of the average house. This outer room was, it is thought, the place frequented mostly by the women of the house.

The next room, entered from the outer room, was commonly the largest room in the house. Its floor was higher than that of the outer room, and its ceiling was higher still, made of palm-logs and thatch, and supported by one or two wooden columns resting on stone bases. The room might have been lighted by a kind of clerestory window set high in the wall separating the first two rooms of the house. A low brick platform or divan marked the place where the house-owner might have sat to conduct business and receive guests, and where he might have laid his bed. The walls of this room contained niches for sacred images, in some cases busts for a cult of ancestor worship which was specially evident at Deir el-Medina. One or more blind, or false, doors might be set, like niches, in the walls also; these too may have had some function connected with the cults of family and of patron deity. In some cases symbolic offerings or the remains of real offerings were found placed before these false doors, the lintels and jambs of which might be inscribed with texts confirming the religious character of these features.[46] In the floor near the divan was a hole covered with a trap-door, leading to a cellar by way of a short stairway, in which the few special possessions of the house were kept. This large room might be distinguished as the place frequented mostly by the men of the family.

Opening off the principal living-room of the house was a small chamber which seems to have been used both as a general store-room and as a place where someone might sleep. Its floor might be higher than that of the principal room, but its ceiling was regularly lower. Beyond this room and reached by a short corridor was the kitchen and also a stairway leading to the roof of the house. It was probably the case that members of the household slept on the roof as a general rule. Families, as recorded on the funerary stelae found in many of the tombs constructed in the neighbourhood, were often quite large, although it may be doubted whether all those recorded members would have been alive, or living at home, at the same time. Nevertheless, substantially sized families could be accommodated in such small dwellings only if sleeping arrangements were of a kind which might now be thought very casual. Bedding could be laid in any room or on the roof as circumstances required, and very little privacy could be expected, except by the house-owner.

The kitchen,[47] frequently the room furthest from the entrance of the house, was lightly roofed with branches and straw, a covering dense enough to shield the occupants from the sun, but open enough to allow smoke to escape. In one corner was the oven for baking bread, fitted internally with a series of pottery stages, and plastered outside with mud. Surviving remains of such ovens show on the outside circular impressions, made apparently by applying the neck of a small pot while the mud plaster was wet. The impressions were not necessarily arranged in a clear pattern, and their purpose—to judge from similar impressions found on modern peasant ovens of almost the same design—was to prevent the plaster from cracking when the oven was heated. The kitchen might also contain stone mortars for pounding grain, set in the floor, and a kneading trough built against a wall and whitewashed. Here again there might be a niche for a divine figure, possibly of one of those household deities favoured by the ancient Egyptians and considered protectors against the common hazards of everyday life—snakes, scorpions, evil spirits. Some houses in addition had a second cellar reached by stairs from the kitchen and used to store provisions.

A visit to Deir el-Medina does not encourage one to envy the living arrangements of the ancient craftsman. The houses are small, crowded and unattractive in their ruined state. Yet there is much to suggest that in antiquity, when the village was in its prime, the houses were of very different appearance. Traces of painting show that the principal rooms were not only partly whitewashed, but also decorated with colourful paintings, quite different from those found in the grander houses of Akhetaten. Divine figures might be found in the areas with ritual characteristics, and others of non-religious themes elsewhere.[48] And a house always looks better when it is furnished.

Very little identifiable furniture was discovered in the houses of the village in the course of excavation, but a very good idea of what might have been found in such a house during the Eighteenth Dynasty is provided by the furniture included in the funerary equipment of the 'overseer of work', Kha, also given the title 'chief', whose unplundered burial chamber was excavated at Deir el-Medina in the hillside over-looking the village in 1906. All the objects found in this chamber are now in the Egyptian Museum in Turin, and they provide the most complete conspectus of the domestic furniture of an artisan's house discovered in Egypt.

Kha lived during the reigns of Amenophis II, Tuthmosis IV and Amenophis III (c. 1440–1370 BC), and died before the religious up-heavals of the reign of Akhenaten. It is not known whether his house was inside the walled village, but it is not unlikely that at that relatively early date in the history of the settlement most of the senior workmen, among whose ranks Kha should be numbered, lived within the walls. Over thirty items found in the burial may be considered as typical pieces of furniture of the kind used in everyday life. Many of these pieces are very simple in materials and workmanship, others are good examples of the joiner's craft; some are decorated with paintings of a non-religious nature; others have funerary texts and scenes. To judge on the superficial grounds of simplicity and appearance, most of the items could have passed directly from house to tomb; even most of those rendered explicitly funerary by texts could have been part of Kha's household equipment, inscribed suitably after his death. A survey of what was found should give a fair idea of what might have been seen in the house of a senior workman at Deir el-Medina in the Eighteenth Dynasty.[49]

The furniture may, very generally, be classified under four headings: pieces to sit on, pieces to lie on, pieces to put things in, and pieces to put things on. Of the pieces to sit on, the most common throughout Egyptian history were stools, i.e. chairs without backs. In Kha's tomb there were nine stools. Four are of the kind frequently shown in contemporary tomb scenes, used by the guests at the feasts which were both celebratory and funerary; they are of fretted construction with shaped, or coved, seats, three of which are made of woven rushes. Two others, functioning as seats in essentially the same way, are differently designed, one with lion legs, the other with shaped legs giving the erroneous appearance of having been turned. The most elaborate stool is of a folding construction with a leather seat, of which only traces remain; its supports end in duck heads inlaid with ivory, grasping in their beaks the cross-bars which provide stability to the piece. This stool, unlike most of the furniture in the tomb, is made of hard wood, imported from tropical Africa—a choice piece which shows no sign of having been made specially for the tomb. Two three-legged stools represent the kind of seat often shown used by craftsmen; they were particularly useful where the floor might not be very level. The most elaborate piece from Kha's tomb is a chair with a sloping back and woven rush seat, painted with gaily coloured designs, some of which represent the kind of intricate inlay in ivory, ebony and glass found on even more expensively produced furniture. This chair may have been specially prepared for Kha's burial, as the inscriptions on it suggest; but in plainer state it may well have been Kha's particular seat in his house during his lifetime.

One further stool-shaped piece was included in the tomb equipment, the piece with a pierced seat, mentioned already in this chapter (p. 227).

It is very sturdily but rather roughly made, and may have been used as a portable easing-stool.

Two beds were found in the tomb, one for Kha and the other, it would seem, for his wife, Meryt, who was also buried in the same tomb. In design the beds are simple but elegant examples of the traditional form: low, with short legs shaped like lion legs walking apparently backwards. The beds rise in a graceful sweep to the head ends; what would in modern beds be described as head-boards are in fact foot-boards. The mattresses are of woven rush supported in each bed by two carefully shaped cross-pieces to prevent sagging. If these beds were actually used by Kha and Meryt in their lifetimes they would have taken up a great deal of room in their house. The larger bed is 1.93 m. long, and the smaller 1.74 m.; neither was apparently made specially for the tomb.

The bed linen needed for these beds was found in great quantity stored in the wooden chests in the tomb. Chests of various designs were used for the storing of all things in the house which needed some kind of protection. Chests of drawers and cupboards were not found in the ancient Egyptian house, although the idea of the drawer was known to the Egyptian joiner, as mentioned earlier, while the typical shrine with doors opening in the side embodied the essential design of the cup-board. There were eleven chests in Kha's tomb, some with flat tops, others with gabled tops; some plain; others decorated in bright colours with geometrical and floral patterns and with scenes showing Kha and Meryt receiving funerary offerings. The patterns on these last chests copy in paint the complicated inlays of fine woods, ivory and faience found on the very best of the chests surviving from royal and noble tombs. Chests used in the house to store linen and other articles would require no decoration, but a few, which might be found in the principal rooms of a house, might have been decorated with painted patterns of the kind found on five of Kha's chests.

Three different kinds of table were included in Kha's tomb equip-ment. Two are simple, but of sturdy construction, about 70 cm. long, 40 cm. wide, and 50 cm. high, and capable of standing considerable use, and carrying substantial weights. Lightweight tables made of dried reeds, with the tops and joints held together with bindings of rush, were used in the tomb to support food offerings for Kha and Meryt. Although these flimsy pieces are not very robust, they could easily be replaced and may well have been used as portable tables to be carried up to the roof of the house, or even out of doors, as occasion required. The third type of table is quite unusual, and is represented by a single example. Its frame is solid; its legs are splayed and braced, all the principal members being circular in section. The top is made of slats, spaced with small gaps between them. Schiaparelli, the tomb's excavator, called it a 'garden table', and indeed it does have some resemblance to the kind of bamboo furniture once commonly found in gardens and conservatories. If it had a special use in ancient Egypt, that use is quite undetermined.

Kha's tomb furniture contained many other objects which might have come straight from his house: vessels of bronze, alabaster and pottery, toilet objects in special boxes, a large chest possibly fitted to hold a wig, lamp stands and lamps. To judge from the contents of his tomb, Kha's house was certainly furnished with a large variety of well-built, well-designed pieces, some of which were painted to copy the fine inlaid furniture of the houses of the great. His house may not have been large, but it was comfortable and made cheerful with mural paintings, coloured textiles and possibly even flowers, although the last may have been hard to come by regularly in the isolation of Deir el-Medina. Things would have been even better in the villas of Akhetaten, but distinctly worse in the crowded tenements of the large towns. It would be wrong to pretend that the average ancient Egyptian house was much more than a place in which the essential acts of life took place. But the possibility of achieving something above the average was not beyond the hope of the talented craftsman.

NOTES

1 A. H. Gardiner, *Ancient Egyptian Onomastica*, II, 10* f.
2 Ibid., 22*.
3 For most see H. W. Fairman in *Town Planning Review* 20 (Liverpool, 1949), 32 ff.
4 But not the workmen's village of Deir el-Medina which was continuously occupied by families for many generations. See M. L. Bierbrier, *The Tomb-Builders of the Pharaohs*.
5 Page 94 above.
6 See B. J. Kemp in P. Ucko, R. Tringham and G. W. Dimbleby (eds.), *Man, Settlement and Urbanism* (London, 1972), 657 ff.
7 H. W. Fairman, op. cit., 37: B. J. Kemp, op. cit., 673.
8 Kemp, loc. cit.
9 See p. 174.
10 British Museum Papyrus 10524; see S. R. K. Glanville, *Catalogue of Demotic Papyri in the British Museum*, I (London, 1939), 20 ff. The translation from the demotic Egyptian text is substantially that of Glanville.
11 Possibly a building connected with the cult of the Buchis bull and its mother; see Glanville, op. cit., xxi ff.
12 U. Hölscher, *The Excavation of Medinet Habu*, V. *Post-Ramessid Remains* (Chicago, 1954), 4 ff.
13 Ibid., 6–7.
14 Ibid., 7.
15 Ibid., 8.
16 See N. de G. Davies in *Metropolitan Museum Studies*, I (New York, 1929), 233 ff.
17 British Museum Papyrus 10471. See Pl. 13 (*above*).
18 T. E. Peet and C. L. Woolley, *City of Akhenaten*, I (London, 1923), 40 f., pl. VI, 4; cf. British Museum no. 63517 which is painted reddish brown.
19 Ibid., 37. Some internal stonework in Amarna houses was painted reddish brown, cf. p. 41.
20 For a drawing, much restored, see Davies in *Metropolitan Museum Studies*, I, 237 (fig. 2), 240 f.
21 Ibid., 234 ff.
22 A good general description by S. Lloyd in *Journal of Egyptian Archaeology* 19 (London, 1933), 1 ff. For detailed descriptions, see *City of Akhenaten*, I and II (details of authors etc. in n. 44 to Chapter 7).
23 For Nakhte's house, see *City of Akhenaten*, I, 5 ff., pl. III; for house V.37.1, *City of Akhenaten*, II, 5 ff., pl. III.
24 For example, the lintel of Hatiay, see *City of Akhenaten*, II, 109, pl. XXIII, 4.
25 Especially, H. Frankfort, *The Mural Paintings of El-'Amarneh* (London, 1929), and particularly 31 ff. for the decoration of the houses. Also see Pl. 14 (*above*).
26 Many examples are described in *City of Akhenaten*, I and II; also H. Ricke, *Der Grundriss des Amarna-Wohnhauses* (Leipzig, 1932).
27 *City of Akhenaten*, I, 29.
28 Ibid., 46.
29 *City of Akhenaten*, II, 47 and pl. XLII, 3.

30 Kha's furniture is more fully described later in this chapter.

31 Identified as such in H. Ricke, op. cit., 35, fig. 34; also illustrated in H. Baker, *Furniture in the Ancient World*, 116, fig. 155.

32 H. Ricke, loc. cit., fig. 33.

33 M. Pillet in *Annales du Service des Antiquités de l'Égypte* 52 (Cairo, 1952), 90 f.

34 The stool is 44 cm. long and 30 cm. high. Its width is not given by Pillet, loc. cit., but from the published photograph it can hardly be more than 35 cm.

35 J. E. Quibell, *Archaic Mastabas* (Cairo, 1923), 29, 31, pls. XXX (tombs 2302, 2307, 2337), XXXI, 3.

36 A brief survey of the evidence is given by D. M. Dixon in P. Ucko, etc. (eds.), *Man, Settlement and Urbanism* (London, 1972), 647 ff.

37 Especially W. M. F. Petrie, *Tell el Amarna* (London, 1894), 15f., where he describes the palace dumps extending over an area of about 180 m. by 120 m.

38 *City of Akhenaten*, II, 3.

39 For example, H. W. Fairman in *Town Planning Review* 20, 39; Dixon, op. cit., 648.

40 H. Ricke, *Der Grundriss des Amarna-Wohnhauses*, 45; *City of Akhenaten*, I, 48; *City of Akhenaten*, II, 61.

41 See B. Bruyère, *Rapport sur les fouilles de Deir el Médineh* (1934–1935), Part III (Cairo, 1939), 33 f.

42 Ibid., 7

43 Generally, see B. Bruyère, op. cit., 50 ff. The measurements are extracted from the detailed map of the village, pl. XXIX.

44 Ibid., 28.

45 Ibid., 54–64.

46 Ibid., 67 ff.

47 Ibid., 72 ff.

48 For example, ibid., 255, 257, 259 for fragments of paintings of the god Bes; see 273–4 for an extraordinary painting of a dancer which has been fully described and discussed by J. Vandier d'Abbadie in *Revue d'Égyptologie* 3 (1938), 26.

49 The furniture of Kha is illustrated and described in E. Schiaparelli, *Relazione sui lavori della missione archeologica italiana in Egitto* (1903–1920), II. *La tomba intatta dell'architetto Cha* (Turin, 1927), 112 ff. It is discussed as a group in H. Baker, *Furniture in the Ancient World*, 114 ff. The textual evidence for furniture at Deir el-Medina is surveyed in J. J. Janssen, *Commodity Prices from the Ramessid Period*, 180 ff.

9

DOMESTIC ECONOMY

In an earlier chapter the plight of the Eloquent Peasant was described. He fell into difficulties when his donkey stepped out of line and sampled the barley crop in the fields of the scheming official Djehutinakhte. The peasant, Khunanpu, was on his way from the Wadi Natrun to the Faiyum to trade the produce of his own small-holding for provisions for his family: 'This peasant said to his wife, "See! I am going down to Egypt to bring back provisions for my children from there . . ." Then this peasant went down to Egypt having loaded his donkeys with reeds' and a dozen or more other products, including plants, hides, wood, natron, salt, birds, 'making up all the good products of the Wadi Natrun'. The named products are mostly of unidentified nature, and it may be doubted whether they represent anything more than a fantasy collection of mostly exotic items. They had in sum, nevertheless, to add up to a fairly valuable consignment, on the one hand capable of being converted into food (of unspecified kinds, but probably grain) for Khunanpu's family, and on the other hand sufficiently tempting to attract the greedy attention of Djehutinakhte.

How then could a value be placed on these goods? How further could Khunanpu set about converting them into provisions to take back to the Wadi Natrun? As the story of the wretched peasant progresses, it tells how his donkey, forced off the path by the wiles of Djehutinakhte, passes by the latter's standing barley crop and eats a trifling quantity, probably one head, of the barley. The landowner reacts strongly: 'See! I shall take your donkey, peasant, for eating my barley.' Khunanpu in outrage retorts: 'My path is all right. One (scrap of barley only) is damaged. For its value[1] shall I buy back my donkey, should you take it for filling its mouth with a scrap of barley.' In so saying Khunanpu expresses a practical solution for the simple matter of his donkey's having eaten some of Djehutinakhte's barley. It is a straight commercial transaction as he sees it. But Djehutinakhte is determined to treat the donkey's eating as a theft, and therefore as a criminal act, to be punished severely by the confiscation of all Khunanpu's property. We have seen how the matter developed in the earlier chapter. Let us here consider how the story might have gone if Khunanpu's solution had been accepted by Djehutinakhte.

How could the two parties arrive at a satisfactory agreement on the proper value of the one head of barley? In what terms would the value be expressed? How, finally, could Khunanpu settle his debt? The specific matter of one head of barley is perhaps too trifling to serve as an example, and indeed Khunanpu's proposal should probably be taken as sarcastic. Yet in a peasant economy, as Egypt's was for the most part in antiquity, small transactions are commonplace and need a machinery for their execution. But size is not of concern here; procedure is what is of interest. In the simplest sense the value of the head of barley needs to be expressed in terms of another commodity which is available to Khunanpu. He may then hand over the proper amount of this second commodity to Djehutinakhte in settlement of the transaction.

In Egypt for practically the whole of the Pharaonic Period money in the form of coinage was not known. It has been argued that a kind of standard metal piece was used from the New Kingdom,[2] and we shall consider this possibility later on. But no coins in the strictest sense were minted in Egypt until the Thirtieth Dynasty (380–343 BC), long after they had been used as common currency in the Greek world. What is more, coins minted outside Egypt before the Thirtieth Dynasty did not generally circulate in Egypt as coins of accepted value even in those places where Greeks and other foreigners worked and traded in numbers. Before regular issues were instituted in Egypt, coins from elsewhere were traded for their bullion value, and many of those of early date found in hoards represent a kind of silver raw material or even waste which could be melted down for purposes other than currency, like the silver cups and jewellery of the Tod Treasure, and the Amarna hoard described earlier (p. 186).[3]

The basis of trade in Egypt before coinage was introduced and accepted was barter, and it may be assumed that even after the introduction of a native coinage the system of barter continued for most practical purposes especially in the simple transactions of the countryside. It has been pointed out that in the last years of the pre-coinage era the use of coins from outside Egypt was wholly one-sided.[4] Coins were silver, and silver had a value in the barter system; goods could be acquired with silver coin because goods could be valued against silver as such. There is some evidence that valuations in terms of metal were being used as early as the Old Kingdom,[5] but the rich evidence for such valuations comes from the New Kingdom, and in particular from the abundant secular records left by the necropolis workers of Deir el-Medina, which have been exhaustively studied in recent years.[6] It may, however, be questioned to what extent—even in small communities within Egyptian society that enjoyed some acquaintance with precious metals—were silver and gold regarded as the standards in establishing an acceptable scale of equivalences for the purpose of trade in daily commerce. They may have been so regarded among the necropolis workers, but not in places away from the metropolitan centres of trade and affairs.

It is most unlikely that Khunanpu, in estimating what he might have to give Djehutinakhte in recompense for the head of barley eaten by his donkey, would have reduced the matter to valuation in terms of metal. If his payment had been uncomplicated by the suggestion of a theft, he could have established some simple equivalent in terms of one of the common commodities used in daily trade. In this same way would he have 'sold' the produce which he had brought from the Wadi Natrun, acquiring in exchange the goods he wanted to take home, either directly by a straight trade between his produce and the desired goods, or indirectly by trading his produce for goods which he could in turn trade for the items on his shopping-list. Evidence of how such transactions were carried out is exceptionally rare from all periods, even from those for which so much information on prices and values is available. Some idea of the process in action can, however, be obtained from the letters and accounts of the small-holder Hekanakhte who lived in the early Middle Kingdom, and whose affairs have already provided us with useful examples in earlier chapters.

Hekanakhte's home and principal holding of land, as it would seem, lay at a place called Nebeseyet, which was probably a few miles to the south of Thebes in the direction of the modern town of Armant. In addition to the land which he farmed himself, he held several plots which he rented out to others, and he further could contemplate the leasing of additional land for the use of his own family. The status of the various plots of land is not made clear, but Hekanakhte talks about them for the most part as if they were properly his own. He might have acquired the plots by inheritance, by purchase, by confiscation, by gift, as payment for services rendered in the form of endowments, or even by renting. His title to any or all of these lands might have been tenuous in the ultimate, but in undisturbed times, provided he paid his taxes (or received immunity from payment), he could treat the lands as his own, to plant as he wished, to rent out, or otherwise to dispose of.

The processes by which land might be rented, and the renting paid for, are set out in the letters written by Hekanakhte to his family. Regrettably, as is commonly the case, not as much detail is provided as we would like. The following passage is perhaps the most explicit:

> Get Heti's son Nakhte to go down with Sinebnut to Perha'a to cultivate [for us] 5 acres of land on rent; and they shall take its rent from the cloth woven where you are. Now if they have collected the value in exchange for the emmer-wheat that is in Perha'a, they shall use it there also. You will have no more concern then with the cloth about which I said: 'Weave it, and they shall take it when it has been valued in Nebeseyet, and rent land against its value'.[7]

Here people from Hekanakhte's household are instructed to go to Perha'a to rent land for cultivation, using either a newly woven length of cloth which would need to be valued for this purpose, or part of the proceeds of a quantity of emmer-wheat for which also a value needs to be obtained. If the emmer-wheat can be used, the cloth could be reserved for some other purpose. Renting and valuation are mentioned as if a monetary system operated: for the land £x, for the cloth £y, for the emmer-wheat £z, none of the sums being identified, although x and y might be almost the same, while z should be more. While x, y, and z are all unknown, so also is the unit of value represented here by £, the sign for pound-sterling in our modern monetary system. What would have been the equivalent unit for Hekanakhte? The quick answer might be that the unit alone was not more important than the medium of exchange, and that the medium might change from time to time or according to the circumstances in which particular transactions took place.

In an agricultural community the commodities available for trading were the products of the field, either directly like the emmer-wheat, or indirectly, through domestic manufacture, like cloth woven from flax, itself one of the common products of Egyptian agriculture in antiquity.

The other regular crop was barley. A little later in the same letter Hekanakhte grumbles: 'When I came hither southwards you had reckoned to me the rent of 7½ acres of land in barley [alone] . . . Do not sow with the barley belonging to it,[8] because you have made the renting of it unpleasant as far as I am concerned, with barley alone and its seed.' Here he complains about the possible misuse of barley, although the precise meaning of his words is uncertain. He writes at a time of shortage when barley in particular was not easily available. It may be that his complaint concerns the use of barley and no other commodity for the renting of land on his behalf, when barley could ill be afforded. But mixed with this annoyance is the fear that Merisu, his son probably, might squander the barley.

In a second letter, in which he follows up some of the topics discussed in the first, Hekanakhte returns to the renting of the 5 acres:

> Now see! I have sent you by Sihathor 24 copper *debens*[9] for the renting of land. Now let 5(?) acres of land be cultivated for us in Perha'a beside Hau the Younger('s land), with copper, or with clothes, or with barley, or with anything else(?), but only when you have collected the value there(?) of oil or of anything else.

Again it is not easy to understand precisely what is being instructed here. The renting of the land can be paid for in copper, clothes, barley or any other commodity, but apparently not directly. First the 'capital' commodity has to be exchanged for oil or anything else and, presumably, the payment is made in this 'neutral' product. The purpose of this intermediate conversion is not made clear; it was possibly a common practice in making a formal transaction like the renting of land. A certain commodity might be specified as the acceptable currency as far as the payee is concerned. The transaction can then be compared with a payment made in one monetary currency for something priced in another currency; the first currency has to be changed into the second, specified, currency before payment can be made. By such specification the payee can be more certain of receiving precisely what he requires than by accepting some roughly equivalent payment in one or more commodities different from what he needs.

If this procedure was regular for all but casual transactions, it would confirm that even in a system based on barter, a fair degree of precision could be achieved. In this particular case of Hekanakhte's renting, the mention of 24 copper *debens* is of special interest, although it might be a mistake to draw too precise conclusions from it. The letter says quite clearly '24 copper *debens*', not '24 *debens* of copper', which ought to signify 24 pieces of copper each weighing one *deben*. They had been sent for the payment of the land rent, not, apparently, because they were a kind of coin, but because they were a convertible commodity, and easily portable by Sihathor. They, like the clothes or the barley, needed to be converted into the right kind of 'currency' to be used for payment. Nevertheless, the idea of pieces of metal to be used for payment comes strangely close to the conception of the coin. It is interesting to see in this case how the idea of metal as a currency carries no special significance.

What does not emerge from the discussions of value and payment in these two letters is the way by which the relative values of standard commodities were established. In the countryside, where the common agricultural products formed the basic structure of the system of barter, some general relationships undoubtedly existed, established by custom and usage, and fluctuating according to the season and the availability and quality of the products. It would be known in broad terms how much barley might be needed to exchange for a quantity of flax or of emmer-wheat. But in any transaction the generally accepted relationship between products probably served as the starting-point in the striking of a bargain. The party to a bargain with the stronger position would inevitably do better in the outcome. In a third letter written by Hekanakhte, but never sent to its addressee, the former states his position, and sets out his requirements in the matter of debts to be collected by Heti's son Nakhte and Sinebnut. Quantities of emmer-wheat and barley are listed by the names of the people in Hekanakhte's debt—they probably represent rents for leased lands—and at the end he says: 'Now he who will give me the equivalent in oil shall give me one liquid measure for two bushels of barley, or for three bushels of emmer-wheat.'[10] Here an alternative method of settling the debts is set out: what is owed in grain can be paid in oil,[11] using comparative valuations which may represent roughly the local, semi-official, rates of exchange; but, in being acceptable to Hekanakhte, they are probably biased towards his advantage. Oil, however, for him is second best, for he adds: 'But see! I prefer to be given my property in barley.' His preference implies that even in the cases where quantities of emmer-wheat are owed, the payment can best be made in barley, using, presumably, the ratio of value 2:3, expressed above.

The preferential position enjoyed by someone like Hekanakhte in transactions designed to favour himself, could be further enhanced by the introduction of conditions potentially disadvantageous to the other parties. Such might be the specification of how the products which served as payment should be measured. He might be owed five bushels of grain. How could he ensure that he received the right amount? No doubt there were measures of length, capacity and weight available in the offices of government or in the temple precincts, checked and calibrated against known standards. Measures used for official purposes might require regular checking against these standards. But what happened in non-official transactions, away from the possible surveillance of the officers of government? Then one side or the other would provide the required measure, which might not be wholly accurate. Of the collection of the grain owed to him Hekanakhte says: 'Now see! I have got them to bring the corn-measure in which it is to be measured; it is decked with black hide.' In an account document found with the letters, quantities of owed grain are listed, followed by the note, 'being what is to be measured in the big measure which is in Nebeseyet'.[12] It is clear, therefore, that Hekanakhte protected his interests by ensuring that his own measuring vessel was used in the collection of what he was owed. It does not follow that his measure was false in any way; but its use served as a kind of assurance for him against fraud by the other parties to a transaction. His declared preference for grain as against oil for the settlement of what he was owed is also made more reasonable: grain could be checked in his own measure, while oil might not so satisfactorily be checked.

The mechanics of trading in the Egyptian barter system indicated by the small-scale transactions of a modest land-owner in the Theban region may seem hopelessly clumsy and even inefficient. But it must be remembered that the system was what the parties were acquainted with; to them it was no more inefficient than the awkward system of calculation which may have been the cause of the lack of advance made in mathematics by the Egyptians in the Pharaonic Period.[13] A society makes use of the equipment available to it, whether intellectual or practical, and the success achieved with this equipment may be taken as an indication both of the efficiency of the equipment and of the intellectual and practical capacities of the members of the society. But a closer look at the Egyptian system of barter may reveal changes and developments over the centuries which brought into certain transactions a degree of precision not found generally in the ancient world until the introduction of coinage. We should in any case bear in mind that in the matter of the acceptance of coinage Egypt lagged behind her Mediterranean neighbours by little more than one hundred and fifty years—a small span when set against the two and a half millennia of Pharaonic history.

In a village society or in the scattered communities of the country-side, the business of obtaining goods for everyday use was no doubt conducted in the manner revealed by Hekanakhte's letters. Produce was available locally for small-scale transactions, and most were probably carried out by simple bargaining in terms generally conform-ing with the local market value of the different farm commodities. If things or services were needed which lay outside the common inventory of items traded, then the bargaining might require the intervention of a third party, although there exists no clear evidence to substantiate this view. It is a pity that the peasant from the Wadi Natrun, Khunanpu, was diverted from his journey to the Faiyum to sell his produce. The story might then have followed his progress to his original destination, and described how he disposed of what he had brought, and how he acquired the goods he needed to take back home. Many of the things he carried were unusual—strange woods, plants and herbs, animal skins—and scarcely the basis for ordinary trade. He would, therefore, have been obliged to go to one or more specialist traders who would know how to dispose of such items in the great city of Ninsu, the provincial capital. If Khunanpu had made similar trips with similar goods on earlier occasions, he would certainly know whom he could trust to give him a good price, and he would also know the merchants from whom he could obtain the provisions he required. There is, however, not much to be gained from such speculation about Khunanpu's methods of trading, apart from considering how he might have acted within the framework of what we have already seen of simple trading.

In large towns the business of buying and selling must, it seems, have been both more complicated and, in some respects, simpler than in the countryside: more complicated, because the commodities to be used by a purchaser might not be easily available, and simpler because the mechanics of trade would be established on a more regular basis. Very little is known about the distribution of produce throughout Egypt, or about the machinery of the commodities market. That there were traders who were involved in distribution is made clear in one of the pieces in the Nineteenth-dynasty *Miscellanies*. They are mentioned among others who came from time to time under the vigilance of the scribe:[14] 'The merchants sail downstream and upstream, busy as bees,[15] carrying goods from one city to another, supplying him who has nothing.' Such a statement does no more than establish the activity of traders who moved freely up and down the river, conveying unspecified goods to be sold here and there to individual buyers. Where did these traders get their supplies? How did they sell them? These questions are almost without answer, although some attempt to provide answers may be made by interpreting certain written and visual evidence. We need also to be cautious in talking of traders and merchants, to avoid the implications of the very words themselves. Trader or merchant suggests private enterprise, and activity free from excessive bureaucratic restraint. The ancient Egyptian word for 'merchant' survived into the Coptic stage of the ancient language (in the Christian era) with a sense close to that of our word for 'merchant';[16] but the status of 'merchants' in New-Kingdom Egypt may have been distinctly less independent. Those who operated in the field of foreign trade— generally thought to have been a royal monopoly for the most part— were probably royal officials under the control of the Treasury; those who conveyed and distributed goods within the country may also have owed their appointments and hence their allegiance to the good offices of the vizir, of the provincial governors and of the great temples. Their status is, however, far from clear.

A study of the sketchy evidence for merchants has shown that some are named as being attached to temples and to individuals, mostly high officials.[17] Others appear to act with some independence, although the content of the texts in which they are mentioned does not specify the status of individuals. A text in the Cairo Museum[18] lists quantities of goods, mostly meat, given to various merchants, all named. The distributions, which are priced, are precisely dated to season, month and day, but unfortunately no year or reign is given. The hieratic script, however, is characteristically of the Eighteenth Dynasty. Sample entries run as follows:[19]

> Second month of inundation, day 24; given to the merchant Minnakhte:
>
> 1 *pesdjet*-vase of wine, worth 3 gold units
>
> Given to the merchant Sherybin:

1 head of long-horned ox, worth ½ unit silver

1 *tepet*-joint, 1 *semes*-joint, worth ½ unit of silver

Second month of inundation, day 25; received from the merchant Baki:

2½ units of gold, in payment for meat

Second month of inundation, day 27; given to Minnakhte:

Head and haunch of a long-horned ox

Haunch of a bull, worth 1 unit silver

The precision of the prices listed in this record might be thought to indicate the reduction of all values to one medium of exchange, namely precious metal. But the payment made by Baki for meat received is stated in similar terms, and it ought to be concluded that he actually paid the quantity of gold mentioned. If he had settled his debt in some other commodity, say barley, the entry would probably have run: 'Received from the merchant Baki: x bushels of barley, worth 2½ units of gold.' The way in which the payments specified in this document were actually made is not clear; and indeed, in spite of the precision of the prices, it would be incautious to conclude that the transactions were carried out in a kind of monetary way.[20] If metal was employed as one of the mediums of exchange how was it used? In brief, the necessary evidence does not exist; but some attempt to reach a conclusion will be made a little later in this chapter.

Within Egypt the distribution in bulk of all kinds of goods was made by river. The written and visual evidence is not extensive, but quite conclusive, and it only confirms what may be thought wholly obvious, both by considering the nature of the land of Egypt—five hundred miles of river bound by narrow areas of cultivation and the spreading Delta threaded with branches of the river and other waterways—and by observing practice in Egypt today, in spite of the existence of a railway and reasonable roads. It was probably the case that most goods conveyed by ship were transported in craft belonging to the great institutions of state, under the charge of crews employed similarly by these institutions. But the men who organized the traffic and concerned themselves with delivery and distribution—the so-called 'merchants', already mentioned—may have had some degree of independence. We have seen in considering other aspects of ancient Egyptian life—particularly the administration of the law and the tenure of land—that the notional autocracy, the all-pervading authority of the king and, by a kind of devolved, unspecified proxy, of the temples, was modified to the point of being ignored. Transactions in the countryside, the village and the family were executed as if the individual parties had the freedom, even the right, to behave with complete independence. There is good reason to believe, therefore, that the merchants in charge of the distribution of goods had the opportunity to trade on their own behalf. They may even have been allowed as part of their terms of service to appropriate to their own use a proportion of the goods under their control. They may also have used the transport at their disposal for the conveying of additional goods for private trading. Payment and perquisite might thus be closely intertwined, with the merchant benefiting in a sense both officially and unofficially.

Some evidence to support this view of the responsibilities and personal independence of the merchant is supplied by two partially preserved papyrus documents of the New Kingdom which have been termed 'ship's logs'.[21] They include lists of goods carried on specific voyages on the Nile, the regular distribution of various commodities to the members of the crew, details of deliveries of goods to specified persons, and indications of daily progress of the voyages. These two documents, if they represent a regular practice of control and record, show that at the top end of the market the conveyance of goods from place to place in Egypt was subject to an extraordinary surveillance.

Fig. 25 Sailors leave their boat and engage in personal trading.

These logs were compiled presumably both to act as records of what occurred, and also to serve as a means of checking the activities of the merchants in charge. Sadly nothing is known of the fate of these logs after they were compiled—where they were deposited, who checked them, who had access to them, whether they were subsequently consulted or were simply consigned to an archive.

While these documents provide a little evidence for the ability of merchants to act with some degree of freedom and enterprise, they also may indicate, although very obliquely, that others who accompanied the goods on their journeyings, whether sailors or labourers, were in a position to benefit from the possibilities of free trade. The modern editor of the logs, in considering the daily distribution to the crew of bread in fairly substantial quantities (their apparent payment), notices the absence of other commodities in these distributions, and concludes: 'Is it not possible that our crew also brought with them products of their native region, perhaps a part of their wages received in kind before the departure, to exchange them for different kinds of food in the local markets? Thus they would not have been condemned to live on their daily bread ration alone.'[22] He draws attention to a scene in the Theban tomb of Ipuy (number 217) in which sailors, just ashore from cargo boats, appear to be conducting private transactions with women attending booths and stalls on the quayside (*Fig. 25*).[23]

This scene, as is so often the case, is not wholly applicable. It has been stated that what the sailors are about in making these transactions is the ill-considered squandering of their wages at the first opportunity when they came to shore. There are five transactions shown, one of which is almost completely lost. In each case the sailor makes his bargain in grain of unspecified kind, to be poured from a sack into a basket placed before the woman with whom he bargains. On the right one woman offers vegetables, and the second deals in bread or cakes; on the left one woman bargains with fish and the second with bread or cakes. Behind this last trader is shown a reed booth sheltering a stand which holds two pots of drink, possibly also available for 'sale'. It was the presence of these jars of drink which prompted these comments: '. . . we see the men spending their wages with female hucksters on the bank . . . it is amusing to trace back by millennia the lure of the saloon for sailors, which is none the less a lure from being as primitive as their appetites'.[24] The point has almost certainly been missed. The transactions shown are scarcely the wild, improvident acts of over-eager sailors, who probably went ashore daily in the course of their voyagings up and down the Nile, and not at all to be compared with the behaviour of sea-going sailors putting into port after many days, even weeks, at sea. They are the regular small acts of barter by which a sailor, or any other workman, might convert his wages of grain into other commodities to enlarge and vary his diet. The booth of drinks may even have been set up not for business but to smooth business, and to celebrate the clinching of bargains. The jars probably contained beer, or beer and water, not beer and wine as has been suggested. Wine was not the drink of the simple Egyptian workman. One of the jars is fitted with an angled pipe, a kind of ancient drinking straw, which was specially used for drawing beer from its jar. The end of the pipe, as is known from an actual example discovered at Akhenaten's city, Akhetaten, and now in the British Museum, was connected to a filter which prevented the solid matter in the beer from being sucked up into the mouth of the drinker.

In this scene from the tomb of Ipuy, then, may be represented the way in which 'shopping' was carried out by ordinary people in ancient Egypt. It is not unlikely that the quay or landing-place where trading boats tied up was commonly the site of a market for small traders; it would be an obvious location because of the large-scale operations connected with the arrival and departure of merchant ships, and the activities of the 'satellite' small-traders, the sailors and other men travelling with the ships, for whom river-traffic provided the ideal conditions for modest private enterprise. The market set up at the landing-place is even better shown in a scene from the tomb of Qenamun, a mayor of Thebes and superintendent of the granaries of Amun (number 162), which is now, sadly, almost completely destroyed.[25] The principal subject of the scene is the arrival and unloading of merchant ships from Asia at a port which should be Thebes. The date is sometime during the reign of King Amenophis III (c. 1403–1365 BC). The bustle of activity is well conveyed within the limitations of the conventions of Egyptian tomb-painting. All kinds of commodities are unloaded— cattle, wine or oil (perhaps both), unusual

Fig. 26 Trading booths on the quay at Thebes.

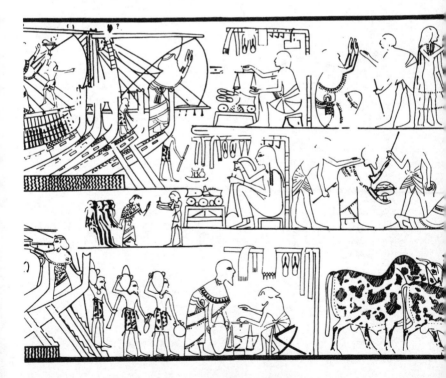

vessels in precious metals—to be set out and presented for inspection to Qenamun. And in the midst of all this official chaos, three small-traders have set up their simple booths for private trading. Their wares are set out on low tables and are also hung from the horizontal cross-members of the booths (*Fig. 26*).

Fig. 27 Marketing scenes in an Old Kingdom tomb.

The goods on offer in the three booths are similar in each case—sandals, cloths, food of various kinds, mostly bread and cakes, and other items which are not easily identified. Two booths are staffed by men and one by a woman; by an interesting and unusual variation not common in scenes of repeated theme in Egyptian art, each shopkeeper

sits on a different type of stool, one three-legged, one with four short legs, and one of folding type—a small indication of the real attempt made by the artist of this tomb scene to enliven his painting.[26] The two men hold balances, which might, it has been suggested, have been used to weigh out precious metal used to conclude transactions or, more probably, for the weighing of small quantities of costly drugs or spices.[27] It is unlikely that any of the goods offered for sale in these booths could have been worth bargaining for in gold or silver. Only one identifiable transaction is certainly shown: in the lowest register a Syrian offers for sale a stoppered jar, probably of oil. He bends forward weighed down by his jar while the trader makes his bargain using his balance, sitting forward on his stool in his eagerness to clinch the deal.

Deficient in descriptive inscriptions, these scenes of market activity in New-Kingdom tombs are, sadly, less informative than we should wish. It appears to be the case, in spite of the presence of scales, that deals were executed by simple barter of commodity or manufactured object against similar goods. There are certainly no signs of the use of metal in these minor market transactions although we shall find shortly that individual transactions might frequently be effected by the use of valuations in metal by workmen and others of modest status, who might be thought to have been more familiar with metal, especially precious metal, in their professional activities than the ordinary countryman. Essentially, however, the barter system of ancient Egypt was one in which goods were traded against goods; and as such it is depicted in the few surviving pictorial representations in tombs.

The most informative scene occurs in a tomb at Saqqara of much earlier date than those of Ipuy and Qenamun. It belonged to Khnumhotpe and Niankhkhnum, two senior officials who lived in the mid-Fifth Dynasty (c. 2360 BC).[28] On a wall to the right of the entrance door to the vestibule the bulk of the decorated area is filled with three rows of market vignettes. Here is shown a busy open-air market with traders, mostly on their own, offering a wide variety of goods: there are at least four different fruit and vegetable stalls; two display fish, one of which offers gutted produce; two separate traders, one of whom is a woman, sell beaker-shaped vessels; a pitch on which cloth is displayed

15 (above) Brick-making in the tomb of Rekhmire.
   (below) Brick-making today at Kom Ombo in Upper Egypt.

has two salesmen. Most of the shoppers, all of whom but one are men, carry small bags or sacks slung across their bodies, thought to represent shopping-bags, and they offer a variety of items to the shopkeepers in exchange for the goods on sale (*Fig. 27*).

At a vegetable stall a man stretches out his hands with a vessel, and the stall-holder says: 'Hand over what you have brought[29] and I shall give you fine vegetables.' At one of the beaker stalls, the shopper hands over a fan[30] for a beaker, and the female trader says: 'See! Something you can drink from.' A young woman with a child offers a bowl, possibly containing something, for sycomore figs. 'Hand over what you have brought for very sweet sycomore figs,' says the salesman, while the woman snaps at the child, 'Do you want to go home?' or something of similar meaning. A jar is bartered for fish, and the salesman accepts: 'Hand over what you have brought for fish, its price.' A craftsman carves a cylinder-seal in exchange for gutted fish, while the pleased trader declares: 'I hand over for it the rest of what I have brought, with contented heart, its price.'

The vignettes of trade are enlivened and interspersed by others conveying something of the flavour of the open-air market. A man with a baboon on a lead, probably an official market attendant, restrains his animal as it steals a fruit from one stall. Another attendant apprehends a shop-lifter, using a monkey who sinks his teeth into the thief's leg. A woman dispenses drink to a man who seems already a little the worse for what he may have drunk. In general, however, the business of this market is conducted in a very orderly way: offers are made, bargains are concluded without too much haggling; exchanges are effected by what may be described as the market instinct for the relative values of different goods. But one scene in particular is of interest in our search for the way by which 'value' could come in time to mean 'metal value', an almost monetary conception. A length of cloth is unrolled for inspection, and the prospective purchaser declares: 'I say this in very truth, it is a god's cloth,[31] of outstanding workmanship.' The two salesmen holding out the cloth make the bargain: '. . .[32] cubits of cloth

16 (*above*) *The Nile as the transport artery of Egypt: a felucca loaded with pots in Upper Egypt.*
   (*below*) *A modern craftsman in stone, carving souvenirs of antiquity in the Theban necropolis.*

in exchange for 6 *shat*'. In this context the meaning of the word *shat* is not at all clear. The transaction values the length of cloth at 6 *shat*, as if a unit of value was intended. All the other transactions shown in these scenes from the tomb of Khnumhotpe and Niankhkhnum are seen to be straightforward exchanges of one lot of goods for another. Here, in the case of the cloth, the purchaser is not shown with any reciprocal object which he can trade against the cloth. He is, in effect, being given a 'price' for the cloth, not in terms of any of the common commodities used in exchanges, but against an apparently abstract unit of value, the *shat*. We may suppose, then, that the purchaser in due course would have completed the bargain (or made the purchase) by handing over in exchange some object or commodity equally valued at 6 *shat*.

This word *shat* with its probable derivatives and successors, such as the *shenat*, *shena* and *seniu* (this last in texts of the New Kingdom was formerly, and perhaps in some instances correctly, read *shaty*)[33] have occasioned much debate in the general consideration of ancient Egyptian commercial practices. The ultimate question asked by Egyptologists in this debate is whether the ancient Egyptians during the New Kingdom had an actual object, a metal token of a fixed weight, known as the *seniu* (or *shaty*) which was used for all practical purposes as a coin. In the instance from the Old-Kingdom tomb which formed the starting-point of this small investigation, there is no suggestion that a metal unit is involved. Of course metals, particularly copper, gold and, to a much smaller extent, silver, must have entered into bargains struck in the Old Kingdom, but it is not probable that they formed part of the generality of commodities required regularly by ordinary people in town or country, and used in the daily barter of the market. In the Old Kingdom, as in later periods, the peasant, labourer, artisan, and to a greater extent all people in receipt of wages, were paid in kind—grain, oil, cloth, sandals, all the paraphernalia of office and existence—if status required it. This 'pay' was food for the individual and for his family, little enough no doubt if he were at the bottom of the social ladder; and what was not consumed in this way could be used for barter, for purchasing essential items for everyday living. In such trade there was no place for a metal piece, and the visitor to a market in the Old Kingdom would surely have been surprised if he had been offered pieces of metal in exchange for what he had brought for bargaining. Yet the idea of 'value' as something separate from actual goods, but applicable to all goods, would undoubtedly have been of use in determining the relative worth of one article against another.

Abstract ideas do not easily reveal themselves in the concrete hiero-glyphic script of ancient Egypt, and the student of this script is in a sense disposed to find concrete meanings for words that are not properly understood. In the word *shat/shenat* the abstract may well have been superseded by the concrete between the Old Kingdom and the New Kingdom; but truly conclusive evidence needs to be found. In the early Middle Kingdom letters of Hekanakhte, to which reference has already been made in this chapter, the word *shena* or *shenat* seems certainly to have the meaning 'value'. The instruction Hekanakhte sends for the renting of land specifies payment 'with copper or with clothes or with barley or with anything else(?), but only when you have collected the value (*shena*) there(?) of oil or of anything else.' There is here clearly an abstract concept, although inasmuch as it is used in an economy based on barter, it must have a concrete element, in fact 'value in terms of goods', has been suggested.[34] We may suppose that an ancient Egyptian sandal-maker had a fairly precise notion of what he might expect to receive in exchange for a pair of his sandals. He could think of this value in terms of many specific commodities—grain, oil, cloth, etc.—but he would not know precisely what he might be offered when he came to 'sell' it. At the point of negotiating a trade for his sandals he would have to set them in one pan of a kind of mental balance, and the offer in the other pan. An equivalence of value could only be achieved if a number of factors were taken into consideration, including the state of the market in the different commodities, and the urgency on each side to conclude the sale. 'Value' or *shenat* would seem to be this variable equivalence, but it would also seem to have been whatever our chosen sandal-maker might have had in mind for the sale at the moment he decided to sell, but before he had met an actual purchaser.

From the example in the tomb of Khnumhotpe and Niankhkhnum, *shat/shenat* could be thought of in numerical terms—units of value. In the renting of his land Hekanakhte could send 24 copper *debens*, but these metal *debens*, in whatever form they came, were not apparently equated with a fixed number of units of value, although they could have been valued in this way presumably. But by the New Kingdom the convenience of having an independent unit of value, not tied specific-ally to one of the common commodities of barter, became so evidently appreciated that in some parts of the Egyptian economy valuations became very common, with the unit often being conceived in terms of silver. In the text quoted earlier in which are listed goods distributed to various merchants, the items are priced or valued in the unit which may be *seniu* or *shaty*, e.g. 'haunch of bull, worth 1 *seniu* silver'. It was pointed out (p. 249) that we should not conclude that payments were actually made in metal as specified. If they were so made, it would suggest that metals, in particular gold and silver, were commonly used as 'currency' in the truest sense; from which it should follow that substantial quantities of these metals were in circulation, available for trading, and regularly passed from hand to hand. It can in fact be well established that in the later New Kingdom at least, the Egyptian word for 'silver' (*hedj*) was also used generally for 'cash' (or 'money', to use a misnomer), although an even more abstract meaning, 'prestation' has been assigned to it when used in certain kinds of transaction.[35] 'Prestation', the payment of money or goods as a kind of toll or feudal requirement, may theoretically convey the idea of the 'payment' made in the ancient transaction, but it could not be said that this is the kind of concept which the ancient Egyptian would have understood.

Scholars who have studied closely the multitude of documents on papyrus and on ostraca from the workmen's village at Thebes recognize that in the very many recorded transactions in which 'values' of objects are given in terms of metal, the metal did not actually figure in the execution of the transaction; it was used usually as a measure of value.[36] But those documents in which the word *seniu* (*shaty*) occurs have an apparently greater specificity in the use of the silver measure, which has led the most eminent of these scholars to conclude that there actually was 'a flat, round piece of metal 1/12 *deben*, that is about 7.6 grammes, in weight, possibly with an inscription to indicate this weight or the name of the issuing authority. If so, the "piece" was practically a coin.'[37] In most of the documents in which *seniu* is used, silver is the metal in question; but in the Eighteenth Dynasty gold also is quoted, as in the document listing distributions to merchants mentioned above and earlier. A further quotation will illustrate its use both with silver and with gold:[38]

> Second month of inundation, day 15: given to the merchant Minnakhte:
> heads of *iwa*-bulls 3, of *ka*-bulls 9
> 1 haunch of short-horned bull: worth 3½ *seniu*

broken *shayt*,[39] worth 1½ *seniu*
Total: silver 5 *seniu*, worth gold 3 *seniu*
Second month of inundation, day 16: given to the merchant Minnakhte:

1 head of *iwa*-bull, worth ½ *seniu*
5 heads of *ka*-bulls, worth ½ *seniu*
broken *shayt*, worth ½ *seniu*. Total 1½

It is attractive to believe that the ancient Egyptians had developed a kind of coinage as early as the mid-second millennium BC, but the truth is almost certainly otherwise. The most comprehensive study of documents of the New Kingdom containing prices, finds the idea of small metal 'pieces' very compelling, and quite consistent with much of the evidence,[40] but points out that nothing vaguely resembling such a piece has ever been found in excavations. 'Objects of silver are not, of course, very likely to have survived, but if the use of these "coins" was anything like as widespread as their appearance in texts would seem to suggest then it seems a little strange that none has ever turned up in the excavations of Deir el-Medina.' It may be added that in Egypt, as elsewhere, coins regularly turn up in excavations in later contexts, casually dropped in antiquity or buried in hoards. Silver scrap of Middle and New Kingdom dates has been discovered, as mentioned in an earlier chapter,[41] but it has never included anything remotely like a coin or fixed piece.

What may most safely be concluded is that the Egyptians of the New Kingdom had no coinage or surrogate coinage, although they were clearly on the brink of developing a kind of coinage. Simple trading in the village and the countryside remained barter; in places where the economics of life were more highly developed, metal—especially copper and silver—was added to the common standard commodities in which values were expressed in the barter system. The convenience of using silver, in particular, for the expression of values, rested probably not on its availability as a material to be used in barter, but in its general stability of value as compared with commodities like barley which would fluctuate in value seasonally. How this worked in practice is demonstrated clearly in the description of a transaction of extraordinary complication by which a Theban woman, Irytnofre, purchased a Syrian slave-girl:

In Year 15,[42] seven years after I had entered the house of the

overseer of the district, Simut, the merchant Reia came to me with
the Syrian slave Gem-ny-her-Imentet, who was just a girl, and he
said to me: 'Buy this girl, and give me her price'; so he said to me. I
took the girl and paid him her price. Now see! I state the price I
paid for her in front of the magistrates:[43]

> 1 wrap of thin cloth: value 5 *kite* of silver[44]
> 1 sheet (?) of thin cloth: value 3⅓ *kite* of silver
> 1 cloak of thin cloth: value 4 *kite* of silver
> 3 loin-cloths of fine thin cloth: value 5 *kite* of silver
> 1 skirt of fine thin cloth: value 5 *kite* of silver

Bought from the citizeness Kafy, 1 bronze *gay*-vessel: value 14
deben (of copper), value 1 2/3 *kite* of silver

Bought from the chief of the store-house, Piay, 1 bronze
gay-vessel: value 14 *deben* (of copper), value 1½ *kite* of silver.

Bought from the priest, Huy-panehsy, 10 *deben* of waste copper:
value 1 *kite* of silver

Bought from the priest, Iny, 1 *gay*-vessel of bronze: value 16 *deben*
(of copper), value 1½ *kite* of silver; 1 *menet*-vessel of honey:
value 1 *hekat* of barley, value 5 *kite* of silver

Bought from the citizeness, Tjuiay, 1 bronze *kehen*-vessel: value
20 *deben* (of copper), value 2 *kite* of silver

Bought from the steward of the Temple of Amun, Tutui, 1 bronze
kebet-vessel: value 20 deben (of copper), value 2 *kite* of silver; 10
tunics of fine thin cloth: value 4 *kite* of silver

Total for everything: 4 *deben* and 1 *kite* of silver

And I gave them to the merchant Reia, with nothing among them
belonging to the citizeness Bakmut. And he gave me the girl whom
I named Gem-ny-her-Imentet.

From the account of this purchase much can be learned about the
conduct of trading in the New Kingdom. For example, it is noteworthy
that the transaction takes place between a married woman and a
merchant who appears to have been offering his goods—a slave-girl—
from house to house. The girl is described as being Syrian, and was
therefore probably the child of a Syrian woman already in service
elsewhere. It would be idle to conjecture how the mother had come to
Egypt, or how the merchant came to have the child in his possession.
No doubt Irytnofre and the merchant Reia bargained for some time
before a price was agreed, and it is clear that this price was expressed in

terms of silver. Irytnofre then had to find acceptable goods equivalent in value to this price of 4 *deben* and 1 *kite* of silver. Again it must be understood that the values given for each of the articles from which the total was aggregated were also the result of agreement between Irytnofre and the merchant. Rather more than half the total was found by Irytnofre in the form of garments and pieces of cloth in her possession, perhaps even woven by herself. The equivalent of 1 *deben* and 8 2/3 *kite* of silver was then made up of various objects obtained from other people, probably neighbours. It will never be known why Irytnofre was obliged to look around to scrape together this balance. It is likely, however, that the merchant did not want the whole of his price in articles which Irytnofre had available. He may have specified *gay*-vessels, waste copper, a pot of honey, etc. as part of his required package. If this last surmise is correct—and it would be natural for a merchant to know what he wanted and to be able to call the tune accordingly—it reveals even more clearly how the use of silver as a medium for valuation was quite independent from the actual use of silver in transactions. Goods of many kinds were also used to effect the bargain. By reducing the value of each to terms of silver, some precision could be achieved.

In ordinary circumstances precious metals would not have passed into the hands of Egyptians except in the smallest quantities, acquired perhaps fortuitously, perhaps by inheritance, or through craftsmen who worked the materials. The existence of gold in burials of quite humble people, usually in the form of a few beads or small ornaments, in no way implies that gold was easily available. But there was surely a ready market for precious metals to meet the demand, which seems to have remained one of the most basic of man's desires, to convert capital into gold and silver. Gold existed in Egypt in large quantities, in burial equipments and in the embellishments of temples and other important buildings. The inhabitants of Thebes have always had a nose for treasure, and an appetite for acquiring it illicitly. The use to which stolen gold might be put is illustrated in the evidence given by priestly thieves after they had been caught removing gold from a temple, probably the Ramesseum, the mortuary temple of Ramesses II. The thefts took place in the reign of Ramesses IX of the Twentieth Dynasty (*c.* 1137–1119 BC), and the record is kept in a papyrus now in the British Museum.[45] The scribe and gardener of the temple, named Kar, describes three visits made with accomplices to the temple, when small quantities of gold were taken from the gilded door-jambs—1 *deben* 3½ *kite*, 3 *kite*, and 5 *kite*. He continues:

> We paid another visit to the door-jambs together with the priest Hori, son of Pakharu, the scribe of the temple, Sedi, and the priest, Nesamun . . . We took away 5 *kite* of gold and we bought barley with it in Thebes, and split it among ourselves. Now some days later, the scribe of the temple, Sedi, came again, bringing three men with him. They went again to the door-jambs and took away 4 *kite* of gold. We divided it among ourselves and him. Now some days later Paminu, our boss, quarrelled with us, saying, 'You have given me nothing.' So again we went to the door-jambs and took away 5 *kite* of gold from them. We exchanged them for an ox and gave it to Paminu. Now the scribe of the royal archives, Sutekhmose, heard a whisper of it, and he threatened us, saying, 'I am going to report it to the High Priest of Amun.' So we took away 3 *kite* of gold and gave them to the scribe of the royal archives, Sutekhmose. And we paid him another visit and gave him 1½ *kite* of gold. Total of the gold given to the scribe of the royal archives, Sutekhmose, 4½ *kite* of gold.

The scribe Kar and his accomplices were quite discreet in their nefarious practice—just a few *kite* on each occasion, not perhaps missed at the next inspection, but in aggregate amounting to a sizeable quantity over a period of time. The gold might be converted at once into goods, or—as emerges from subsequent depositions—be divided and melted down and hoarded for use at a later date. This account of theft and bribery is of universal kind, and, as is so often the case, it ended in the apprehending and punishment of the criminals. We are here, however, not concerned with the morality of the priests' behaviour, but with the economic aspects of the case. The only price mentioned in the passage quoted is 5 *kite* of gold for an ox, that is 60 *deben* of copper according to the rate of equivalence between the two metals at that time.[46] It is impossible to say whether this was an average price, or one 'adjusted' by the seller of the ox, who must have known directly or indirectly that the gold had not been honestly acquired. Records of the sale of cattle in the Theban area during the Nineteenth and Twentieth Dynasties show great variations in the prices reached.[47] They range from 127 *deben* of copper at the top end, down to 20 *deben* at the bottom end. Some of the variations reveal the difference in price between male and female animals, others between young and old beasts. We are not told what kind of ox was bought by the thieves with their gold, but it is reasonably certain that they did not get a real bargain. The trader from whom they purchased it was probably a 'fence', a receiver of stolen goods, who was prepared to handle the gold, knowing it to be stolen, and who knew equally how to dispose of it where no questions would be asked. Both in acquiring and in disposing of the gold he would act to his own advantage. He would also be a significant figure in ensuring the distribution of a commodity which in normal circumstances should not be held in any quantity by private persons. Through his agency small amounts of precious metal could be worked into the private domain and distributed to individuals for conversion into jewellery, etc. At that point in the recycling of the metal it was surely treated as one commodity to be traded as such against other commodities and manufactured articles.

In this transaction and in the acquisition of an unspecified quantity of grain for 5 *kite* of gold, also admitted in this deposition by the priest Kar, we are faced with barter in which precious metal is used against ordinary trading commodities, and in circumstances very different from those in which daily domestic economy was practised in most of Egypt during antiquity. A sharp division undoubtedly existed between the practice of domestic economy in the countryside and in the town. In the countryside the produce of the fields was easily available for food and for the manufacture of most of the articles required by a household. Pottery might be made locally; leather tanned; even some small-scale metalwork might have been carried out in villages. Families living in the countryside were almost self-sufficient, provided that exchange and barter operated on quite a simple level, accompanied by a degree of charity for those who worked on the land but owned none. In the great cities and towns, however, circumstances were very different. Ordinary workmen, artisans, craftsmen and others who had no direct access to the produce of the countryside, were dependent on the wages they received for their work, and on whatever articles they might be able to make by exploiting their trades. With any surpluses a household might build up, other foodstuffs could be acquired by barter in the markets; household articles and clothes could similarly be obtained from specialist craftsmen and from friends and neighbours who might have articles to trade. It should be remembered that the diet of the average Egyptian was relatively simple and unvaried, except at festival times, and that houses were very modestly equipped. Needs therefore were not very great.

Much of the produce of the land of Egypt fell by various requirements to the temples throughout the country. Vast numbers of cattle and fowl were provided for the offerings to the gods, and most of what was offered reverted to the priests, and through them to their families and to the many workers and dependants of the temples and the temple estates.[48] In the great cities like Memphis and Thebes where there were huge temple complexes with a multitude of divine figures to be entertained daily with lavish banquets, the reverted offerings were probably sufficient to feed very large numbers of people, including the poor at the gate. Such people might have been adequately fed, but in other respects were poorly provided for the remaining needs of daily life. Without income in goods, and without the ability to make things for trading, the poor of ancient Egypt were unable to advance beyond a level of simple subsistence. But throughout the lowest levels of a society in which the economy was based on barter, there would have been difficulties over the making of even simple bargains. How do you pay for some necessity? How do you recover a bad debt? All transactions could not have been settled on the spot by the simultaneous exchange of goods. Egyptians were surely no better than other peoples, ancient or modern, in concluding honourably all bargains. Consider, for example, the case of the scribe Amennakhte who failed to settle his side of a bargain before he died. His opposite partner to the bargain was obliged to write to the widow:[49]

> The scribe, Amennakhte, your husband, took from me a coffin, saying that he would give the calf for it, but he has not given it down to this day. I mentioned it to Pa-aa-akhet, and he said: 'Give me a bed in addition to it and I will bring to you the calf when it has grown up'; and I gave him the bed. There is neither the coffin nor the bed down to this day. If you give the calf, send it, and if there is no calf, send back the bed and the coffin.

In this case the writer, probably a carpenter, had made the coffin, and had traded it to the scribe Amennakhte for him in turn to paint. His loss had subsequently been made worse by the intervention of Pa-aa-akhet who had additionally deprived him of a bed. No doubt resort to law would settle the matter. We do not know the outcome. But the hazards of trading in goods may not appear to us too dissimilar from trading with money. While the Egyptian system is only partly made clear to us, it yet emerges as one that worked well and met the needs of those who operated it. And so must have been the case generally in all communities where barter was used. It so happens that through documents and representations we know so much more about its working in Egypt than in other ancient societies. New discoveries of private documents will certainly enlarge this knowledge; but we shall never know precisely how the housewife went shopping, or how bargains were made between two craftsmen disposing of their respective wares. Undoubtedly the success of the system depended to a great extent on the trust which might exist between the parties to a bargain; the accepted morality, preserved in the wisdom compositions, certainly required honesty in business practice. As Amenemope said:[50]

> Do not make the scale uneven or render the weights false or reduce the parts of the grain-measure . . . Do not make a measure of dual capacity for yourself; then will you descend to the depths. The measure is the eye of Re; one who defrauds is its abomination. He who uses a measure, making many its inaccuracies, his [i.e. Re's] eye will shut tight against him.

NOTES

1 There has been some dispute over the Egyptian word used here (*šn'ty* var. *šn'*). For the sense 'value', see E. F. Wente in *Journal of Near Eastern Studies* 24 (Chicago, 1965), 105 ff., and also below p. 258 ff.

2 In general, see J. W. Curtis in *Journal of Egyptian Archaeology* 43 (London, 1957), 71 ff. The coin of Teos of the Thirtieth Dynasty, cited there (p. 73 bottom), is now known to be of the Persian King Artaxerxes III (359–338 BC), whose rule over Egypt was scarcely more than nominal. For the correct identification, see A. F. Shore in *Numismatic Chronicle* 7th Series, 14 (London, 1974), 5 ff.

3 See the remarks of M. Price and N. Waggoner, *Archaic Greek Coinage. The Asyut Hoard* (London, 1975), 117 ff.

4 Price and Waggoner, op. cit., 125.

5 J. Černý, in *Journal of World History* I (Paris, 1954), 904, n. 5.

6 Especially J. J. Janssen, *Commodity Prices from the Ramessid Period*.

7 T. G. H. James, *The Hekanakhte Papers*, 13; Letter I, ll.3-6. The word conventionally translated 'acre' here and in other passages, represents the Egyptian *setjat* (in Greek *aroura*), 100 cubits squared, about 2/3 of the English acre.

8 Probably 'the barley from this land'.

9 See n. 26 to Chapter 1. The estimated weight of 91 grammes for the *deben* may not have obtained in the Middle Kingdom.

10 James, *The Hekanakhte Papers*, 46; Letter III, ll.8 f.

11 No specific kind of oil is mentioned. The word used (*mrht*) is generic. The various kinds of vegetable oil possibly available in Egypt in antiquity are discussed in A. Lucas, *Ancient Egyptian Materials and Industries*, 327 ff.

12 James, *Hekanakhte Papers*, 63; text VI, ll.12 f. This matter of the personal measuring vessel has been touched on in Chapter Four, see p. 126 above.

13 See the remarks of G. J. Toomer in J. R. Harris (ed.), *The Legacy of Egypt*, 45; but see also the somewhat more favourable assessment by R. J. Gillings, *Mathematics in the Time of the Pharaohs* (Cambridge, Mass., 1972), 2 f. and generally.

14 A. H. Gardiner, *Late-Egyptian Miscellanies*, 103.

15 Literally 'occupied like copper', a fairly common expression.

16 J. Černý, *Coptic Etymological Dictionary* (Cambridge, 1976), 253 bottom.

17 J. J. Janssen, *Two Ancient Egyptian Ship's Logs* (Leiden, 1961), 101 ff.

18 Cairo 58070, known as Papyrus Boulaq 11. It is studied by T. E. Peet in *Mélanges Maspero*, I (Cairo, 1934), 185 ff.

19 From column 3, ll.1-10.

20 I have deliberately used the colourless word 'unit' in the translation, rather than the often used 'piece', because the latter bears distinctly a suggestion of coinage.

21 One in Leiden and one in Turin, published in J. J. Janssen, *Two Ancient Egyptian Ship's Logs* (Leiden, 1961). Chapter III, 'Trade and Transport' (96 ff.), brings together much useful evidence on these topics, and very sensible conclusions are reached.

22 Ibid., 8.

23 N. de G. Davies, *Two Ramesside Tombs at Thebes* (New York, 1927), pl. XXX.

24 Ibid., 57.

25 A drawing made from traces and from old photographs is published by N. de G.

Davies and R. O. Faulkner in *Journal of Egyptian Archaeology* 33 (London, 1947), 40 ff.

26 The three-legged stool would have a solid seat; the four-legged stool, a woven rush or string seat; and the folding stool, a leather seat. For the different types, good examples of which are known from the Eighteenth Dynasty, see H. Baker, *Furniture in the Ancient World*, 133 ff.

27 Davies and Faulkner, op. cit., 46.

28 See A. Moussa and H. Altenmüller, *Das Grab des Nianchchnum und Chnumhotep* (Mainz, 1977), pl. 24, fig. 10.

29 He actually says, 'Give your property', meaning, apparently, the object brought for barter. The same word is used elsewhere in the scenes in this tomb.

30 For fanning fires.

31 'God's cloth' was, presumably, cloth of the finest quality.

32 The quantity number is not preserved on the wall.

33 The more probable reading, *seniu*, is reasonably established by J. J. Janssen, *Commodity Prices from the Ramesside Period*, 102 ff.

34 T. G. H. James, *Hekanakhte Papers*, 113.

35 On *hedj* as 'cash' see T. E. Peet in *Studies presented to F. Ll. Griffith* (London, 1932), 124. For 'prestation', see S. Allam in *Orientalia* 36 (Rome, 1967), 416 ff. Also J. J. Janssen, *Commodity Prices*, 499 ff.

36 J. Černý in *Journal of World History* I (Paris, 1954), 906 f.; J. J. Janssen, op. cit., 545 ff.

37 J. Černý, op. cit., 912.

38 Papyrus Boulaq II (Cairo 58070), column I, ll.1–9.

39 In many documents 'broken copper' is mentioned in transactions; it clearly is 'scrap copper'. *Shayt* is a kind of cake or loaf. The commodity must be scraps of bread ('broken biscuits'?), and most unlikely goods for trading.

40 J. J. Janssen, op. cit., 105.

41 See p. 186 above.

42 Of Ramesses II, *c.* 1275 BC. This extract comes from Cairo Papyrus 65739 ll.3 ff.; it is published by A. H. Gardiner in *Journal of Egyptian Archaeology* 21 (London, 1935), 140 ff. Simut was Irytnofre's husband.

43 The document is the record of a law-suit concerning the purchase of the slave-girl.

44 The *kite* was one tenth of a *deben* (about 91 grammes).

45 British Museum Papyrus 10053. The passage in question is on the verso, page 3; see T. E. Peet, *Great Tomb-Robberies of the XXth Egyptian Dynasty* (Oxford, 1930), 118, pl. XX.

46 See J. Černý, op. cit., 906.

47 J. J. Janssen, op. cit., 173.

48 On the extraordinary quantities involved in servicing the temples, see H. Kees, *Ancient Egypt*, 89.

49 Part of a letter on an ostracon in Berlin (no. 12630) of the reign of Ramesses III, published by S. Allam, *Hieratische Ostraka und Papyri* (Tübingen, 1973), pls 10,11. The translation is that of J. Černý in *A Community of Workmen at Thebes in the Ramesside Period*, 351.

50 From *The Instruction of Amenemope*, 17, 17–20; 18, 21–19, 3. See F. Ll. Griffith in *Journal of Egyptian Archaeology* 12 (London, 1926), 191 ff. For a good modern translation of the whole text, see M. Lichtheim, *Ancient Egyptian Literature*, II, 146 ff.

A BRIEF CHRONOLOGY

(The system of dates followed here is that proposed by J. von Beckerath in *Abriss der Geschichte des Alten Ägypten*, Munich-Vienna, 1971)

THE EARLY DYNASTIC PERIOD (Dynasties I–II), *c.* 3000–2635 BC
The foundation of the Kingdom and the beginnings of Egyptian culture

THE OLD KINGDOM (Dynasties III–VI), *c.* 2635–2155 BC
A time of great central control and of the building of the pyramids

THE FIRST INTERMEDIATE PERIOD (Dynasties VII–XI), *c.* 2155–2060 BC
The disintegration of central authority; a time of uncertainty, socially and politically

THE MIDDLE KINGDOM (Dynasties XI–XIII), *c.* 2060–1700 BC
Reunification of Egypt under kings supported by a strong bureaucracy

THE SECOND INTERMEDIATE PERIOD (Dynasties XIII–XVII), *c.* 1700–1554 BC
The time of the Hyksos domination; native kings rule in Thebes

THE NEW KINGDOM (Dynasties XVII–XX), *c.* 1554–1080 BC
The rise and decline of imperial Egypt

Eighteenth Dynasty (selected rulers)

Amenophis I	*c.* 1529–1508 BC
Tuthmosis I	*c.* 1508–1493 BC
Tuthmosis II	*c.* 1493–1490 BC
Hatshepsut	*c.* 1490–1470 BC
Tuthmosis III	*c.* 1490–1439 BC
Amenophis II	*c.* 1439–1413 BC
Tuthmosis IV	*c.* 1413–1403 BC
Amenophis III	*c.* 1403–1365 BC
Amenophis IV (Akhenaten)	*c.* 1365–1349 BC
Tutankhamun	*c.* 1347–1337 BC
Horemheb	*c.* 1332–1305 BC

Nineteenth Dynasty (selected rulers)

Sethos I	*c.* 1303–1290 BC
Ramesses II	*c.* 1290–1224 BC
Merneptah	*c.* 1224–1214 BC

Twentieth Dynasty (selected rulers)

Ramesses III	c. 1193–1162 BC
Ramesses IV	c. 1162–1156 BC
Ramesses IX	c. 1137–1119 BC
Ramesses XI	c. 1110–1080 BC

LATE DYNASTIC PERIOD (Dynasties XXI–XXX), c. 1080–332 BC
A divided kingdom, afflicted by foreign conquests and alien rulers

PTOLEMAIC PERIOD, 332–30 BC
Macedonian Greeks occupy the throne of the Pharaohs

ROMAN PERIOD, after 30 BC
Egypt becomes a province of the Roman Empire

SELECT BIBLIOGRAPHY

C. Aldred, *The Egyptians*, 2nd edition (London, 1983).

J. Baines and J. Málek, *Atlas of Ancient Egypt* (London, 1979).

H. Baker, *Furniture in the Ancient World* (London, 1966).

M. L. Bierbrier, *The Tomb-Builders of the Pharaohs* (London, 1982).

J. H. Breasted, *Ancient Records of Egypt: Historical Documents*. 5 vols. (Chicago, 1906).

Cambridge Ancient History, 3rd edition. Vol. I. Part 1 (Cambridge, 1970), Part 2 (1971); Vol. II, Part 1 (1973), Part 2 (1975).

E. Brovarski, S. K. Doll and R. E. Freed (eds.), *Egypt's Golden Age* (Boston, 1982).

J. Černý, *A Community of Workmen at Thebes in the Ramesside Period* (Cairo, 1974).

N. de G. Davies, *The Tomb of Rekh-mi-Rēʿ at Thebes*. 2 vols. (New York, 1943).

A. H. (Sir Alan) Gardiner, *Ancient Egyptian Onomastica*. 3 vols. (Oxford, 1949).

Egypt of the Pharaohs (Oxford, 1961).

Late-Egyptian Miscellanies (Brussels, 1937).

J. R. Harris (ed.), *The Legacy of Egypt*. 2nd edition (Oxford, 1971).

W. C. Hayes, *The Scepter of Egypt*. 2 vols. (New York, 1953, 1959).

T. G. H. James, *The Hekanakhte Papers and other Early Middle Documents* (New York, 1962).

(ed.), *An Introduction to Ancient Egypt* (London, 1979).

J. J. Janssen, *Commodity Prices from the Ramessid Period* (Leiden, 1975).

H. Kees, *Ancient Egypt* (London, 1961).

M. Lichtheim, *Ancient Egyptian Literature*, 3 vols. (Berkeley, Los Angeles, London, 1973, 1976, 1980).

A. Lucas, *Ancient Egyptian Materials and Industries*. 4th edition, J. R. Harris (ed.) (London, 1962).

A. Mekhitarian, *Egyptian Paintings*. 2nd edition (London, 1979).

D. B. Redford, *History and Chronology of the Eighteenth Dynasty of Egypt* (Toronto, 1967).

E. Riefstahl, *Thebes in the Time of Amunhotep III* (Norman, Oklahoma, 1964).

W. K. Simpson (ed.), *The Literature of Ancient Egypt* (New Haven and London, 1972).

INDEX